CHINESE THEOLOGY IN CONSTRUCTION

CHINESE THEOLOGY IN CONSTRUCTION

Wing-hung Lam

William Carey Library

Library of Congress Cataloging in Publication Data

Lam, Wing-hung, 1946 -
    Chinese Theology in construction.

    Bibliography: p.
    Includes index
    1. Theology, Doctrinal - China - History -
20th century.   2. Persecution - China - History -
20th century.   3. China - Church history - 20th
century.   I. Title.
BT30.C6L35   230'.044'0951   81-15483
ISBN 0-87808-180-1   AACR2

Published by
William Carey Library
1705 N. Sierra Bonita Ave.
P.O. Box 40129
Pasadena, California 91104
Telephone: (213) 798-0819

In accord with some of the most recent thinking of the academic
press, the William Carey Library is pleased to present this
scholarly book which has been prepared from an author-edited
camera-ready copy.

PRINTED IN THE UNITED STATES OF AMERICA

Contents

Preface

Has there been any genuine Chinese theology worthy of its name after the numerous missionary attempts, at various times, in importing the Christian Gospel to the Chinese people? This question has, for many years, aroused my curiosity that drove me to a more thorough historical and theological investigation during my graduate studies in the United States.

The present work is a modest effort to share with western scholars some of my findings on a theological case study of the Chinese Church in the era of Anti-Christian Movement of the 1920's. It was originally a doctoral dissertation written for the Church History Department of Princeton Theological Seminary.

I am indebted to Dr. Charles West and Dr. Frederick Mote who granted me valuable suggestions and criticisms for the manuscript. Although I acknowledge their help, I am responsible for any errors and omissions that remain. I am grateful to Dr. Herbert Kane and Dr. R. Pierce Beaver for introducing me to the field of Chinese Church studies. Reverend Jonathan Chao also spent time with me in many fruitful conversations during the early stage of my research.

An article entitled, "Patterns of Chinese Theology", based on Chapter Three of this volume, was published in the *Occasional Bulletin of Missionary Research* in January 1980.

I must express my gratitude to the editor and the publisher of William Carey Library for their willingness to publish my manuscript. My special thanks are due my wife, Shirley

Chua, who typed the entire manuscript and often reminded me
that there are other interesting things in the world apart
from writing a book for publication.

Wing-hung Lam
China Graduate School
of Theology, Hong Kong

Introduction

The present study is an historical investigation of the response of the Protestant Christian Church to the challenge of the anti-Christian movement in modern China during the 1920s.

Anti-Christian activities are not new in the history of Christian missions in China. The religious persecution in T'ang Dynasty (around A.D. 845), the opposition to the Jesuits by the literati and officialdom in Ming Court, the struggle for authority during the Rites Controversy in early Ch'ing, and the antiforeignism in the nineteenth century--all reflect in one way or another the hostile reception of the Christian faith by the Chinese people. However, there is a marked difference, both in scope and in nature, between the anti-Christian movement before and after 1900. Previously, Christianity was opposed from the standpoint of Chinese culture, but in 1920s from that of Western ideology. Before 1900, Christianity was regarded as not Confucian enough; after 1900, it was regarded as not modern enough to be compatible with the rapid process of westernization of the society. During the twenties, the Christian faith and the Christian community became the target of unprecedented nation-wide criticism.

In the early years of the Republic, the nation was searching for her identity in the midst of various intellectual currents and political adversities. The May Fourth Movement (ca. 1917-23) epitomized the intellectual transformation in which Confucianism was under relentless attack

when Western ideas flooded the market. The unsatisfactory
settlement of the Shantung question at the Paris Peace
Conference led to the upsurge of nationalistic sentiment
which came to a climax in the crisis of the May Thirtieth
Tragedy in 1925. Warlordism and imperialism became the two
foes of young China. The successful Northern Expedition
led by the Kuomintang, in nominal collaboration with the
Communists, seemed to promise the Chinese people a new day.
However, their feelings were mixed when the Kuomintang
liquidated the Communists and exalted the Party rule.
Against this background of political instability, social
upheavals, and intellectual diversity, the anti-Christian
movement is to be viewed.

The outbreak of the anti-Christian movement occurred in
1922 when the World's Student Christian Federation decided
to hold its conference in Tsing Hua University near Peking
in April. It sparked a chain-reaction of emotion-filled
campaigns against Christianity over the country. Demonstrations, speeches, telegrams, and pamphlets were employed
to oppose it as the tool of imperialism and agent of
denationalization. Numerous *hsüeh ch'ao* (student strikes)
occurred in Christian schools, supported by political
parties, that crippled the function of the institutions.
The government restoration of educational prerogatives
from mission schools challenged the place of Christian
education, both as a mediator of Western culture and as a
means of religious proselytism. The anti-Christian force
was of such magnitude as seemed to threaten the existence
of the Christian movement. Evidence of such possibility
was seen in the exodus of foreign missionaries after the
Nanking Incident in March, 1927. The Chinese Church was
caught in the turmoil, puzzled about the viability of its
message and perplexed with the uncertainty of its future.
For the first time in the history of Chinese Christianity,
indigenous leaders significantly stood to defend the
Christian faith. The success of their effort has to be
carefully evaluated.

This historical study is motivated by a curiosity in the
writer which has been stimulated by the recent missiological
notion of 'indigenization' or 'contextualization' of theology.
How could the Chinese Church manage to survive the onslaught
of anti-Christian antagonism? What kind of apology did they
give to "account for the hope" that was in them? Was there
any 'contextualized theology' worthy of that name? Christian
activities in this volatile decade are comparatively unex-
plored in the history of Christian missions in China. The

anti-Christian movement in the 1920s has been variously
interpreted by scholars in Chinese studies. Despite their
differences in presupposition and method, their common
interest lies in the actions taken by the anti-Christian
intelligentsia and the government toward the Church. There
is as yet no comprehensive treatment of the Christian
reaction to the anti-Christian opposition.(1)   It is hoped
that the present project will fill out a dimension of modern
Chinese intellectual and religious activities that has often
been neglected.

The structure of the book is based on several related
questions asked in the period. The first chapter deals with
religion itself at a time when science and democracy were
popular in China. The various approaches to religion are
analysed with respect to the urgent needs of the nation. Is
Christianity suitable to modern China? To answer this question, Chinese Christians were engaged in a diligent search
for a viable message that could speak to the nation in turmoil. And Chapter Two will take up the dialogue between
Christians and anti-Christians from which we see the shape
of the contemporary Christian message.

In the third chapter we examine the relation of the
Christian faith and the cultural crisis of the time. To
present Christianity acceptable to the people, Chinese
Christians attempted to develop a theology in the context
of the Chinese tradition. Their efforts gave rise to
several patterns of indigenous thought.

The indigenous Christian movement was largely a reaction
to the challenge of nationalism. From both the communist
and the nationalist standpoint, Christianity was criticized
as imperialistic. Chapter Four will study the various
impacts of the anti-Christian movement on the Chinese Church,
and Chapter Five will present the Christian answer to the
charge of denationalization.

From the discussion of these chapters, we will see that
in the struggle of the Chinese Church with the anti-
Christian movement during the twenties, there emerged a
Christian apologetics, Christo-centric in both orientation
and application, with which they faced the contemporary
problems.

1

The Religious Issue

The study of religion in the early decades of our century is
important to the understanding of modern China. Religion
was so much intertwined with the socio-political situation
of the day that many forms of activities were directly or
indirectly connected with it. For example, the revival of
Confucianism as state religion, the controversy over the
problem of religion in the Young China Association, the
formation of the Anti-Christian Federation, the campaign
for the revision of the Unequal Treaties, and the massive
withdrawal of missionaries from China—all happened in the
two exciting decades after the establishment of the Republic
in 1912. In seeking to define New China, an important question was, What is the role of religion? Does China need any
religion? What is the nature of religion itself?

The religious problem drew the attention of many Chinese
intellectuals who, involved in the revolution of the New
Culture Movement,(1) devoted themselves to the investigation
of the issue. To them, it seems, belonged the task of
setting the patterns and the direction that young China
should follow. As Chan Wing-tsit puts it, "If the masses
are the body of Chinese religion, the intellectuals are the
mind".(2) Various patterns of religious thought were
recognizable which laid the ideological foundation of the
anti-Christian activities in the 1920s. In the Chinese
Church some Christians felt the need of rethinking the nature
of Christianity and its relevance to the nation. They hoped
to construct a religion in a way suitable to the modern
Chinese mind.

RELIGIOUS CONTROVERSY: DID
CHINA NEED ANY RELIGION?

Anti-religious activities in this century were first
directed against Confucianism. As early as 1898, K'ang
Yu-wei proposed to the Manchu Emperor to make Confucianism
the state religion, hoping that it would be the means of
national salvation.(3)   In 1912, the Confucian Society was
established in Shanghai under the leadership of Ch'en Huan-
chang, Chu Tsu-mou and others. In February 1913, K'ang
founded the magazine *Pu-jen* (Compassion) to be the organ of
the Confucianist campaign. In his zeal, K'ang proposed to
the Government in 1916 that "since the people of all nations
have some kind of religion and only the aborigines and wild
people have none, China would be admitting herself to be a
country without religion and a country of aborigines and
wild people if the Chinese do not worship the founder of
Confucianism".(4)

They were criticized from different sides. Religious
groups saw this act as suppression of religious liberty
stated in the Constitution of the Republic. Leaders of the
New Culture Movement repudiated the Confucianists as still
holding to the declining heritage of the past which was a
hindrance to national modernization. In his *Diary of a
Madman*, Lu Hsün, the popular satirical essayist, ridiculed
the entire Confucian ethics as unconscious cannibalism
practiced by the Chinese for centuries. Ch'en Tu-hsiu,
editor of the influential magazine *Hsin Ch'ing-nien*, argued
that Confucianism is not a religious system and should not
be exalted as state religion.(5)   The attack on the
resurgence of Confucianism was immediately extended to
antagonism against religion in general.

The first organized anti-religious activities were
connected with the Young China Association, which was a
main force in the New Culture Movement. The purpose of the
Association was to dedicate itself to "social service,
under the guidance of the scientific spirit, in order to
realize our ideal of creating a young China".(6)   In August
1920, the executive committee of the Association in Peking
approved the recommendation by Li Huang and others of the
Paris branch to limit membership to those without religious
belief. This act aroused controversy among the Association
members. T'ien Han, a well-known dramatist, protested
against the resolution saying that religious freedom was
provided in the Chinese Constitution and that religious
faith was not incompatible with the material and cultural

life of society.(7) As a result of such protest, the
Association in the Nanking Conference in July 1921 cancelled
the previous resolution and regarded religion as an issue
for future investigation.

    Some members in France, led by Li Huang, wrote to the
professors at Paris asking for comment on the following
questions: 1.) Is man a religious animal? 2.) Is there
any value of the survival of old and new religions? 3.)
Does New China need any religion?(8) Their responses were
all negative. Marcel Granet, professor of Chinese History
at Sorbonne, remarked that it is unnatural for a nation to
set up a religion. And it is unfruitful to copy others'
religious practice. China is a non-religious society whose
national spirit comes from ethical teachings rather than
from dogmas or legends. Henri Barbusse, a famous novelist,
commented that the missionary enterprises in China were
not beneficial to the country, but they were a tool to
develop commercial and political power. For the salvation
of China, Chinese youths should be independent and should
unite themselves with the current ideologies of the world.(9)

    Different lecture series were arranged in Peking and
Nanking to discuss the problem of religion. Scholars who
were invited by the Young China Association were divided in
their opinions. Opposers of religion included Wang Hsing-
kung, Li Shih-tseng, and Bertrand Russell; advocates of
religion were Liang Sou-ming, T'u Hsiao-shih, Chou Tso-jen,
Liu Po-ming, and Lu Chih-wei. The opposite view points in
these lectures were expressed from a diversity of background
and with different degree of philosophical sophistication.
Seldom before had the problem of religion been discussed
with so much intellectual objectivity and competence. These
arguments had formulated the intellectual climate in which
the different sides of the anti-Christian movement expressed
their positions in later years. An analysis of the various
approaches to religion will enable us to appreciate the
rationale behind the ideological confrontation during the
movement.

Emotion as a Starting Point

    To some scholars, the origin of religion is primarily
located in the emotional constitution of the human being.
Liang Ch'i-ch'ao,(10) a prolific scholar and foremost
intellectual leader in modern China, viewed religion as the
object of faith of an individual. In his opinion, there

are two characteristics about such faith. First, it is a
product of emotion, not of reason. Secondly, it is an end,
not a means, because "one can sacrifice other things for
faith but not faith for other things".(11)   And "any one
who has absolute faith in an ideology, that ideology becomes
his religion".(12)   From this perspective, a Marxist
believer has his own religion while many nominal Christians
in the Roman Catholic Church have actually no faith. The
anti-religion movement itself is a religion if the participants commit themselves to this end.

For Liang, religion is not due to man's weakness in
seeking dependence and comfort in times of fear and despair.
It is positively the "crystallization of affection". He
remarked, "Only when emotion rises to white-heat intensity
can great things be accomplished. . . . The progress of
mankind consists in the achievements made possible by the
white-heat emotion of mankind. Such white-heat emotion,
since it cannot be named satisfactorily, may be called
religion".(13)

Liang felt that it is important for the Chinese people
to have some form of religious thinking which will offer
them noble ideals to live for and a moral means of social
reform.(14)   His career as a political statesman and
propagandist explained his emphasis on emotional commitment
in life. The answer to the critical situation of the nation
required no less than a strong faith, political and social
in outlook, that would mobilize the Chinese people to serve
the national goal.

The emphasis on emotion was also central to the well-
known philosophy of aestheticism of Ts'ai Yüang-p'ei,
Chancellor of National Peking University (1916-26) and
advocate of the anti-Christian movement.(15)   To Ts'ai,
traditional religion has undergone an evolutionary process
in three stages of human development delineated by Auguste
Comte: theological, metaphysical, and positivist. The law
of growth is in the positivist direction. As Ts'ai saw it,
religion comes from the psychological activity in man's
life, including intellect, volition, and emotion. Primitive
beliefs in creation and final judgment are myths and legends with no scientific warrant. Appeals to unknown deity
to account for blessing or misfortune are superstitious.
Modern man should avoid reading religious meaning into
natural phenomena or human relations which could be explained
with science and reason.(16)   New discoveries in sociology,
psychology, and biology have enabled man to make ethical

decisions in life, resulting in his volitional independence
from religious standards.

However, the emotional nature of man, as Ts'ai asserted,
has a most intimate connection with religion.(17)   He
observed that in the history of Chinese religion, the development of art had become a form of cultivation for
emotional expression. Various religions might give rise to
conflict and confusion, but appreciation of artistic beauty
went beyond religious differences. It nourished the noble
nature of man and transcended selfish ambitions. Beauty was
universal and accessible to all, assisting men in pursuit
of the ultimate reality.

Ts'ai isolated religion from the realm of morality and
education, and suggested that aesthetic education should
replace it in the spiritual cultivation of the Chinese
intellectuals.(18)   This was "in line with the typical
Chinese philosophy of naturalism and humanism, for education
through art presupposes nothing supernatural or superhuman".
(19)   Ts'ai's view drastically reduced the functional role
of religion in the Chinese society and logically inclined
toward its elimination altogether.

Tendency of Transcendence

A different approach to religion dealt with man's innate
tendency to get beyond his mundane life. Some Chinese
intellectuals pursued this line of argument to affirm the
necessity of religion.

Liu Po-ming, professor of South Eastern University,
attempted to define man's religious instinct as the need to
resolve the conflict between the actual and the ideal existence. He defended the objective existence of spiritual
values, for example, the achievement of mankind down the
centuries.(20)   Employing the Platonic analysis of religion,
Liu pointed out, in a strong moral language, the dichotomy
between the world of senses and the world of ideas. The
latter should be the pattern to be emulated by the former.
Man's goal in life is not to be enslaved by the present
existing order but to unshackle himself to the higher sphere
of spiritual reality. Man's religious time is the moment of
dissatisfaction with temporal life and followed by the
ambition to transcend it. Though a critic of Ts'ai's
aestheticism, Liu Po-ming agreed that artistic appreciation
can cause temporary psychological transference to another
state of existence, which will reduce man's internal conflicts.

Seeking to define religion properly, Liang Sou-ming,
professor at Peking University, (21) asked, "What is the
common condition of all religions"? If there is no answer,
as Liang remarked, we have only different religious phenomena but not a religious conception.(22) In his view,
religion refers to that which goes beyond the realm of knowledge and gives comfort and encouragement to man's emotion
and volition. Liang claimed that his definition is based
upon objective evidence and the inductive method. Both the
task and the basis of religion are contained in it. The
task--to comfort and encourage--is indispensable in all
religions, primitive or modern, for it holds life together
in a disintegrating world. Therefore, religion becomes a
"cultural necessity". Its basis, established beyond man's
knowledge, carries a transcendent and mysterious dimension.
And religion often draws on the dimensions of deity for
assurance of hope and confirmation of faith.

However, in Liang's view, the genuine need for religion
does not lie in the intensity of man's emotion, in the
resolution of guilty conscience, or in the search for the
meaning of life. It is the Buddhist way of proceeding above
the life cycle of birth, senility, sickness, and death to
the realm of tranquillity and bliss.(23) Liang Sou-ming's
interest in such other-worldliness was regarded by Liu
Po-ming as a Buddhist form of resolving the conflict between
the practical and the ideal.

T'u Hsiao-shih, an influential critic of religion in the
twenties, began his discussion from human experience.(24)
To him religion is not ethical theory, like Kant's cate-
gorical imperative, which requires intellect to control
emotion without experiential motivation. Religious believers
who are inspired by the desire to avoid misfortune and to
gain blessing will oppose such ethical theory. Nor is
religion a metaphysic of Hegel's sort. In different
religious experiences, such as ecstasy in Medieval mysticism
and meditation in Zen Buddhism, there is absence of conceptual knowledge. T'u regarded Schleiermacher's "feeling of
absolute dependence" as a more realistic, though inadequate,
starting point.(25) The right approach is to place religious nature in man's internal experience. Man is a spiritual being whose activities are not mechanical responses to
environment alone but expressions of creativity. He has
the inner desire to free himself from all restrictions of
natural existence. There is the inborn urge to search for
the unchanging principle to account for the changing experience. T'u was aware that the principle would be subject to

modification with new information in the future, yet the
disposition toward the absolute and ultimate was undeniable.
The possibility of religion lies in the tension between
restriction and emancipation, between relative and absolute.
According to T'u, the final goal of all religions is to unite
the self with the transcendent reality, which produces a
direct subject experience beyond rational analysis.(26)
Such experience, concrete and intuitive, is not subject to
value judgment for it is itself ultimate.

Exponents of the position that religion is a form of
inner tendency of transcendence were mostly affirmative of
the need for religion among the Chinese people. Their
argument moved from universal validity in human life to
particular social environment and from individual necessity
to cultural necessity. Science and knowledge can improve
the material condition in life, they held, but they do not
reduce the problems. When hardship comes, man wants comfort
and encouragement offered by religion. The human aspiration
to go beyond mundane concerns is undeniable by the intellect
or emotion. Religion draws on the mysterious and the transcendent dimension for the assurance of hope. It is a form
of social cohesive force that helps maintain the communal
order. Scholars of this type of religious persuasion
attempted to give a functional interpretation of religion as
suitable for the Chinese people. Their shortcoming lay in
the failure to formulate a feasible program to meet the
national crisis. Most of their exhortation was individualistic in orientation.

Science, A Way of Salvation

The decade of the New Culture Movement was characterized
by the emphasis on science and reason. The anti-intellectual
bias of religion ran counter to the basic way of thinking
among the "new youth". In the minds of many Chinese, the
scientific spirit of the West had replaced the Confucian
spirit of the Chinese tradition. It was in the name of
modern science that religion received the most vigorous
opposition. Never before was religion attacked from such a
standpoint.

The popularity of science was well expressed by Hu Shih,
a most articulate spokesman of the New Culture Movement. (27)

He said,

> In the past thirty years there has been a name
> which has almost gained a status of incomparable
> dignity in the country. No one whether informed or
> uninformed, conservative or progressive, dare to
> show publicly an attitude of disrespect or scorn.
> This name is Science. Whether this nation-wide
> worship has any value or not is another question.
> But we can at least say that since the national
> reform movement began, no one person who regarded
> himself a modern man has openly disparaged Science.
> (28)

Hu was a keen disciple of John Dewey's pragmatism, Thomas
Huxley's agnosticism, and Charles Darwin's evolutionism. To
him, the scientific method is the correct approach to search
for truth and the only adequate way of solving problems. He
said, "We may not easily and lightly admit that God is omnipotent, but we certainly can believe that the scientific
method is omnipotent and that man's future is inestimably
large".(29)   In his view, due credence must be given to
facts and evidences in any process of study. One must be
courageous in formulating hypotheses and cautious in seeking
their empirical proofs. Impressed by the scientific
achievements of the West, Hu did not hesitate to exalt
science even to a cultic status. Science is not confined in
its application to the physical universe but to all areas of
life.

As a well-known scientist in Peking University, Wang
Hsing-kung delivered a speech in the Young China Association
that gave support to the anti-Christian cause in the 1920s.
(30)   To him, the unverifiability of religious claims is
the primary reason for its unacceptability. Religions often
attempt to offer an overall simplistic answer to problems in
life, asserting theistic claims instead of going through
logical investigations. This dogmatic approach is not intellectually responsible.(31)   Wang refused to accept an
unbridgeable gulf between the known and the unknown. In
his view, what is purported to be unknowable virtually does
not exist because in the course of time man's knowledge will
inevitably increase. From this premise, the realm of
religion is automatically reduced with the growth of scientific discoveries. Thus, Wang challenged the ideological
construction in religion as lacking the support of empirical
evidence. For he felt that human knowledge cannot be established
on a mystical, subjectivistic basis. This was undoubtedly a

serious challenge to the validity of religious experience.

The advent of science questioned the viability of the
entire tradition of the Chinese people. Critics in the New
Culture Movement were ready to identify anything religious
with primitive superstition. According to Ch'en Tu-hsiu,(32)
the hypotheses of God and spirit are superfluous in modern
society. Religions are merely human inventions. An important function of science is to break down myths and legends
that have captivated the Chinese for centuries. He said,

> If the existence of Gods and spirits of heaven
> and earth cannot be proved accurately, all forms of
> religion are nothing but deceitful idols: the god
> Amida is false; Jehovah is false; and the Supreme
> Lord of Heaven (head of the Taoist Pantheon) is
> false. All kinds of Gods, Buddhas, Immortals,
> Spirits revered by various religions are useless,
> cheating idols and must be destroyed.(33)

As science became a 'sacred cow' in the thought of the
Chinese youth, they imagined that the nation could be saved
through science. And "K'e-hsüeh wan-neng" (Science is
omnipotent) and "K'e-hsüeh chiu-kuo" (National salvation
through science) were slogans shouted by the students. The
formation of such scientific mentality had little room for
religious possibilities. The Western battle between science
and religion was imported to China and took on a local
appearance.

During the anti-Christian movement in the twenties,
religion was virulently opposed from the vantage point of
science. For example, in the telegram of the Great Anti-
Religion Federation issued at Peking on March 21, 1922,
religion was spoken of as "divisive", "deceptive", "hypocritical", and "hynoptistic".(34)   The Federation was devoted
to the goal of "sweeping the obscuring fog from mankind on
the basis of human conscience and showing forth the light of
human progress according to the spirit of science".(35)   It
welcomed people of all political and social background to
join its task force in opposing the propagation of religion
in the country. The reason for its hostility toward religion
was spelled out in the manifesto of the Federation on the
same day. It said, "The poison of religion is a thousand
times worse than that of disastrous floods and ferocious
animals. The existence of religion threatens the welfare of
mankind. If there is mankind, there should not be any
religion. Religion and mankind cannot exist together".(36)

The doctrines of religion, it continued, have captivated
man's thought, have provoked warfare, and have exploited
human personality. The fictitious nature of religion will
be revealed under the judgment of science. "Religion is
ridiculous as it cannot reconcile with science and obnoxious
as it completely contradicts the way of humanity".(37)   Any
person having flesh and blood should support truth by de-
porting religion. In modern society, religion is already
out-of-date, and its role has been replaced by science and
philosophy.(38)

The emotional thrust in these accusations was easily
recognizable. The surprising thing in this campaign was to
see the subscription to the manifesto by not a few notable
scholars. In the comment of a Christian observer, "the
standpoint of this movement is based on the thought that
science is omnipotent. Therefore they felt that all religions are unscientific superstition, depriving man's rational
ability and binding his freedom. This is the greatest
barrier to human progress".(39)

The supremacy of science which undergirded the revolt
against religion did not go unchallenged. In Liang Ch'i-
ch'ao's *Ou-yu hsin-ying lu (Impressions of Travels in
Europe)*, he argued that the materialistic and mechanistic
world-view of European civilization has proved to be inadequate for modern man. The West should now wake up from the
"dream of the omnipotence of science". The spiritual tradition of Chinese culture will have a message to offer to
the suffering Continent.(40)

Liang's exhortation was a prelude to the Great Debate
over the question of science and metaphysics in 1923.(41)
The central issue of the Debate was whether science is
sufficient to formulate a viable philosophy of life. Most
scholars argued to and fro over such possibility, but few
had attempted to establish a scientific philosophy of life.
(42)   The weakness of the Debate, as pointed out by Hu
Shih, is the scarcity of effort to investigate what philosophy of life will emerge if science is put to use.(43)
Toward the end of the year, all related significant writings
were collected in a volume entitled, *Science and the
Philosophy of Life*, which was widely read by Chinese students.

Weighing the quantity and quality of the arguments, we can fairly say that the results of the Debate were in favor of science. However, the question of religion received more attention than before among Chinese intellectuals. It precipitated a ponderous challenge to the Chinese Christians in facing up to the issue of science and religion in the modern era. In the midst of anti-religious ideologies and hostilities, the Chinese Church stood like a reed in the stormy wind. Could Christianity, a religion having its historical root and Western heritage, defend itself before its foes? How did the Chinese Christians conceive of Christianity as a suitable religion for China?

CHRISTIAN ALTERNATIVE: WHAT KIND OF RELIGION DID CHINA NEED?

The New Culture Movement and Christianity

Before we can properly examine the response of the Chinese Church to the religious issue, a prior question has to be discussed. What was the impact of the New Culture Movement on Christianity?

The New Culture Movement was marked by the freedom of expression and the attitude of criticism. All schools of classical literature were under scrutinous examination. All patterns of thought and customs were relentlessly criticized. In the past, thought and expression were shaped by the Confucian tradition. The intellectual had definite lines to follow and models to emulate in the way of scholarship. The New Culture Movement gave him independence and individuality. He felt free to articulate his reaction to problems of his concern.

Moreover, the vernacular language had removed the former restrictions in grammar, vocabulary, and style in literature. Many of the technicalities in composition and antiquated forms of delivery were abandoned. A new dignity was given to what was previously regarded as the vulgar language. The language of the people was popular among the educated elite. Prevalent at the time was the spiritual emancipation of the Chinese intellectuals that gave rise to an avalanche of new literature. This sentiment of liberation from the shackles of the past was well expressed in the first issue of *Hsin Ch'ao* (New Tide Magazine):

Through this magazine we desire to cooperate with students of all middle schools throughout the

country to fight for spiritual emancipation. Our
hope is that all students of the country will interest themselves in scientific thought that they
will give up a subjective mind and fixed ideas in
order to be objective and critical; that they will
have personality enough to conquer our society
rather than to be conquered by it. The spirit of
our publication is the spirit of criticism.(44)

The literary revolution gave stimulus to the Christian
intellectuals to express boldly the Christian views on contemporary issues. The new intellectual climate also influenced the formation of the Apologetic Group at Peking, which
sought to interpret Christianity to the Chinese intelligentsia.(45)   A number of Christian magazines came out
during this time including *Sheng-ming, Chen Kuang, Ch'ing
nien Chin-pu, Chung-hua Kuei-chu, Wen-she, Chen-li, Chen-
tao,* and *Cheng-tao.*

The Chinese intellectuals seemed to rebel strongly against
the traditional concept of individual which was closely tied
with the family-clan system. The Western emphasis of individual personality and value greatly affected the man in the
New Culture Movement.(46)   Hu Shih denounced the four evils
in the Chinese family: selfishness, dependence, hypocrisy,
and cowardice.(47)   He recommended Ibsen's individualism
of freedom, expression, and self-determination to replace
the family-centered view. The "new youth" was challenged to
rebuild a society of the future from the ruins of the past.
The conception of the individual, of the family, and of the
nation all required redefinition.

The wave of criticism could not be conducted apart from
the presence of alternative positions and presuppositions.
In the aftermath of the severe rejection of Confucianism,
the Chinese intellectual faced an ideological vacuum. There
was a spectrum of reaction to the iconoclasm of the traditional heritage and the acceptance of Western doctrines.
Some were rationally convinced that Confucianism must go,
but they were emotionally tied to the time-honored tradition.
After World War I, some Chinese scholars who witnessed the
cultural bankruptcy of the West wanted zealously to reha-
bilitate Confucian values. Others were uncompromising in
their opposition against the futility of the Confucian
structure and advocated the all-out imitation of the Western
way. Any conscientious Chinese student who was informed of
the volatile situation would find it difficult to decide a
position.

An orthodox Confucianist took no interest in investigating
the realm of the supernatural. Most leaders in the New
Culture Movement were unanimous in their judgment that Confucianism was not a religion but an ethical system. The
agnostic element, however, was still vividly present in the
subconscious mind of the intellectual although the Confucian
tradition had declined. The psychological disposition to
resist the religious was easily recognizable. When K'ang
Yu-wei and others were trying to assert Confucianism, the
modern intellectual saw in this act a twofold error--the
misunderstanding of Confucianism as religion and the retention of a dying culture.

In the era of the New Culture Movement, the intellectual
milieu was not favorable to the development of Christianity.
Western thinkers who were widely read and discussed included
Descartes, Voltaire, Bentham, Larmarck, Comte, Darwin, Marx,
and Kropotkin. These writers understood Christianity in
their own ways, and many of them espoused an anti-religious
outlook. Many Chinese leaders of the time were trained in
Western schools and absorbed the anti-religious philosophy
of their predecessors. Ch'en Tu-hsiu's historical materialism, Hu Shih's social immortality, Ts'ai Yüan-p'ei's asthe-
ticism, and Li Shih-tseng's anarchism--all were impatient
with religious beliefs and institutions. They were respected
scholars and professors who easily gathered a multitude of
followers, and their opinions drew attention. Anti-
Christian ideologies were imported from the West and were
broadly disseminated in classrooms and in newspapers and
magazines. Students, especially in government schools, were
caught in this chaos of ideas and were looking for direction
from someone who offered viable guidance for both the nation
and the individual.

The 1920s were an age of forward-looking excitement. The
political uncertainty and the ideological diversity un-
settled the mind of the students who were responsive in
action and less sophisticated in their consideration. To
see the nation suffer from foreign exploitation and from
internal rivalry among the warlords was impossible to bear.
The traditional image of a scholar-official still lingered
in intellectual circles. Education and politics were not
regarded as independent of each other in their social
functions. The students might well imagine that, being of
the privileged and qualified elite who received education,
they were responsible for the political destiny of the
nation. Nationalistic fervor rose high during and after the
May Fourth Movement. The Chinese intellectuals were united

in spirit by the common goal to save and strengthen the
nation although their involvements in practical politics
were different. The victory of the May Fourth Incident was
still fresh in the mind.(48)   They saw that a task force
could be formed among themselves to exert pressure on the
government through the technique of demonstration, strike,
and boycott. Success to bring about changes in national
policy through protest and petition to the government during
the May Fourth event had led to more radical activities in
the twenties. They were ready to take any form of patriotic
action and to utilize available opportunity to show forth
their frustration and dissatisfaction. The same concern for
China's destiny was expressed in Christian circles; for
example, the slogan used by the China For Christ Movement
was "Religion saves the Nation". The theme of social reconstruction was much discussed in contemporary Christian
literature.

How did the Chinese Christians interpret the New Culture
Movement?

The humanistic outlook of the Movement was obvious to
many. A fair comment was uttered by Lo Yün-yen (49) that
"the New Thought Movement might be called a 'humanistic'
movement, for its aims and its chief interest is in the man,
his welfare and progress. It is a many-sided movement,
touching various aspects of life and placing a new valuation
on them.(50)   Liu T'ing-fang,(51) professor at Yenching
University, remarked that the primary concern of the Movement was "in the present world and in the immediate future".
(52)

Most Christian spokesmen gave a positive interpretation of
the Movement, though aware that its humanistic orientation
in the context of modern science and democracy might have
little place for religious consideration. Lo Yün-yen saw no
conflict between the New Culture Movement and Christianity.
In his view, both had the same motive of searching for truth
and the same concern for improving personal and social life.
If openness and objectivity were practiced in criticism and
research, the Movement should not repudiate religion but
should possibly benefit from it.(53)

Hsü Pao-ch'ien,(54) another professor at Yenching, regarded the movement as a necessary instrument to bring
changes. According to Hsü, this is "a movement in the realm
of thought, a process or phenomenon, characterized by
criticism and dissatisfaction on the one hand, and recon-

struction on the other".(55)   In this respect, he acknowledged a mutual supplementing function between Christianity
and the Movement. The new freedom in expression and criticism introduced by the literary revolution would assist the
spreading of the Gospel. In turn, the Christian ministry in
schools, hospitals, and social welfare continued to be helpful in improving the quality of human life. In Liu T'ing-
fang's opinion, the Movement had given "impetus to a constructive Christian social message. If the platform of the
Movement is carried out to its logical conclusion nothing
short of a satisfactory program for social reconstruction
can satisfy the longings of the spirits that are back of
this movement, . . ." (56)

Some cautious observers warned of the unorganized nature
of the Movement. Behind the clamor of voice there were no
creeds or hierarchy. The disorderliness and spontaneity of
it anticipated similar confusion during the anti-Christian
movement in the twenties. Several Christian critics examined the roots of the Movement and thought that, strictly
speaking, there was no new social theory, political concept,
or religious doctrine coming from it. Most of the ideologies were imported from the West and took on a local significance.(57)   However, this remark did not mean to minimize
the elements of novelty and creative contribution to the
Chinese society. The effort of indigenization of Western
thought and practice in modernizing national life was commendable. The search for an indigenous Christian message was
a product of the age.

In general, the Chinese Church welcomed the Movement,
despite the fact that most of the Movement's leaders were
not favorable to religion. It was a reform movement in
modern China whose goal seemed to be compatible with the
social outlook of Christianity even though its humanistic
presuppositions had made the Christian uncomfortable. As a
movement that emphasized ideological and practical relevance
to the immediate national situation, it offered to the Christian Church an agenda to reconsider the function of Christianity in China today. The Chinese Church was challenged to
meet this intellectual movement with a rational expression
of Christianity and to go through a process of self-exami-
nation regarding its internal problems and external relationships.

A New Religion in Construction

Some prophetic voices urged that Christianity should seek
to provide leadership to the Movement by establishing a new
religion for the Chinese people that took into serious consideration the contemporary intellectual and social forces.
An editorial in *Christian China* summarized it fairly well.
In the reconstruction of old China,

> What is urgently needed is a religion capable
> of preserving the morale of the people, of main-
> taining the fundamentals of living, and of satis-
> fying the deep spiritual yearnings of the millions.
> It must be a religion that will break down the sway
> of fear and superstitions, . . . that will stand
> the acid test of intelligent examination, reasonable
> doubts and rational inquiries, . . . that will dis-
> regard minor points concerning creeds and beliefs,
> and will, on the contrary, emphasize most strongly
> the fundamentals of life. (58)

The philosophical trend in the early twentieth century
gave priority to life itself. Bergson's creationism,
Darwin's evolutionism, and Dewey's pragmatism sought to
promote life. The most popular view of religion among contemporary Chinese Christians was that religion serves life.

According to Chien Yu-wen, (59) "The most important enterprise in human life and the most earnest desire of human
heart is the pursuit of a nobler, more peaceful, more abundant, more harmonious, more perfect, and longer life". (60)
In the process of life, man employs different means of
accommodating to environment. And in Chien's view, religion
is a most effective way of accommodation. For it will lead
man to realize the presence of a power beyond in the universe and enable him to form personal relationship with it.
From Henry Churchill King's *Religion as Life*, Chien got the
impression that life is not absolute and static but is a
process of evolution and development, manifesting itself in
different areas. As life changes, religion is subject to
changes in time and space, according to the needs of life.
No inflexible form of belief and unalterable norm of practice
could contain religion which should be constantly informed
by modern science and philosophy. (61)

A similar position was espoused by Wei Ch'üeh, (62) eminent educator in the Nationalist Government. Wei saw life as "a continuous process of adjustment with the cosmic and social forces". And religion is a way of life that seeks to establish proper relationship with them. (63) Wei regarded religion as servant and life as master. Therefore, it is "invariably conditioned by the concrete social, economic, and political conditions of the life-process". Consistent with his definition of religion as a technique of life, Wei did not claim the finality of Christianity but saw it as "a very efficacious and unique religion". (64) In man's interaction with environment, Wei noted four characteristics of religious experience: the sense of dependence upon God, social solidarity, guilt from moral imperfection, and the value of the person.

As a working definition, Mei Yi-pao, (65) professor of Yenching University, viewed religion as human awareness, adjustment, and improvement of life values. It embraces all areas of activities, instead of being one aspect of life. In human experience there exist the real and the ideal, the now and the future, the potential and the actual. The purpose of religion is life itself, dealing with its possibilities and opportunities. (66) Man in his weakness and limitation often calls upon the Power of the Universe for help, resulting in varieties of religious experience. In other words, the pursuit of religion is not life hereafter, eternal or transcendent as taught by some institutional religions, but life in the present. From this perspective, Mei pointed out the dual function of religion: integrative and motivative. (67) Religion attempts to bring together isolated and confused experiences into a holistic picture, thus imparting meaning to life. Not only does it satisfy the intellectual quest, but it also establishes the relation between the individual and the universe. Religion offers a dynamic to life in accomodation to circumstances and in improvement of its quality. Herein lies the ethical function of religion to usher man to higher and nobler ventures.

In a comprehensive manner, Chao Tzu-ch'en (68) conceived of religion as the communication between man and the universe, focused on the center of the universe and scheduled according to its plan. Man believes this reality, follows its principle and is intimately related to it. This would help him to be conscious of his position in the universe. (69) Such universal consciousness is the core of religious life. Religion therefore has to keep pace with life in its cosmic and mundane progress. As Chao said,

> Life is like the running water in the mountain
> stream, constantly flowing. Without flowing, it
> is not water. From the time of old, the same
> flowing, the same stream of water. We cannot say
> the water is no longer the water, and the flow is
> no longer the flow. Religion and all the com-
> ponents of a culture are in the same situation.
> Therefore even until today, religion is still
> religion, yet it is not the religion of the past.(70)

In Chao's view, religion in practice links man to the
universal spirit above and humanity below, leading him to
an abundant life in a particular physical and spiritual
environment. (71)

This new religion had several characteristics. First,
there was the emergence of a social consciousness in religious values. The former individualistic message of personal
salvation was modified into a social doctrine. Religious
individualism, parochial in interest and other-worldly in
outlook, could easily lead to social escapism which was
contrary to the ethos of the age. The salvation of China
needed involvement, rather than detachment, of the people.
The individual and the society should be inseparable in
purpose and in function.

Religion should have an ameliorating effect on social
life which had been exposed to various corrosive forces of
the modern age. The growth of production due to scientific
advancement made life more materialistic. The search for
wealth and power increased competition and exploitation.
Modern China required the right path to combat social evils
left by previous centuries of tradition and caused, directly
or indirectly, by the influence of Western culture. Religion
needed the cooperation of many factors to fulfill its social
mission in improving life and culture.

The social interpretation of Christianity by the Chinese
was closely connected with their eschatology. Conservative
Chinese Christians had comparatively little interest in the
practice of social reform. The theology of natural depravity
hindered them from entertaining the hope to rebuild a better
human society. Their activities mostly lay in evangelization
of individuals with a message of supernatural regeneration
for repentant sinners. Wang Ming-tao, a well-known pastor
at Peking, denied the possibility of establishing an ideal
society due to the doctrine of human sin. Man and society
had deteriorated in wickedness and corruption to the stage
beyond remedy, only awaiting the final judgment of God. (72)

Nothing short of a spiritual transformation could enable the sinner to renovate his life. This theological order explained the primary interest of Wang in evangelistic activities instead of in social reform. (73) In Wang's view, the kingdom is largely a future realm brought into existence through the operation of divine power. Wang conceived the kingdom of God as a qualitatively different state of existence that would replace the present world order. In his promised return, the Messiah will enrapture the Church of true believers and introduce a new heaven and new earth.

Advocates of the new religion, on the other hand, held a different eschatology which was not "futuristic" or "realized" but humanistic. Man is the sole agent to bring out the kingdom of God from the existing world system. The ideal society is to be the collective achievement of men in the present. The time to realize the kingdom is now. As Wei Ch'üeh said, the new religion "does not follow the traditional view which believes in the destruction of the present world and the supernatural creation of another, but it seeks to change and reconstruct the present social order with the end to gradually establishing the Kingdom of God, . . ." (74) Formation of such social ideal should be the common cause for all.

Science and democracy were the most important intellectual and social forces that shaped the era of the New Culture Movement. The value and necessity of science were almost accepted as a "heavenly mandate" in the modernization of China. It was the effort of some Chinese Christians to employ the method and the spirit of science for the defense of their faith. For example, the aim of the Peking Apologetic Group was to "make use of modern conceptions of science and philosophy in order to clear up the religious misunderstandings and doubts of the present generation, and with a view to proving the truth of the claims of Christ". (75)

Scripture itself was scientifically censored. Higher and Lower Criticism invented by Western scholars were now employed in the interpretation of Scriptural texts and the evaluation of the documents. As Liu T'ing-fang said, "The only way is to use the scientific and historical method, being willing to acknowledge the eccentric mistakes and illusions of our Christian forefathers together with their inventions and hair-splittings, and our cowardice with regard to modifying or changing them". (76) The figure of Jesus Christ was to be studied by historical method. Not as the

Son of God but as Jesus of Nazareth was Christ more relevant
to the Church and society.

The scientific mentality led to theological repudiation
of many traditional doctrines previously held to be central
by Christian orthodoxy. The supernatural dimension of
Christianity was depreciated, if not eliminated, in the
formulation of the new religion. The doctrines of miracles,
Virgin Birth, and Resurrection were no longer espoused as
important. In some quarters, they were simply removed from
theological consideration. The biblical story of creation
and human depravity were regarded as unsupported by modern
evolutionary and psychological theories.

These were various reactions from local Christians to the
charge that Christianity contradicts modern science. It
was a source of embarrassment to many who had inherited
the attitude of their fundamentalist missionaries who in
general were not trained in science and were unable to
answer their critics. They retreated from the controversy
and took a depreciative attitude toward science. Many
Chinese Christians gave up science for the Bible when they
found contradictions. Some saw the conflict as impossible
because, in their views, science and religion operate in
two different spheres of nature. The former is related to
the objective, material, visible, and finite universe. The
latter deals with the subjective, spiritual, invisible, and
infinite. As Lo Yün-yen remarked, both of them, strictly
speaking, should not be named together for discussion as
their paths are different. (77) Others would regard the
conflict inevitable. Since the two disciplines are separate,
any effort to force them together will provide undesirable
quarrel. In Chao Tzu-ch'en's word, "Conflict is hard to
avoid, for religion conserves value and science criticizes
value. We do not wish religion to be not conservative and
science to be not critical. But it depends on us to keep
the balance". (78) The search for balance had led a small
group of Christian intellectuals to study the relation of
the scientific enterprise and the Christian faith.

Most of them were cautious to distinguish science from
scientism which was the philosophical tendency in the New
Culture Movement. They recognized the limitation as well as
the utility of the scientific method. In theoretical formulation, the explanation of reality must not be identified
with reality itself. Christian apologists were not willing
to allow science the exclusive interpretation of life. The
unconditional claim of the omnipotence of science is only
unscientific dogmatism.

The hope to reconcile the conflict between science and religion was entertained by some Christians. They believed that the God of Christianity is also the God of nature. Science and theology will serve one another in understanding the intelligent design of the universe. Through scientific knowledge certain interpretation of nature by Christians will be modified. Through Christian theology the scientific enterprise receives a metaphysical structure which offers purpose and meaning to the silent nature. (79) Both of them are interrelated in the formation of a more complete epistemology of human experience.

The scientific attitude also excluded the finality of any religious claim. The changing conditions of life and experience would subject religious hypotheses to continual verification. In this scientific process, religion was an open system flexible and alterable with a self-improving ideological mechanism. Although not every Christian truth was testifiable in experiment, the Christian should have the scientific spirit to practice it. The Church and the Christian schools were laboratories to experiment these principles. Christianity should be made scientific if it was to appeal to the intellectual audience and to be accepted by modern China. In this way the new religion would be divested of its superstitious and speculative content which were a stumbling block to a progressive faith. Although science was not to be deified as scientism, any modern religion which contradicted it had no value of existence.

Moreover, the prevalent democratic spirit was at odds with any form of authoritarianism. The concepts of "state religion" and "religious state" were denied their institutional relevance in the present generation. Religious domination, political or ecclesiastical, would be obnoxious to the ethos of the age. Religion served life, and its final authority rested with individual experience. The idea of individualism, popular in the New Culture Movement, was turned into good use in the definition of the new religion. In the communication of the Christian faith, any dogmatic approach was to be avoided. An objective, intellectually sound message must be given so that believers came to accept the new religion not by blind faith or by mere adherence to authority. The weakest area of the Chinese Church was the absence of a rational Christianity that could gain a hearing from the secular intellectuals. (80)

Respect for the dignity and value of the person was the
constitutional element of a democratic religion. The affir-
mation of human personality in Christianity was closely tied
with the teaching of the Fatherhood of God and the Brotherhood of man. One's status before God as His child helped
restore one's worth in the Confucian society in which women
and the delinquent were lowly estimated. This became the
basis of different forms of humanitarian involvements by the
Christian Church in the Chinese society. What China needed
most was altruistic love and sacrifice for the neighbourhood
without favoritism or parochialism. The new spirit was "not
to be ministered unto, but to minister". (81) Humanitarianism
in the nineteenth century social philosophy was undoubtedly
contributive to the new spirit. With it was the shift in
theological emphasis from divine decree and authority to
divine morality and personality, from the miracles of Jesus
to his character. (82) The contemporary religion was
strongly ethical in emphasis.

The question of human value, when extended to a broader
scope, was directly related to the issue of nationalism
which could be regarded as the exaltation of one national
value over another. Patriotism and racial superiority were
enemies of universal brotherhood. Religious wars in
previous centuries had abandoned the moral imperatives of
"Do not murder", and "Love your enemy". The new religion
had to re-assert them with the exhortation for national
repentance and advocate internationalism as a possible
remedy for nationalistic extremes.

Advocates of the new religion were eager to see that it
would be compatible with the ethos of the time and acceptable
to the Chinese intellectual. They spoke from both religious
conviction and apologetic concern that such religion could
meet the needs of young China. It gave a message vibrant
with life that promoted the task of reconstructing the nation.
In their view, Christianity, the religion centered on Jesus
Christ, would supply an ethics and a dynamic to this effort.

2

A Christo-Centric Message

CHANGING EMPHASES IN THE CHRISTIAN MESSAGE

What was the shape of the Christian message in the 1920s that the Chinese Christians sought to preach? To answer this question, a brief historical sketch of the evangelistic message from the late nineteenth century will be in order.

In the conviction of most Christian missionaries in the previous century, they came to China in response to the great commission of Christ to declare the Gospel to the dying heathen world. There were two assumptions in such evangelistic approach: the divinity of the Christian message and the superiority of Western civilization. The first impression the missionary gained from the Chinese society seemed to confirm these assumptions. The Confucian tradition betrayed increasing signs of decline in the second half of the nineteenth century. (1) China to the foreigner was a country of undesirable social practices and weak political structure. Taoism and Buddhism, though philosophical in their doctrines, were mingled with cultic activities. To the missionary, the pagan Chinese urgently required the redemption by the Gospel.

As Griffith John, a representative figure of the London Missionary Society, said in his speech in the General Conference of Protestant Missionaries at Shanghai in 1877,

As missionaries we believe that we are in China
in obedience to the command of our Lord; and the
purpose of our mission is to disciple, or make Christians of, this great nation. Whatever others may do,
this is our work. We are here, not to develop the
resources of the country, not for the advancement of
commerce, not for the mere promotion of civilization:
but to do battle with the powers of darkness, to save
men from sin, and conquer China for Christ. (2)

Griffith John expressed the theological position of the majority of Western missionaries in his generation, a position
still held by the largest section of missionaries in the
1920s. His strong military language was characteristic of
their negative approach to local religions and traditions.(3)

The exclusive concern for direct evangelism constituted
the program of J. Hudson Taylor, the founder of the China
Inland Mission. In the second national missionary conference
in 1890, Taylor appealed for a thousand new missionaries to
enter the China field in the next five years. (4) He aimed
at a rapid evangelization by presenting the Gospel to the
Chinese, though not necessarily converting them to become
Christians. This missionary movement was well described by
the slogan, "the evangelization of the world in this generation". (5) Christianity was looked upon by the missionaries
as the final religion and criterion of judgment for other
faiths. They took a condemnatory attitude toward the heathen
culture and religions in China. Their evangelistic message
was largely individualistic and other-worldly in orientation.

Contacts led to knowledge; knowledge to appreciation.
Existing side by side with this conservative missionary outlook was a cultural respect for the ancient land in a small
but enlightened section of the missionary body. James Legge,
the famous translator of Chinese Classics, spoke highly of
traditional Chinese ethics. In commenting on the problem of
human nature in the General Missionary Conference in 1877,
Legge thought that Christianity could supplement the Confucian doctrine. (6) Without disparaging the status of the
Christian revelation, Legge was concerned with the possibility
of truth elements in Chinese culture. Chinese religions, as
Legge commented, "are still to be tested according to what
they are in themselves. We will approve what is good; we
will note what is defective; and we will disapprove what is
wrong". (7) Other missionaries were cautious that a depreciative attitude toward Chinese civilization might be harmful to the propagation of the Gospel. As F. S. Turner said,

"Let us not denounce Confucius as a foe, but welcome him as ally and use him as a schoolmaster to lead men to Christ". (8)

The more liberal effort in relating Christianity to the Chinese society was closely associated with a new phase of missionary policy which did not gain prominence until the last years of the nineteenth century. With prophetic vision some early missionaries had seen the inadequacy of mere religious proselytism. Conversion must be accompanied by Christianization. To W. A. P. Martin, mission consisted in the "conversion of the total cultural life of China" through science and Christianity. (9) Both Timothy Richard and Young J. Allen similarly insisted on the introduction of Western civilization to China.

With the turn of the century, there was a strong emphasis on the spirit of social service in the liberal wing of mission. It was thought that this approach would render the Christian message more acceptable to the Chinese mind which was practically and socially oriented. The numerous Christian institutions--schools, hospitals, and orphanages-- were physical signs of cultural mediation. No longer did they look upon the Chinese as merely heathen to be redeemed with the Gospel. There was the concern to extend Christian humanitarianism to various aspects of social life. A. R. Kepler, General Executive Secretary of the Church of Christ in China in 1927, argued that the social approach was able to maximize the points of contact between the ethical ideals of Confucianism and those of Christianity. (10) The attempt to create a Christian social order was rooted in the shift of theology that the Kingdom of God was not a future existence of bliss but an ideal community to be constructed on earth. The dimension of social service was regarded as a practical apologetics, seeking to reduce the distance between Christian theory and action.

This sketch of the development of the Christian message in relation to the increasing appreciation of the Chinese culture will help us understand its shape in the 1920s and after. Most of the views mentioned so far are missionary writings. Not until the second decade of the century can we see more significant contribution by indigenous authors. By that time, secular intellectuals could no longer oppose Christianity out of ignorance nor neglect it as a foreign religion. The impact on national life produced by missionaries and local Christians became a "social problem" they had to study.(11)

THE EMERGENCE OF A CHRISTO-
CENTRIC APOLOGETICS

In the previous chapter, we have seen the way in which
Chinese Christians constructed a scientific and democratic
religion for young China. They regarded Christianity as a
religion for human life which would offer a solution to the
national crisis. After the First World War, their message
emphasized the return to the "pure and simple Gospel of
Jesus himself". (12) Christo-centricity became the basis in
the formation of indigenous theology. As one Christian
leader put it, "We must go back to the simplicity and un-
assuming attitude of the preacher of the Sermon on the
Mount". (13) How did the Chinese Christians define the
Christian faith?

Chao Tzu-ch'en saw Christianity as the subjective appro-
priation of an objective reality. He said,

> Christianity is Christ. The term Christ has
> two senses, viz.the Jesus of history and the
> Christ in spirit. The historical Jesus did come
> to an end, but the spiritual Christ is everlasting.
> The living Christ is all in all. He is salvation,
> the regeneration and the reconciliation. The
> Christian religion may be submitted to varying
> conditions but Christ remains our sole and uni-
> versal object of faith.(14)

In this way the accessibility of the spiritual Christ was
universal, not confined by time and space. In Chao's
previous writing, he gave more attention to the subjective
consciousness of the Christ reality. Christianity was

> . . . a type of consciousness, a definite personal-
> social experience and a new life that has its origin
> and realization in the person of Jesus Christ. In
> other words, Christianity means a Christ life, or a
> Christ consciousness, the content of which is a de-
> finite relation of men as children to God as Father,
> with all that it involves. (15)

This understanding of Christianity enabled Chao to define
the task of the Christian mission in China: "to give the
Christ-life to China, that she may also be received into
this kingdom or brotherhood". (16) The ultimate aim of all
Christian endeavor was to glorify Christ in every area of
life.

Wu Lei-ch'uan, (17) a former *chin-shih* and radical Christian thinker, also equated Christianity as Jesus Christ through whom the true knowledge of God comes. To be a Christian is to imitate Christ, his faith and morals. In Wu's view, the personality of Jesus alone is adequate to be the focus of the Christian belief. (18) However, Wu was not willing to accept the uniqueness of Christianity, for he thought that the Christian religion and other faiths were of the same origin. His theology was deeply intertwined with the major concern in his career to deal with the problem of national salvation through Christianity. In Scripture, Jesus said, "I must be about my Father's business" and "For this cause came I unto the world, that I should bear witness unto the truth". To Wu Lei-ch'uan, this 'business' and 'witness' must be decided "in the light of the needs of our own age, as well as of our ability". (19) Christian regeneration, though legitimately begun with the individual, should end in social transformation. To accept Christianity is not just to receive the grace of salvation but to be collaborators with Christ in the redemption of mankind. From Christ we obtain strength to reform society and to share the great ministry of social progress. (20)

A similar "imitation of Christ" motif was found in Hsü Pao-ch'ien. To him, "Christianity without Christ ceases to be Christianity". Being a Christian is "to understand Jesus and to be like Him. That is, we have to make a constant effort in discovering what Jesus means to us". (21) Christ's life was a perfect synthesis of his mystical experience in union with God and his sacrificial living in love and forgiveness for men.

The Christian religion, in Hsü's view, consists in a similar synthesis of two related aspects: spiritual experience coming from God and man's effort to live according to the moral light. (22) Apart from the theological core of emulating Christ, other tenets of the Christian faith are "working hypotheses" which have to be revised "in the light of new experiences and new truths". (23) Beside the vertical dimension of Christianity, Hsü stressed the horizontal which deals with the relationship of the Christian individual to the community. As a modern religion, Christianity must put "equal emphasis on service and spiritual cultivation, which makes service possible". (24)

In Chien Yu-wen's opinion, Jesus set to his followers an example of necessary accommodation in transforming the Israelite tradition into a new religious experience. Later

on St. Paul, the Apostle to the Gentiles, integrated the
Jewish view of ethical personification and the Hellenic idea
of metaphysical absolute to produce an infinite-personal
deity in Jesus Christ. (25) The Christian religion down
through the centuries has been a constant process of adaptation in both theory and practice to the needs of life environment. Chien said, "Every age has a Christianity of its
own. The characteristic depends on the demand of the question peculiar to that age . . . Christianity is always in
the making". (26) Christianity has its primary concern for
the value and improvement of life, its flexibility in adjustment to circumstances, its moral dynamic in strengthening human relationship, its cultivation of character after
the example of Christ, and its built-in organism of growth.

These four figures probably represented a general picture
of the theological effort to present the Christian message
focusing on the person of Jesus Christ. (27) Chao's
"consciousness", Wu's "imitation", Hsü's "service", and
Chien's "accommodation"--each tried to define a significant
aspect of the message. The question remained, How did this
message answer the Anti-Christian Movement?

The Character of Jesus

The formation of the Christ-centered theology met with
both opposition and commendation. Anti-Christians of
various motives and backgrounds took issue with the doctrines of the Christian faith.

An earlier antagonism was launched against the character
of Jesus in an essay entitled, "What a thing is Jesus"?
written by Chu Chih-hsin, (28) a leader of the Kuomintang
and manager of the magazine *Chien-she (The Construction)*.
In Chu's description, the historical Jesus was "an idol whose
mouth uttered what his heart did not conceive, and who was
narrow-minded and self-seeking, easy to anger and ready to
revenge". (29) Chu knew some Scripture and church history,
but superficially. His scandalous way of interpreting Jesus
provoked the contemporary Christian apologists.

Chu tried to show the contradictions within Scripture and
its suspicious authorship. Concerning the existence of
Christ, there was, in Chu's view, little warrant from extra-
biblical evidences. Influenced by the German biologist,
Ernst Haeckel, Chu saw Jesus as the illegitimate child of
Mary and a Roman soldier. Jesus was said to be a revolutionary figure among the Jews struggling against the Roman

authority. His twelve disciples were comparable to those
characters mentioned in a Chinese legend, *Feng Shen Ch'uan
(The Coronation of Deity)*. The parable of the Virgin in
Matthew 25 was regarded as a selfish story contrary to the
principle of "Love your neighbour as yourself". The cursing
of the fig tree in Mark 11 further revealed the revengeful
spirit in Jesus' life. The same inconsistencies were found
in the history of the Christian Church when, under the dis-
guise of freedom and love, there were numerous persecutions
of other religions and heavy loss of human lives in religious
wars.

A different evaluation of Jesus' character was given by
Ch'en Tu-hsiu, whose writings about Christianty were often
quoted by both Christians and anti-Christians. Ch'en did
not overlook the impact of Christianity on China. Christianity must not be regarded as heterodox as in the past and
then rejected. (30)

Ch'en was highly selective in his approach to the Christian
religion. He liked the personality of Jesus but not the doctrines, a selectivity hardly acceptable by the Christian apologists. In Ch'en's view, scientific studies in history and
nature have rendered incredible the theories of Creation and
the Trinity. Christianity was reduced by him to a religion
of faith and love as manifested in the life of Christ. He
said, "The noble character and fervent emotion of Jesus Christ
should be developed and cultivated in our blood, to save us
from the pit of darkness, filth, and coldness." (31) The
Chinese people would benefit if they imitated the example of
Jesus in the spirit of sacrifice, forgiveness, and equity in
love.

Chu Chih-hsin's writing called out specific response from
the Chinese Church in the attempt to reconstruct the historical figure of Jesus. Liang Chün-mo (32) took to answer
the defamatory article in *Chen-kuang tsa-chih (The True
Light Magazine)*. (33) His apologetic approach was typical
of Christian writers of the time. He demanded adequate
evidence for argument, fair interpretation of Scripture, and
unbiased treatment of Church History. According to Liang,
the Virgin Birth was made possible by the operation of the
Holy Spirit, which was beyond human reasoning, like the
origin of life. Chu's allegation of Jesus' illegitimate
birth had little support from biblical data. (34) Liang defended the superb character of Jesus as uncomparable and his
achievement unmatchable by any human being that had ever
lived. Ch'en Tu-hsiu's favorable remark on Jesus was used

to refute Chu's blasphemy in calling Jesus an idol. Along
a similar line, Chien Yu-wen argued that Chu's insult was
not justified. (35) Jesus should be judged not according to
his family background or tradition but on his own merits.
How he was born had nothing to do with his personal morality
and achievement. The absence of valid criticism among the
Pharisaic circles and the dedication of his close disciples
bore witness to his irreproachable character.

According to Liang Chün-mo, Chu has distorted the meaning
of Scripture. The parable in Matthew 25 refers to the
eschatological judgment when every individual is to be responsible for himself. And the curse in Mark 11 is Jesus'
warning to the people against unfruitfulness in life. Liang
disapproved religious persecutions in history, but he regarded the persecutors as political opportunists using
Christianity for their own ends. Believers should live up
to their belief. He quoted the examples of Lincoln's emancipation of slavery and Livingstone's mission to Africa.
Liang criticized Chu that "if a man's heart is filled with
hostility, he won't be able to distinguish right or wrong
under heaven." (36)

When Chu's essay was circulated in the evangelistic rally
in Canton area in December, 1920, the anti-Christian propaganda was interpreted as jealousy of the success of the
meeting and as hostile opposition to the Church. (37) Chang
I-ching,(38) editor of *Chen-kuang,* gave a point-to-point
response to Chu's notorious criticism. Chang argued that
Jesus' life was consistent in word and practice, altruistic
in spirit, impartial in attitude, sacrificial in conduct, and
philanthropic even to enemies. Since Chu Chih-hsin recognized the excellent teaching of Jesus, his accusation was
blind and his statement illogical. In Chang I-ching's view,
the weakest area in Chu's critique was the lack of historical support. Chang then continued to establish the
existence of Jesus and the development of the Christian
movement by referring to the records of Josephus and Pliny
the Younger. Josephus discussed the life of Jesus including
his judgment before the court, the crucifixion, the resurrection, and the growth of the Early Church. Pliny's document described how the Christian believers spread to cities
and villages and refused to worship the Roman Emperor. As
they met, they honored Christ as God. (39)

The significance of Chu's scandal against the character
of Jesus could hardly be exaggerated. Its popularity and
theological distortion had given the Chinese Church a diffi-

cult time to rebuild the people's confidence in the historical founder of the Christian religion. While the Church was seeking to advocate "salvation of the nation through character," Chu's criticism shook the moral foundation upon which Christian character was to be established. From the standpoint of apologetics, Liang, Chien, and Chang had quite successfully dismantled Chu's antagonism. But to what extent their rational defense had repaired the bad impression outside the Church is a question hard to answer historically.

Supernatural Dimensions in Jesus' Life

Another line of opposition dealt with the supernatural elements in Jesus' life and ministry. Although Ch'en Tu-hsiu was impressed by the noble character of Jesus, his attitude turned from friendliness to animosity in a later essay entitled, "Christianity and the Christian Church". Here he took a two-pronged attack on the Christian beliefs and practices. (40)

Ch'en disowned the possibility of the supernatural in saying that the Virgin Birth, the miracles, and the resurrection of Jesus had little warrant from historical and scientific evidence. Jesus' moral doctrines of equity of love and self-sacrifice, previously held by Ch'en as praiseworthy, were not challenged regarding their practicality in a time of national crisis. He asked, how is one to define the object of love and sacrifice in face of imperialism and capitalism today? Ch'en's criticism could have reflected his Marxist thinking.

In Chang I-ching's response, he based his argument on Biblical records, extra-scriptural evidence, and testimonies of early Christians. (41) He distinguished between the scientific approach and the historical approach to investigate the reality of the past. And it was the latter method which would do justice to the examination of Jesus' life. What did happen in history had happened and was recorded in documents. (42) The historicity of the life of Jesus was supported in the words of Josephus:

When Pontius Pilate was the governor of the Jews, there was a man of wisdom named Jesus, who was known for his miracles and wondrous deeds purported to be performed for the people's sake. He was fond of teaching the people to do good, including mostly the Jews and the Gentiles. He was also called Christ. At that time Pilate mistook the counsel of prosecu-

tion by the Jewish leaders and crucified him to death.
But his disciples persisted in following him, unwilling to scatter themselves. After three days of
burial he came to life and appeared, according to
the words of the prophets. His wondrous works
were numerous and his disciples grew in number and
came to be called Christians. (43)

The birth of the Messiah was long before indicated by
Isaiah, and the fulfillment of the prophetic promise was
recorded in the Gospel of Matthew. In Chang I-ching's view,
the greatest miracle was the Incarnation of Christ. If this
was accepted as factual, it should be less difficult to
believe the miracles. The evidence of the empty tomb and
the physical appearance of Christ testified to the reality
of the resurrection. The theory that Jesus' body was stolen
was considered as inconsistent with the explicit record of
the Gospel of St. John and the Book of Acts. The swoon
theory that Jesus did not actually die on the Cross but just
fainted away was rebutted by Chang. For if Jesus did not
resurrect, his feeble bleeding body, even though he may
have crept outside the tomb, could have never been a source
of inspiration to his followers in the later propagation of
the Gospel. (44) It would be physiologically impossible,
were there no resurrection, for Jesus to have left the tomb
and appeared to his followers. It was also psychologically
unbelievable that his disciples, having witnessed the
crucifixion and burial of their master, came to deceive the
crowd by preaching a resurrected Christ. How could Saul of
Tarsus, a persecutor of the Early Church, be converted into
a preacher of the Truth if he had not actually confronted
the Christ of Easter?

From a theologically conservative background, Chang I-
ching sought to establish the divinity of Christ by appealing to a literal interpretation of Scripture. His writings
reflected a sensitivity to the Modernist-Fundamentalist
debate in the West over the supernatural possibility in the
Bible. Most conservative writers and evangelical missionaries would regard divinity as categorically different from
humanity. They maintained the traditional Western theology
that both natures were united in the person of Jesus Christ.

Christian intellectuals of liberal leaning took a different position. Few explicitly admitted that Jesus was
divine in the traditional sense but rather held that he was
the most perfect expression of God. Many scholars of the
Life Fellowship *(Sheng-ming she)* and of Yenching University

were of this viewpoint. To them it was the humanity of
Christ to which they gave theological priority.

Hu I-ku, (45) a leading Christian voice in the Y.M.C.A.,
respected the personality of Jesus as a renowned historical
figure described even in non-Christian literature. However,
Hu denied the Virgin Birth as unscientific. There was no
contemporary record of this event until the second century
when the divinity of Christ became an issue. (46) He pointed out the lack of evidence of the Virgin Birth in the
Gospel of Mark, in the words of Mary, and in the epistles
of Paul and Peter. In Hu's view, divinity and humanity are
not qualitatively different but consistent and harmonious.
"God" is the important element of "man", and the highest
achievement of man is "God".

Hu's theology attempted to domesticate the traditional
concept of God as the First Cause or the Absolute One into
the mundane ethical realm. Instead of seeking God in nature
as previous philosophers did, man now finds God in human
life. The summit of moral pursuit and human spirituality
is itself divinity. The question that concerned Hu was:
What kind of man was Jesus? Jesus was a full man, equal to
every human being. He reformed the Jewish religion and fulfilled the Law and the Prophets after reinterpreting them
in his own way. In him was noticed the profoundest awareness of the special mission of God, unmatched by and inscrutable to the common people. He was the supreme manifestation of divine love. These qualities earned him the
status of Godhead.

Much shaped by Confucian thought which presupposed a
humanistic starting point, Chao Tzu-ch'en had a similar view
of Jesus Christ. While traditional theology stressed the
dichotomy between humanity and divinity, Chao saw a continuity. The comprehension of man's own reality should precede
the apprehension of God's deity. And Jesus of history was a
perfect expression of humanity itself. Chao said,

It was not as God or the Son of God that Jesus
attracted me: rather He commanded my attention and
interest because He was a thoroughly human being.
... Consequently, when Jesus declared Himself to be
the Son of Man, whatever else that term may mean, I
was glad, because here I could have ground for assurance that what He taught was true, for He was human.
(47)

Chao parted company with many Western scholars who, he thought, had isolated the reality of God from the context of human relationships. William James' encounter with the divine in our exalted consciousness, Karl Barth's inaccessibility of God apart from revelation, Rudolf Otto's mystical experience, A. N. Whitehead's religious activity in solitariness -- all had made similar mistakes. (48) Consequently, many areas of social life had now been separated from religion: law and government, art and science, philosophy and politics. Christianity had thus lost its appeal to the modern mind. Chao's theological intention in featuring the humanity of Jesus and his inseparable life from the community was to restore the Christian religion from being "one of the many" spheres in life to being "the one in all" spheres. This undoubtedly helped formulate Chao's theological basis in his program of social reconstruction of national life. God was the "objective reality of our life" transcendent yet immanent in the entire universe. Jesus, the supreme revelation of the divine reality, saw God "in all men and in all things." (49) According to Chao, the Virgin Birth, the Incarnation, and other stories of nativity had the effect of obscuring the believers from perceiving the full humanity of Jesus, which was "the very stuff of divinity itself." (50)

In Hsü Pao-ch'ien's Christology, the uniqueness of Jesus lay in his moral and spiritual perfection. Jesus' life was sinless and sacrificial, dedicated to human service. His altruistic life style directly contributed to his tremendous influence on his contemporaries. His deep religious consciousness unfolded his close union with God. However, Hsü had little mention of the deity of Jesus. Hsü commented that, "If God means a being who is entirely different from me, or, in other words, if there is no divine element in me, then Jesus is not God to me." (51) The "divine element" in man must be developed by following the footsteps of Jesus to experience God and to serve man. In this manner, the promise of the Kingdom would be achieved in our midst. And thus, "man and God become more and more identical." (52) Hsü's "service motif" was conspicuous in his theology which was expounded in the light of the Incarnate Christ as a man for others.

Another articulate Christian scholar who gave a humanistic interpretation of Jesus was Wu Lei-ch'uan. Wu's reason for accepting Christianity was to learn how to be a man by imitating the example of Jesus. His concern for the regeneration of China through Christinaity led him to give priority to the social principles and involvements seen in Jesus' earthly pilgrimage. In Wu's view, Jesus' ministry developed

in two stages. Starting as a layman, Jesus found it difficult to achieve the purpose of the Jewish Messiah after two
years in Jerusalem and Galilee. He failed to obtain the approval of the leaders for His teaching and was often mis-
understood by the crowd. (53) Jesus then became aware of the
sinful world, and, in order to fulfill the commission of God,
he began to reform the society, not through inferior ways or
by compromising with the leaders, but by preaching the truth.
Therefore, Jesus' understanding of the mission did not come
from a priori revelation but through progressive interpretation of the circumstances. (54)

The theological focus on Christ's humanity, rather than
his divinity, and on the historical Jesus, rather than the
Son of God, was the crucial element of the new religion. In
defining divinity as a continuation of humanity, the distance
between God and man was reduced. By making divinity more
acceptable to man, a form of ethical motivation was imparted
to the Christian program of "national salvation through
character." In the age of science and reason, many apologists stopped to defend the supernatural aspect of Christ's
life and ministry, and others discarded that from their credo.
Only the Christians from conservative denominations who
stood for the infallibility and authority of Scripture
traditionally maintained a literal hermeneutics of the
supernatural account of Jesus life.

The Mission of Jesus

As expected, the earthly mission of Jesus could not have
escaped the notice of the anti-Christians. From the viewpoint of an educator, Wang Ching-wei, (55) then Chairman of
the Kwangtung Educational Association, took Christianity to
task. Incensed by an evangelistic poster in the First Public
Park in Canton, Wang wrote a short essay, trying to expose
the "three big errors" of Christianity. The poster had the
words: "Believers in Jesus will enjoy life in paradise; un-
believers will suffer in hell." (56)

Wang accused Christianity of being theologically narrow
and ideologically intolerant. The exclusive alternatives of
heaven and hell had no room for other religious faiths and
practices. The liberal Buddhism and the filial ancestral
worship were antagonized by the Christian way of redemption.
This was unacceptable to the Chinese tradition of religious
toleration. Why was Jesus the only way to God? The second
alleged error lay in the claim of Jesus as the true Son of
Heaven, the King of Peace in all nations. Such autocratic

rule was distasteful to China which was in the process of
modernization along democratic lines. (57)   In Wang's view,
the dogmatic theories of Christian mission were contrary to
the principles of education in modern society.

A similar criticism was launched by another writer who
used the pseudonym *Ling Ken* (the root of the spirit).   The
essay was named, "The Place of Jesus in Modern Time," intended perhaps to "counteract the spreading influence of the
custom of Christmas among educated people." (58)   In his
view, Jesus was no more than a religious reformer in ancient
history.   He was a deceived and deceiving individual whose
stupendous claim in his mission to be the Son of God was a
sign of his self-assertive authority over others.   Jesus'
philosophy of life was absolutistic, compelling obedience by
giving false promises to his followers.   His demand for sacrifice from others to himself, instead of to the welfare of
society, indicated his egocentric conceit.   The Christian
enterprise based upon the mission of such a person was a
form of intellectual suicide.   It was just "compulsory, mystical (and) illogical" religious policy.

Wang's "three big errors" were confronted by Chang I-
Ching, the apologist of the South.   He charged Wang with
being unfair to regard the little poster as representative
of the Christian faith or the Christian Church.   Wang's
personal grudge against Christianity was revealed in his
words, "If he asks me why I have written this essay, I will
ask him back why he has drawn up the poster". (59)

Concerning human destiny in relation to faith in Jesus,
Chang clarified the theology of heaven and hell.   These
names designate the eschatological state of existence, an
ultimate way of reward and punishment for human morality.
It is the impartial judgment of God which is inscrutable by
man.   No preacher or missionary can have the authority to
send people to heaven or hell.   And Jesus came not to con-
demn but to redeem sinners.   The poster should be seen as a
well-intended warning rather than a cause for scandal.
Jesus' salvation for mankind was founded on His love and
sacrifice.   Chang remarked: "Every person is the son of
God by creation and everyone should receive the salvation
of the designated Saviour.   So we have to preach the Gospel
without reservation.   If there is no preaching, there is no
love". (60)

In answering the charge of the monarchical disposition of
Jesus, Chang urged to separate Christianity from politics,

especially from current Chinese politics. The Jews had made the mistake of exalting Jesus to be the political Messiah in order to restore the Davidic Kingdom. The kingship of Jesus consisted in the spiritual reign of God in man's heart, a qualification for heavenly citizenship. Chang reversed Wang Ching-wei's criticism by asserting that Western democracy took root from the Christian concept of servanthood, as taught by Jesus in the Gospel of Matthew, "I come to serve not to be served, even to give my life as a ransom for many" (chapter 20).

The theology of heaven and hell in relation to the mission of Jesus was given a material interpretation by liberal Chinese Christians. Many considered it from the position of social utility. Jesus' mission offered a model for social transformation. The distinction between heaven and hell, instead of being two states of eternal existence, depended on the degree of such transformation. Their concern for social reform seemed to have consigned to oblivion, if not to non-existence, the theological interest in matters of the next world. To entertain the hope of life after death in paradise was just a "pleasing yet unrealizable dream". (61) Chang Ch'in-shih urged that the achievement of the Kingdom relied upon whether the individual and the community followed the sacrificial life style of Jesus. (62) In his comment of the Five Year Movement, Wu Yao-tsung, secretary of National Y.M.C.A., advocated the goal of the Kingdom as the ideal human society in which material inadequacy and social injustice were eliminated. The mission of the Church was to bring about such social existence. (63)

In Wu Lei-ch'uan's theology, the mission of Jesus for the Kingdom was expressed in three major principles: to do the work of God, to be of service to others, and to bear witness to the truth. (64) These practical dimensions constituted the philosophy of Jesus' ministry with which he taught and exhorted his contemporaries to participate in the work of the Kingdom. Without any trace of monarchical tyranny, Jesus, in Wu's view, admitted that there is the highest Lord in the entire universe, the Father of all mankind. This means that all men are brothers together enjoying the status of sonship. Even Jesus confessed that he was the Son of God. (65) As brothers in the family, we share the love of our Heavenly Father on the condition that we recognize Him and know to love Him. The perfection of Jesus' character was due to his profound knowledge of God and to his moral cultivation. Therefore he claimed that, "I am the way, and the truth, and the life; no one comes to the Father, but by me". (66)

The theology of the Fatherhood of God and Brotherhood of
men was espoused by a number of Chinese Christians, especially those educated in the West. They regarded this as
coming from the pure doctrine of Jesus Christ, who identified
himself with the whole human race without qualitative difference in his person from them. His moral excellence sur-
passed ours, not in kind but in degree. In this way, Jesus
was imitable and was to be imitated in his character and
mission.

The Relevance of Jesus' Teaching

Many Chinese Christians who defended religion for life
were seeking to establish Christianity as a religion of
relevance to the Chinese people. They viewed religion not
as one aspect of life, like science or art, but as the to-
tality of life. Their concern was to work out the Christian
solution for the national problems. On the one hand, they
spoke from their conviction that Christianity was the answer
to China's predicament in the 1920s. On the other hand,
they had burdened their religion with the responsibility of
providing the answer since they defined religion as embracing
all areas of life. The tension emerged between theological
conviction and existential application of the Christian
faith. Was Christianity really able to cope with the situation?

The quest for relevance was centered on the ethical
teaching of Christianity. Not many anti-Christians or non-
Christians had opposition to the ethics of Jesus. The doctrines of sacrifice, forgiveness, and love were welcomed by
many with enthusiasm. Ch'en Tu-hsiu considered them as the
"most precious elements in Christian teaching". Chou Tso-
jen, (67) famous essayist and advocate of religious liberty,
spoke highly of these qualities. "Love your enemy" and
"Pray for your persecutors" could be regarded as the source
of modern humanitarian thought. (68) And Ch'ien Hsüan-t'ung,
(69) professor at Peking University, looked upon Jesus as
one of the few greatest figures in history of a commendable
revolutionary spirit in transforming the Hebrew religion.
The Sermon on the Mount represented to him the central ethics
of the religion.

However, antagonism was directed to the practice of the
Christian Church in history and the practicality of Christian morality to the current situation in modern China.

The misdemeanors of the Christian Church in the past in-

vited a lot of virulent criticism from the anti-Christians.
Some called the history of Christianity a "history of
slaughter and bloodshed". Others remarked that the evils
committed by the Church were "heaped up like a mountain".
How could the lofty moral doctrines of Jesus Christ be reconciled with the enormity of Christian failures in history?

In an article, "Christianity and World Reform", a writer
by the name Ch'ih Kuang (70) listed the historical blunders
of the Church in a strong communist language. The mission
of the crusades and the religious persecutions between the
Roman Catholics and the Protestants were the most ugly epi-
sodes. The suppression of scientific discoveries and the
murder of scientists in the so-called Christian nations
could hardly be justified. During the wars, the pastors, in
the name of the same God, prayed for success of their own
country and the defeat of their Christian enemy. How inconsistent were theories and practices in Christian circles?
(71) The hypocrisy of the "rice Christians" and the para-
sitic missionaries in China would hinder the reconstruction
of the national life. (72) Ch'ih Kuang commented that in
reforming the Chinese society Christianity must be abandoned.
It was a bondage to human thought in preaching theistic
dogmatism and was responsible for the cultural inactivities
of the Dark Ages before the European Renaissance. If
Christianity had committed so many mistakes in the past,
how could it be given any opportunity now?

Responding to these accusations, Chang I-ching tried to
present more accurate historical information. The problem
of the Crusades belonged to the Roman Catholic Papacy in
previous centuries. The Christian Church today should not
be held responsible for their failures. Ch'ang Nai-te (73)
urged that the anti-Christians should have a proper concept
of time, for it is unfair to hold the past against the
present. (74) As in the Boxer Uprising, a large number of
innocent foreigners were murdered. Now there are no more
cases of manslaughter by the Church or the Inquisition
court for suppressing heresies. Liang Chün-mo explained
that the evil of the religious wars was due to the destructive nature of human beings not yet tempered and disciplined
by the Christian religion. (75) The conflict between the
Roman Catholics and the Protestants came from the errors of
both, for they had abandoned Christ. Both the systems of
"religious state" and "state religion" were contrary to
Scripture.

According to Chang I-ching, it is important to distin-

guish the Christian belief from believer. The credibility
of the former should not be dependent upon the latter. The
hypocrisy of the pastors during religious wars among Christian nations must not impair the Christian faith that promotes the virtues of peace and love as exemplified in
Christ's life. In Ch'ang Nai-te's observation, such distinction would have saved a lot of unnecessary and unsound
rebuke by the anti-Christians. The blunders of a few should
not be ascribed to the whole Christian Church. For if a few
can represent the majority, why do not the anti-Christians
mention the good works of the Christians in hospitals and
schools? It is prejudice to take notice of evil things only
while neglecting the good. (76) The intellectual unproduc-
tivity in the Middle Ages was largely due to the misunderstanding of the Christian duties to society and culture. (77)

Another major line of opposition dealt with the modern
relevance of the Christian religion. T'u Hsiao-shih in his
lecture on the problem of religion argued that it is unten-
able to use history to defend religious belief. (78) In
history, there is no unalterable theory or absolute exemplary
morality. Historical religions only pertain to a particular
age. Religious truth is only temporal and relative, rather
than eternal and ultimate. Among higher religions, their
doctrines are established on the experience and character of
their founders, such as Jesus Christ, Buddha, and Mohammed.
Their words and works became final criteria for their followers in subsequent generations. Nevertheless, these religious
figures were historically unique. And they could not dictate
a behavior pattern without ruining the freedom of personality
and the right of individual expression. In T'u's view, truth
consists in the upward progress in life, not conformity of
subjective experience to an objective static model. The
individual's character and activity are one aspect of the
whole historical process. He is a subject of history itself.
How can Christians in the modern age be followers of a historical person who happened to walk the streets of Jerusalem?
Religion was a product of the primitive time, an obsolete
exercise for the twentieth century man.

Like T'u, Ch'ien Hsüan-t'ung pointed out the relativity
of morality and emphasized the importance of its applica-
bility. (79) Even Jesus was a man of the past with imperfect
knowledge. His morality must be subjected to the test of
utility to our society. Modern man should formulate their
own principles for ethical decisions. The possibility of
immutable moral normatives is precluded as life and society
are constantly changing.

These charges were directly or indirectly dealt with when the Christian leaders sought to apply Christianity to the current national problems. What was the identity of China in the midst of external aggression by foreign nations, internal corruption by the warlords, and the disunity between North and South? How to save the nation in this social and political turmoil?

Regeneration of China through Christianity was the belief of many Chinese Christians. But, in what way? Many affirmed that it was through the cultivation of Christian character that China was to be saved. This belief came from the conviction that Christianity was the most vibrant, lively, and flexible religion that could adapt itself to the modern culture. Christianity was believed to be a religion of life that would rehumanize the mechanical and depersonalized society. Some secular scholars seemed to endorse this possibility. Once Ch'en Tu-hsiu encouraged the Chinese to "knock directly on Jesus' door, asking to be united with his noble, supreme character and fervent, genuine emotion". (80) And Chou Tso-jen regarded Christianity as suitable for "the making of a new heart" among the Chinese people. (81) In Chien Yu-wen's comment, the Christian character imitative of Jesus consists in "loyalty, sincerity, kindness, righteousness, altruism, sacrifice, humility, purity, cooperativeness, unity, responsibility, faithfulness, persistence, hopefulness, striving to the point of death for the country and truth". (82) These qualities do not come from man's effort but from the life of God. The life power promised by Christianity is none other than the life of Jesus Christ, whose character gives us ethical normatives to follow and whose spirit fills us with a moral dynamic to act accordingly.

In conjunction with character formation, Christian leaders pointed out the urgency of a spiritual revival. The moral bankruptcy that went widespread in the country had caused them to emphasize this necessity. They realized that the problem of China today was the problem of the people. And regeneration of the people must precede the reconstruction of society. Chao Tzu-ch'en believed that, "The heart of the problem of reconstruction, beyond any doubt, is the creation of a new spirit in man". (83) In his view, Jesus of history has come to an end, but Christ in spirit is everlasting and constantly available to all. In Chang Ch'in-shih's comment, the possibility of moral reform depends on the development of the good element in man to enable him to lead a productive life for the community. (84)

The emphasis of national reconstruction did not only come
from the social dimension of Jesus' doctrine but also from
the traditional concern. In Chinese thought, heaven above
and society below are in strong relationship. The invisible
Tao of Heaven is believed to be expressed in the context of
human affairs. Among the intellectuals there is not much
interest in religious matters which are other-worldly in
outlook. Christian involvement in social reform is to be
seen as an attempt to make Christianity visible to the
Chinese world. The reality of the spiritual Christ has to
be expressed in concrete, tangible actions in order to gain
the attention of the agnostic and pragmatic Chinese.

Chinese Christians understood that the program of national
reconstruction was primarily a cultural process that involved
all levels of society. Regarding the magnitude of the
problem and the gravity of resistant forces, their expectation was marked by a cautious optimism. Cold metaphysics
and futuristic theology should be avoided. Individualistic
spirituality could only result in various forms of escapism
from the actual world. Indigenous theology must go beyond
the conceptual level. (85) It seemed that an applicable
Christian message in the twenties was inseparable from an
effective participation in the national task. And to the
Chinese Christians this task was a Christo-centric effort
in which divine activity and human responsibility cooperated.

A THEOLOGICAL ASSESSMENT

As we have seen, the construction of a Christo-centric
apologetics in the 1920s was due to the interplay of two
factors. The external stimulus of the intellectual and
social circumstances had forced the Chinese Church to think
of a viable solution to the pressing problems of the time.
The internal dynamic of the Christian faith, as expressed
in the life and works of Jesus Christ, confirmed the conviction of a relevant Christianity.

This apologetics served several purposes. The identification of Christianity with Jesus Christ was a theological
retreat to the minimum essential of the Christian religion.
It offered a direct and concise message for the large,
unevangelized population. Western credalism and ritualism
had to some extent clouded the Gospel, and imported denominationalism gave it a confusing presentation. Theological
differences had accompanied the missionaries in coming to
China and created disagreement in the Church. Conscious of
these difficulties, Chinese Christians were zealous to pre-

serve the purity of the Gospel by returning to the message
of the Early Church. In the significant effort to coordinate
various church bodies to establish the Church of Christ in
China, the doctrinal principle of integration was Christ.
According to this principle, the need to simplify and the
will to cooperate were strongly felt. (86)

During the early years of the 1920s, the Western controversy between the Modernists and the Fundamentalists had
already reached China's shore. Conservative missionaries
organized the Bible Union of China to combat liberal theology and to uphold the literal interpretation of Scripture.
D. E. Hoste, Director of China Inland Mission and representative of theological conservatism, declared his reason for
joining the Bible Union: "It is my conviction that the
Modernist movement, as a whole, is a departure from the
Christian faith as revealed in the Bible". (87) Some
Chinese leaders saw this as "an attempt on the part of those
missionaries to repeat the sad experience of the churches
in the West. It is nothing short of suicide". (88)

Apart from the two opposing parties with their Chinese
followers, there was a third group of "sympathizers" who
were more concerned with practical issues of church life than
technicalities in theology. The imported battle from the
West was regarded as a serious hindrance to the progress of
the Christian movement in China. They believed that a
common platform could be worked out between the Conservatives
and Modernists by resorting to the centrality of Christ.
As Chao Tzu-ch'en said, "The realization of Christ in life
is the first and last aim we have. Both the Social Gospel
and the Individual Gospel culminate in this point". (89)
The embarrassment of the situation was well expressed in
these words:

> The fact is that, in view of the complexity of
> the Christian work in China today, the missionaries
> are even more needed than before. The only con-
> dition is that we need more missionaries of the
> right type. We need men who will present them-
> selves on a united front, not as 'fundamentalists'
> and 'modernists'. In other words, we do not want
> men whose minds are merely engaged with the for-
> mulating of eternal dogmas or the promoting of
> theological controversies. (90)

To preach Jesus Christ was a protective as well as uni-
tive theology of the day. It would defend the Christian

religion from the anti-Christian campaigns launched against
the historical blunders of the Church and the undesirable
behaviors of the Christians by separating the Christian
belief from believers. The life of Jesus was conceived as
the model of social service and object of moral imitation.
This reinforced the ethical emphasis of the social dimension
of Christianity and came to terms with the practical side of
Chinese thought.

Significant to the formulation of indigenous theology was
the conviction that Christ was the universal principle of
divinity at work in every culture. As Ch'eng Ching-yi, (91)
General Secretary of the National Christian Council of China,
said:

> The essential nature of the Christian religion
> is the same in China as anywhere else. Our Chinese
> people need to return to God through Jesus Christ,
> as do the people of all other nations. The central
> message of the Christian religion, which is that
> humanity needs Christ, is the same yesterday, today
> and forever. (92)

Chao Tzu-ch'en's "Christ consciousness", Wu Lei-ch'uan's
"imitation of Christ", and Chang I-ching's "historical Jesus"
sought to present the Christian faith which operates in
individuals and society, in history and culture. Chinese
Christian leaders believed that Christianity understood in
this Christo-centric manner would have a real message for
China in her present crisis and that, in turn, they could
make definite contribution to the understanding of the
Christian faith from their cultural experience.

The return to the Gospel of Jesus seemed to be the best
ideological device to dewesternize the Christian message
brought by the missionaries. To remove the cultural baggage
of the West which had been loaded on the historical Jesus
for centuries was the first step toward indigenization.
After this 'decoding', the ensuing step was to 'encode' it
in the Chinese culture. This process of deculturalizing and
reculturalizing was the basic theological presupposition in
the various patterns of indigenization by the Chinese
Christians.

3

Indigenization of the Christian Faith

The problem of indigenization (1) is intrinsic to the task of evangelism. When the missionary attempts to communicate the Gospel of Christ to his audience, a process of indigenization begins which involves the psychology, the language, and the culture of both parties. The Western missionary is brought up in a culture which has been for many years closely associated with Christianity and whose content and expression are alien to the non-Christian country. His very presence in the mission field, his life style and values are often identified, rightly or wrongly, with the religion he advocates. This inevitably imparts to the Christian message a foreignness that easily becomes a source of irritation to the local people. If the dislike for foreignness is to be regarded as constitutive of human nature, such dislike is easily recognizable among the Chinese people.

The necessity of indigenization was long ago felt by the Jesuit missionaries to China. In their effort of preaching Christianity, they were sensitive to the Chinese ethnocentrism and were culturally conciliatory in their approach. (2) They put on a Chinese appearance in their activities and mingled with the Confucian intelligentsia. Using Western scientific knowledge to establish the Chinese confidence in their message, they sought to accommodate their religion to the local civilization. Over the delicate issues which later provoked the Rites Controversy, the Jesuits took a

moderate position, respecting the traditional practice of
the Chinese. (3) How successful was the Jesuit mission is a
question outside our discussion, but it is undeniable that
they had won the hearing and admiration of the Chinese
literati.

The 1920s were a unique period in the history of Chinese
Christianity when there were a host of experiments to indigenize the Christian faith. A series of significant events
happened in this decade that gave momentum to the indigenous
church movement.

Since the controversy over the problem of religion in the
Young China Association, Christianity began to gain the
attention of the educated Chinese. Anti-Christian activities
from 1922 onward made Christianity both popular and notorious. Ch'eng Ching-yi described the situation in these
words:

> At one time Christianity was largely disregarded
> by the more intelligent people of China. Their
> indifference constituted a real obstacle to the
> spread of the Christian faith among the common
> people. Today the situation is changed. Christi-
> anity is both more appreciated and more condemned
> than ever before; it is becoming the best liked
> and best hated religion in China. Many of China's
> most intelligent sons and daughters have declared
> their allegiance to Christ, while on the other
> hand many of her best minds are doing their utmost
> to oust the religion of Christ from China's shore.
> (4)

After the suppression of the Boxer Uprising, the government and the people held a certain respect for Western
missionaries. The Chinese Church enjoyed a brief period of
growth, and its membership registered a rapid, unsurpassed
increase. (5) Although Western ideologies became popular,
the majority of Chinese intellectuals were still indifferent
or hostile toward the foreign religion. The Christian message had little appeal to the humanistic and practical mind
of the Chinese. (6) However, during the era of the anti-
Christian movement, their opposition to Christianity, from
whatever motive or background, required them to study the
religion, its doctrines and organization. Most Chinese
Christians regarded this as more helpful to the propagation
of the Christian faith than the previous negative detachment. Some took the opposition as an opportunity of

purifying the Church of its undesirable elements and re-
pairing its internal failures. The anti-Christian activities
served as catalyst to the Chinese Christians to rethink the
Christian faith and its suitability in contemporary China.
(7) The National Christian Conference held in May 1922 was
a good expression of theological reflection.

The National Christian Conference was a milestone in the
development of the Chinese Church. (8) About half of the
total 1185 participants were Chinese, the highest representation of local churches in all national conferences organized in the past fifty years. (9) The theme of the Conference was none other than "The Chinese Church". The Chinese
Church had long suffered from the stigma of being a foreign
institution and from the chaos of denominationalism. The
recent theological conflict between the modernists and the
fundamentalists in the West had its Chinese counterpart.
The keynote that struck in the National Christian Conference
was a prophetic echo of the time--the desperate need for
unity and cooperativeness in establishing an indigenous
church. The ideal of a "coordinated and cooperative Church"
was upheld in the whole Conference and set the direction for
the future ministry.

In its theological aspect, the outstanding opinion of the
Conference was, "Christian belief must be so expressed as to
reveal more clearly and keep open the road to common expression of Christian unity". (10) Both the interpretation of
the Christian faith and the administration of church life
were regarded as indigenous responsibilities. As Liu T'ing-
fang said, "the rapidly changing conditions of the country
all demand an indigenous church which will present an indigenous Christianity, a Christianity which does not sever the
continuity with the historical churches but at the same time
takes cognizance of the spiritual inheritance of the Chinese
race". (11) Amidst political and social instabilities of
the time, the Conference could be seen as a joint Christian
manifesto to the world that the Chinese Church helped, rather
than hindered, the achievement of national progress and reconstruction. As Frank Rawlinson put it, the "greatest
Christian apologetic is the Chinese Church of 1922". (12)
Could this apologetics stand the stormy wave of nationalism
in the twenties?

The decade of anti-Christian movement was marked by the
pervasive consciousness of national solidarity. During the
era of the May Fourth Movement, this consciousness built up
its intensity among the Chinese intellectuals and expressed

itself in concrete political actions. They were united in
spirit by the common goal to save the nation although their
involvements in practical politics were different. (13) But
they were disappointed internally by warlordism and government bureaucracy and externally by the imperialism of foreign
countries.

The year 1924 saw the founding of the Great Anti-Imperialism Federation with its avowed aims: to repudiate all unequal treaties and to join with other oppressed nations of
the world in opposing imperialism. Subsequent to this, a
number of patriotic groups joined themselves to form the
Association of Nationalistic Organizations, publicly declaring their goal to defend the rights, economy, and culture of
the nation against any form of foreign transgression. (14)
A most unfortunate event that marked the summit of the upsurge of nationalism was the May Thirtieth slaughter at
Shanghai in 1925. (15) The whole nation was caught in the
heat of anti-imperialistic sentiment.

Where did the Chinese Church stand in such traumatic
times? Nationalism was the supportive force behind the anti-
Christian hostilities. Its great impact on the Church was
seen in the restoration of educational rights by the government. The Christian Church was accused of usurping the
educational authority of the government and of forsaking the
cultural heritage by the religious curriculum. All these
expressions of nationalism had driven the Chinese Christians
to evaluate the relevance of Christianity to the national
life and had given impetus to the task of indigenization.

The Gospel comes through the missionary to the Chinese in
their own culture. The Chinese recipient should bear the
responsibility of interpreting the message. The missionary
cannot do it for him, for he is culturally different. Nor
should the missionary force his own understanding of the
Gospel to the local recipient, knowing that his theology is
mixed with Western elements. The foreignness of Christian
theology in China is due to its Western framework and expression. Western theologies owe a good deal to the philosophy of Aristotle and Plato for their structure and logic.
Later secular thinkers, such as Kant, Hegel, and Leibniz,
have tremendously influenced the Christian faith. The Chinese
are a product of their own world, and Christianity should
come to them through their thought and language pattern. A
number of contemporary Chinese Christians saw the need to
shake off the theological as well as the economical dependence on the West. As Ch'eng Ching-yi mentioned in the

opening address of the National Christian Council, the most serious aspect of the problem was "not the dependence of the Chinese Church upon the liberality of Christians in other lands. Its dependence upon the thoughts, ideas, institutions and methods of work of others is even more serious". (16)

The Gospel does not negate all of culture as God is working, directly or indirectly, in every civilization. Each civilization has its own right to exist. However, many missionaries, consciously or unconsciously, preached a culture of the West instead of the Gospel of Christ. (17) The Gospel is to be appreciated in a definite social setting and personal experience but not as a foreign theory imposed from outside. Indigenous theology is theology developed in a definite context and in dialogue with the problems that come from it. The search for relevance of Christianity to contemporary issues is a basic force that sustained the indigenous enterprise of the Chinese Christians in the 1920s.

A most representative effort was the formation of the Peking Apologetic Group with its chief organ, the *Shengming yüeh-k'an*. With the conviction that the principles of Christianity are "all inclusive and eternal", they sought to employ modern science and philosophy to express the Christian message. Moreover, emphasis on the universal characteristic of Christianity was to be accompanied by its particular application in historical situations. As the Statement of the Peking Apologetic Group said, "The development and the spread of Christianity cannot be the same in all countries and under all circumstances. Consequently, the people of China must have a special explanation of the Christian religion". (18) The Asian Church should decide the priority and emphasis of its theology which might not be relevant to the Western Church. The dominant problem of the Chinese Church in the twenties was not the infallibility of Scripture but the salvation of the nation.

The majority of the church people did not trouble themselves with the problem of indigenization. Many already felt comfortable with the denominational life style in the church. Others accepted what the missionaries taught them as signs of social prestige and traditional value. Chinese Christians of more liberal theological persuasion were more sensitive to the urgency of the task. Some of them organized the *Chung-hua Chi-tu-chiao Wen She*, a leading literary effort that dealt with national problems from a Christian perspective. The *Wen-she yüeh-k'an* was devoted to these

purposes: 1.) to reform contemporary life and develop new
life in the future; 2.) to present a new Jesus to the
generation; 3.) to express truth for its own sake; and 4.)
to advocate an indigenous church. (19) This magazine made
no small contribution to creating an indigenous Christian
faith.

Indigenous church movement was the central issue facing
the Chinese Church in the 1920s due to the combination of
these various forces. The attention of this chapter is to
examine the ideological aspect of the movement. What was
an indigenous Gospel?

ATTITUDES TOWARD TRADITIONAL CULTURE
IN THE MAY FOURTH ERA

The problem of indigenization must be seen in the broader
context of cultural relations between East and West. Before
we examine the various patterns of indigenous theology, it
is helpful to know the contemporary climate of ideas regarding the Chinese culture.

Christianity was only one among other things brought to
China since the nineteenth century. As merchants, diplomats,
and missionaries were seeking to fulfill their respective
ambitions in the age-old country, they felt the cultural
reaction from the Chinese people in one way or another. The
introduction of Western ideas through literature and the
return of Chinese students from overseas contributed to a
process of cultural confrontation and assimilation. What
were the representative positions in the cultural debate
during the May Fourth era?

As Ch'en Tu-hsiu pointed out in a provocative article in
Hsin Ch'ing-nien, a major difference in the development of
the Chinese and the Western society lies in the way of
thinking, which decides the pattern of social behavior and
the outlook of values. The Chinese traditional way of thinking, Ch'en argued, is inferior to that of the West and obsolete for a modern nation. (20)

Confucian ideology and practice were under attack in the
early years of republican China. Ch'en was a leading figure
among the iconoclasts against tradition. The Confucian
ethics was regarded by him as a product of traditional
feudalism which was incompatible with a democratic society.
The system of filial piety which had controlled the lives
of the people perpetuated the autocratic politics. To Ch'en

the only hope to modernize China was to introduce Mr. Science
and Mr. Democracy to the nation. (21) The renewal of the
country was dependent on how far the people could adopt the
Western way.

A most prestigious proponent of "total modernization" was
Hu Shih. In his view, the position that Oriental culture is
spiritual and Western culture material is only a means of
saving the face of a declining civilization. For "modern
Western civilization is not at all a material civilization.
Rather, it is idealistic and spiritual". (22) The difference
between Eastern and Western culture is like that between
rickshaw and motorcar, separated miles apart in the path
toward modernization. Hu admitted that Chinese culture has
its unique qualities, but uniqueness is not necessarily a
virture. The Chinese are inferior to the Westerner not only
in science and politics but also in ethics and arts. "Go
West" characterised Hu's cultural outlook. (23)

As Hu commented, "The most outstanding characteristic of
the Oriental civilization is complacency; that of the modern civilization is dissatisfaction". (24) The ambition of
the Western people largely explains the success of their
civilization in combating the evil of poverty and illiteracy
and in improving the material condition of life. He was
confident that the scientification and democratization of
China in the future was certain. (25)

On the other side, there were scholars who defended the
Confucian culture and who held a relatively low view of the
West. Their slogan was, "Go East". Liang Sou-ming expressed
his expectation that the future of the world culture would be
a renaissance of the Chinese culture. To Liang, Western
culture is well illumined by the "dazzling lights" of science
and democracy which are based on reason and utility. These
two premises, however, give rise to a culture which is pre-
occupied with material achievements and troubled by a spiritual exhaustion. Life in the West is now threatened by de-
humanization. (26)

In his philosophical work, *Tung Hsi wen-hua chi ch'i che-
hsüeh*, Liang analyzed the progress of world civilizations
into three successive phases, with the intention of explaining the essential differences between the West and the East.
Western civilization is in the first stage of the cultural
movement, characterised by its aggressive, forward-looking
attitude toward life. Chinese civilization belongs to the

second phase, having a passive view and seeking to accommodate to the immediate environment instead of struggling
against it. The final stage is found in Indian culture with
the attitude of retreat from conflict and frustration and of
denial of their existences. (27) In Liang's view, the
success of Western culture is due to its adaptation to life
problems, and the present failures of Chinese and Indian
culture are due, not to their intrinsic weaknesses, but to
their being not suited to their times. However, the West
has moved in the first course to its end and has suffered
from its social and economic crises. It should turn to the
Chinese path for cultural remedy. (28) Liang disagreed
about the possibility of cultural synthesis because of the
essential disparities between the East and the West. The
Confucian way of life will gain ascendency, and China is
therefore ahead of the West.

A neo-traditionalist of a different emphasis was Liang
Ch'i-ch'ao. His effort in the contemporary debate was to
assert the place of Chinese culture in which he was nurtured.
This largely accounted for his devotion to the study of
Chinese History in the 1920s, seeking to evaluate the past
and to preserve what was of enduring values. (29)

After his return from his postwar visit to Europe, Liang
gave a pessimistic description of the decline of Western
civilization. (30) In his comment, instead of improving the
qualities of life, scientific advancement had contributed
to the disaster of the recent war. Material science, as
Liang continued, has usurped the place of human spirit in
the formation of values in life. (31)

To this Western crisis, Liang claimed that Confucian
China might come to help. He wanted to purge the ancient
heritage of its distortions and outdated forms of life in
order that the better portion of the Confucian culture
could be preserved. However, a true appreciation of the
Chinese culture would also require the methods of Western
scholarship. Liang's belief in the partnership of scholarship was guided by his vision of a "new culture", synthesizing the best in both the West and the East. He called
upon the Chinese youths to undertake the urgent task of
cultural cooperation:

> Our beloved youth! Stand firm. March forth.
> Across the ocean there are thousands of people
> suffering from the bankruptcy of their material
> civilization and crying desperately for help.
> They are waiting for you to deliver them! (32)

Another middle roader who was concerned with cultural assimilation was Ts'ai Yüan-p'ei. Ts'ai's combined educational backgrounds of both East and West seemed to have prepared him for such a job. In his view, the European renaissance had its Chinese counterpart which had just begun. The introduction of Western science and philosophy made possible the renovative experience in China. (33)

Ts'ai saw culture as a flexible, synthetic force ready to undergo interaction with its environment. Cultural absorption and exchange through continual contact in modern societies were an educational necessity. In Ts'ai's promotion of a "world education", he believed that both East and West were able to make their contribution. No cultural frontier should be set up as if culture were vulnerable. Intellectual openness must be exercised by modern China to welcome Western ideology and technology with discernment and to evaluate the national tradition with objectivity. The essence of the Chinese cultural inheritance should be subject to the test of scientific inquiry. In admitting that China had to learn from Western colleagues, Ts'ai seemed to be more concerned with universal values and creativity than with the preservation of Chinese national dignity. (34)

We have examined the range of ideas, in cross-section and not in chronological sequence. By the 1920s, this full spectrum of attitudes toward Chinese and Western cultural values was being vigorously debated in China. It is against this background that the concerns with theology developed.

TOWARD THE MAKING OF AN
INDIGENOUS THEOLOGY

The formation of Chinese Christianity is a task that involves two kinds of loyalty in the mind of the Chinese Christian. As Chinese, he wants to be faithful to his cultural tradition; as Christian, he has to present his religious message without diminution. Indigenization of the Christian faith can be regarded as an intellectual movement between the two loyalties. Some contemporary Christian scholars felt the conflict between Chinese traditional values and the Christian ethos. Their indigenous effort became a competition of commitments. Others were at home with both, confessing that Christianity and Confucianism are different names of the same truth. Most Chinese Christians stayed in between these two positions, sympathetic with the ethnic culture and critical in relating Christianity to it. A

recurrent question should be kept in mind when the patterns
of indigenization are examined: Is the effort meant to
render Christianity more acceptable to the Chinese or to
preserve the Chinese cultural values?

What was the identity of Chinese culture in the 1920s?
Chao Tzu-ch'en has a handsome definition of the amorphous
term 'culture' which may serve our subsequent discussion.
Chao said:

   The culture of a people is the result of long
   periods of experience, thought, and discipline.
   It is the sum of ideas, attitudes, and habits
   acquired and continuously active in relation to
   their social self-consciousness, sharpest in outline at the top and gradually settling into a
   mist at the bottom, where the mass of the unedu-
   cated depend upon their cultured leaders for
   articulation. (35)

Chao made the distinction between culture (*wen-hua*) and
civilization (*wen-ming*). Culture is spiritual; civilization
is material. The former is substance; the latter is application. In Chao's view, civilization presupposes culture
and is the expression of it. (36)

Similarly, Wei Cho-min (37) remarked, "Civilization is
the accumulated sum total of the achievements of a people up
to a given time in their dealing with the physical environment and in trying to live together in a community; and
culture is the spirit of that civilization embodied in human
personalities". (38) The majority of Christian intellectuals
did not make such distinction and employed both terms inter-
changeably.

Contemporary Chinese Christians took Confucianism as the
mainstream of Chinese culture. The school of Lao Tzu and
Mo Tzu were regarded as side currents. Buddhism and Taoism,
though they may have been quite popular in the religious
experience among the mass, did not gain as much intellectual
attention among the students as Confucianism. (39) Most
indigenous literature of the period presupposed Confucian
tradition as the cultural entity to be related to Christianity.

During the current debate on cultural relations between
East and West, most Chinese Christians took a middle position
such as Ts'ai Yüan-p'ei's or Liang Ch'i-ch'ao's. They did

not "go East" because Christianity came from the West and
claimed their allegiance. They could not "go West" because
the upsurge of nationalism in the era of the anti-Christian
movements stigmatized Christianity as foreign. A main line
of apologetics was to assert that Christianity was not denationalizing. Yet, to them, nationalism posed an ideological dilemma. On the one hand, nationalism was "somehow
linked with the disintegration of Chinese civilization". (40)
On the other hand, the Chinese Christians had to witness to
the hostile intellectual world that Christianity does not
betray the culture of the country. The attempts at indigenization were influenced, consciously or unconsciously, by
the dilemma. A viable solution seemed to be a sympathetic
criticism of the Chinese culture with a calculated accommodation of the Christian faith. Many Christian intellectuals
adopted this path toward indigeneity although their stations
on the journey were different.

What, then, is indigenization? Amidst the vast Christian
literature of the decade, we can construct a general con-
sensus of opinions offered by the representative figures
in the indigenous church movement. Indigenization is not a
retreat to the ancient culture (*fu-ku*), imitating traditional
customs and practices. Nor is it reluctance to cooperate
with the West, following a form of anti-foreignism. Also it
is wrong to conceive of indigeneity as the abandonment of
the rich Christian experience of the past and the establishment of a new Christianity by merely fusing it with the
Chinese culture, which would become, as one contemporary
Christian scholar said, neither a horse nor a donkey. (41)
Christianity is to be expressed in a cultural setting, but
it does not depend upon a culture for its existence. (42)

Positively speaking, indigenization, in Ch'eng Ching-yi's
view, is "to render Christianity suitable to the needs of
the Chinese and to accommodate it to the customs, environment, history, and thinking of the Chinese culture". (43)
Local people should be responsible for all aspects of the
church ministry--financial, ministerial, and intellectual--
yet without neglecting to learn from the Western churches.
Chao Tzu-ch'en defined the indigenous church as "one which
conserves and unifies all truths contained in the Christian
religion and in China's ancient civilization and which thus
manifests and expresses the religious life and experiences
of the Chinese Christians in a fashion that is native and
natural to them". (44) Similarly, Liu T'ing-fang commented,

As the Chinese Christians have received the
imported gift, they themselves need to extract the
fundamental elements from the synthetic and mingled
product, so that, in the guidance of God, these will
be freshly combined with the history and experience
of our nation to become a Chinese indigenous Christian faith of our own. The same should be said about
the documents, ceremonies, rituals, and organization
of the church. (45)

Indigenous Christianity must be a local growth, subsequent
to the transplant of the Western religion, that absorbs the
nourishment of Chinese culture and is suited to the spirit
and psychology of the Chinese people. (46) From the several
definitions, it is easy to perceive the urgency and importance of the indigenous task. Few would doubt the necessity
of the indigenous movement. The question is not why to indigenize, but how. (47)

Presence of Classical Precedents

Proponents of this pattern of indigenization had intimate
knowledge of the Confucian tradition. Their love for it and
confidence in it did not flag although Confucianism was
under attack in the May Fourth Movement. Even their pro-
fessed allegiance to Christianity did not weaken their
emotional and intellectual tie to the ancient tradition.
Instead, Christianity offered them opportunity to defend its
value in the time of adversity. They sought to maintain the
double loyalties, though it sometimes was hard to tell which
was higher, without betraying any conflict between them. If
there were areas of tension, they either ignored their existence or explained them away. Their conviction was that the
Chinese heritage was good and deserved our continued respect
in the modern age. Its values had to be preserved not
because they were Chinese but because they were universally
true. They saw Christianity not as the ultimate and absolute religion to substitute for the time-honored deposit of
cultural excellences but as a collaborator for mutual service. Christianity and Chinese culture would enrich each
other. Christianity was interpreted from the standpoint of
Chinese culture, seeking elements from the Christian doctrines that would agree to certain classical precepts.

A key representative of this pattern was Wu Lei-ch'uan of
Yenching University. Wu came from a strong Confucian back-
ground and was well-versed in the knowledge of the Four
Books and Five Classics. He earned the traditional degrees

of *hsiu-ts'ai, chü-jen,* and *chin-shih,* and became a member of
the Hanlin Academy. (48) He made numerous efforts to create
an indigenous thought in the 1920s and 1930s until his most
systematic work, *Chi-tu-chiao yü Chung-kuo wen-hua (Christianity and Chinese Culture)* came out in 1936.

To Wu Lei-ch'uan, indigenization of Christianity was
necessary to its development in China. In *Chen-li chou-k'an,*
a magazine dedicated to this purpose, Wu said,

> In the propagation of any popular religion from
> one place to another (popular religion can also be
> regarded as world religion that has no racial or
> national boundary), if it does not go through a
> process of mutual absorption and accommodation with
> the local culture, it cannot progress and develop.
> It is like a transplant. If the soil and climate
> of the new environment are not suitable, even though
> it can temporarily be nourished through artificial
> means, the growth of its seed will not prosper for
> a long time or will even change its original nature.
> (49)

Furthermore, he commented,
> We acknowledge that Christianity will reconstruct
> China. First, it requires a thorough knowledge of
> the Chinese academic tradition and an assimilation
> with it. Then, the establishment of the indigenous
> church will be closely related to the needs of the
> time. Therefore, our *chou-k'an* (weekly) hopes that
> in the future, apart from the exposition of the
> Christian faith, we will, from the Christian per-
> spective, critically study Chinese literature,
> ritualism, and customs in order to prepare the
> way for the indigenous church. (50)

The theological presupposition of Wu's indigenization lay
in the identity of the sources of truth. Truth is one and
its expressions are many. In Wu's view, Christianity and
Confucianism are different expressions, due to their backgrounds and cultures, of the same truth, the *Tao.* Wu said,

> I believe that the truths of the Christian
> religion do not come in conflict with the truths
> of science and philosophy . . . I believe espe-
> cially that the source of Christianity and that
> of all other religions, even of all systems of
> thought, are one, and all religions and systems

of thought are not far different from each other
in the great fundamentals. In the good future
all the tributaries and the great river will run
together into the sea. (51)

Whether it is Christianity absorbing Confucianism or
Confucianism accommodating Christianity, the true *Tao* will
bear its fruit in China. With this belief, the uniqueness
and finality of Christianity had no place in Wu's system.
And his indigenous effort was governed by the intention of
establishing continuity between Christianity and Chinese
culture.

To Wu, the main line of Chinese culture is *Ju Chia*, which
embodies the doctrines of Confucius as inherited largely
through the traditions of Mencius and Hsün Tzu. But after
centuries, the *Tao* has been obscured and distorted in both
Confucianism and the Christian Church. The way to restore
its true expression is to expound it anew. Wu's approach
was to go back to early figures and examine their original
doctrines. He was not surprised at all to find that many
basic Christian concepts already had their classical counter-
parts in the teaching of the Chinese sages. (52) And the
Chinese should welcome Christianity as a like-minded friend,
instead of as an ideological foreigner, who would vindicate
the worth of its culture.

In Wu's mind, there is no conflict between the Christian
and the Confucian concept of God. In Christianity, *Shang-ti*
is the highest Lord of heaven, the only cosmic reality
operating in the universe. *Shang-ti* is also the heavenly
Father of all mankinds who are united in one brotherhood,
sharing a kind of family love. The term 'Shang-ti' is mentioned in *Shih Ching (Book of Odes)* and *Shu Ching (Book of
History)*, apart from 'T'ien'. But in the sayings and writings of Confucius, Mencius, and Hsü Tzu, *T'ien* is mostly
used. According to Wu, during the time of the Spring and
Autumn Era (ca. 722-481 B.C.), Chinese intellectuals altered
their idea of deity and the personified *Shang-ti* ceased to
be used. In accommodating to the understanding of the
people, the sages adopted a contemporary term to express the
idea of God who had will and reason as well as power in
nature. (53)

In discussing the primitive state of creation, Wu drew
the analogy between Genesis chapter two and the *Chung Yung*.
In a symbolic language, Wu continued, God is described as
breathing life into the nostril of man (Gen. 2:7). *Chung*

Yung 1:1 shows the same event but in a more inclusive way: "The heavenly decree is called nature, . . ." Following the interpretation of Chu Tzu, the famous neo-Confucian scholar in the twelfth century, Wu regarded the entire creation as having sprung from the activity of *Yin Yang Wu Hsing* (i.e., the bimodal cosmic force of *Yin* and *Yang* plus the "Five Agents" of the cosmic dynamism). Will and reason were imparted according to the heavenly decree. In the human realm, 'nature' designates the gift of rationality and morality. Wu argued that the story of creation in Genesis was present in the ancient Chinese literature. (54)

Isaiah's prophecy of the Messiah in the Old Testament (Isa. 11:1-10) was identified by Wu with the expectation of the coming saint as seen in the *Chung Yung* (chapter 31). The Holy One was to arise and rule the nations in peace and to manifest an example of perfect virtues. In Wu's view, both accounts were written in the hour of crisis when political unrest provoked the people to look for a savior to rectify the situation. Thus, Tzu Ssu, author of this chapter in the *Chung Yung*, and Isaiah shared the same thought, even their styles of expression were similar. To the Israelites, Isaiah was a prophetic voice; to the Chinese, Tzu Ssu was an optimistic theoretician. Their difference in outlook was due to their social and political circumstances.

According to Wu, Jesus' messianic self-consciousness was not absent among the great sages of the Chinese past. It was a common feature in history that many significant individuals possessed and expressed such consciousness. Jesus regarded himself as doing the will of God and witnessing to the truth (John 18:37; 5:17). In Wu's interpretation, Mencius also said of himself:

> In five hundred years a kingly figure must arise and in such period some renowned individuals will appear. . . . Unless Heaven does not desire to rule *t'ien-hsia* in peace; if it wants such rule in this time, who else beside me is to make it? (55)

Jen, the central doctrine in Confucianism was, in Wu's argument, equivalent to the Holy Spirit. When Confucian scholars referred to *jen*, a dimension of spirituality was present. We should pray in order to receive *jen*, and when *jen* is applied, it will prevail over the nation. (56) Confucius once told his disciple, "To discipline oneself to conform to *li* (propriety) is *jen*. When this discipline

becomes a daily exercise, heaven and earth will be ruled by
Jen". (57) This is the same with the work of the Holy Spirit
in relation to the kingdom of God (Matthew 12:28). When
people are submitted to the guidance of the Holy Spirit, the
peaceful reign is not far. As Wu said, "*Jen* is in the heart
of men. If *Jen* does not exist in human society, the world
cannot stand. Therefore, it is said, 'The Kingdom of God is
in your heart'". (58)

It is wrong to regard Wu's program as merely an effort to
fuse Confucian and Christian concepts together, as if a third
amalgam would emerge, or to seek modern relevance for certain
ancient teachings. Wu acknowledged the value of Confucian
culture and its meaning for China. But Wu's primary concern
was not conformity to the Chinese past but to transform the
present. Social reform, as Wu declared, is a universal
principle for human life, a goal which Jesus followed closely
in his ministry. This is the way to bring in the kingdom of
God which demands unreserved sacrifice and service. The
same ideal is found in the Confucian program from self-
cultivation to the rule of the nation, until the great harmony (*ta-t'ung*) is achieved in *t'ien-hsia*. (59) Wu's progressive and evolutionary ethos in correlating Christianity
with Chinese culture is unmistakable. The nation must be
reconstructed, and the society likewise reformed. Wu Lei-
ch'uan's indigenization is forward-looking, instead of
dwelling in the Confucian past, in order to create a new
China from its political and social ruins. Jesus offered
the best example and principle of such reform in human history. And the Confucian sages gave their classical sanction
for the enterprise.

Harmonization of Cultures

A second approach to indigenizing the Christian faith
emphasized the possibility of harmonizing it with Chinese
culture. Harmonization did not mean a passive attitude
toward the weakness in traditional China. Nor was it compromise, surrendering the cultural characteristics in order
to come to terms with another ideology. (60)

In the understanding of Wang Chih-hsin, (61) culture is
a world property which is not to be monopolized by any one
nation, though it may be expressed in it. Culture itself is
subject to constant changes and exchanges. History is full
of examples of cultural absorption and assimilation. Western civilization emerged from the contact between the Greco-
Roman and the Hebrew cultures. Neo-Confucianism in the Sung

and Ming dynasties was the integrated product of Confucianism and Buddhism. In Wang's view, Christianity is a universal culture into which Western and Eastern cultures can
be synthesized. The possibility of such harmonization has
the scriptural warrant in Jesus words: "I have other sheep,
that are not of this fold; I must bring them also, and they
will heed my voice. So There shall be one flock, one shepherd". (John 10:16). Wang considered China as a sheep outside the fold to be gathered to the Good Shepherd in the
future. His indigenous effort was directed by the vision of
a universal Christian culture, a vision tempered by nationalistic flavour. And Christianity offered a rallying point
for cultural unity among different civilizations in the
world.

To Wang Chih-hsin, an indigenous church must be established on the "characteristics and inheritance of the Chinese
people". And indigenous message must be suited to the ethos
and psychology of the Chinese. (62) In discussing the conditions for producing an indigenous literature, Wang pointed
out that such literature should come from the assimilation
of Chinese thought and "be baptized in the ethical tradition".

Wang took Confucius as the representative of Chinese
thought, and attempted to find cultural kinship between
Christian and Confucian teaching. The common point in both
systems which can serve the purpose of harmonization is the
emphasis of *t'iao-ho* , the closest meaning of which is the
middle way or harmonious amalgamation. Wang seems to have
been inspired by Liang Sou-ming in recognizing that the
spirit of the Chinese people is characterized by *t'iao-ho*.
He dissented from the view that Western civilization is
material and that Eastern civilization is spiritual. Confucian doctrines express a smooth combination of both dimensions. For example, equal emphasis is given to learning
which is external and material and to thinking which is internal and spiritual. (63) To be a *chün-tzu* or "superior
person" in the Confucian tradition, one's thought should be
trained in scholarship and one's conduct disciplined in propriety. According to Wang, Christianity expresses the same
unity in the activities of the soul and body. Jesus prayed
to God in the mountains and ministered to the sick in the
villages. He taught Nicodemus and the Samaritan woman the
highest spiritual doctrine and distributed bread and fish to
feed the audience.

Confucian thought, Wang continued, contains both conservative and progressive elements, as seen in the life of
Confucius himself. A non-competitive attitude is perceived
in his contentment with the state of poverty. Yet the
Master also travelled from nation to nation, seeking to be
employed by contemporary rulers. For "if we miss the middle
way, we may go to the extreme of either over-aggressiveness
or total inactivity". (64) Similarly, Jesus taught his
followers that they were in the world but not of the world.
They should not withdraw from the sinful world but should
seek to save the people from sins. They were told to involve themselves in the world without being contaminated by
it. The ethos of the middle way penetrates the teaching of
both systems and provides a viable point of cultural harmonization.

In Wang's view, Chinese culture is ethical in orientation,
and its ethical structure is established on filial piety.
As the *Hsiao Ching* (i.e., *Classic of Filial Piety*) says,
"*hsiao* begins with service to parents and ends with the
cultivation of self". (65) *Hsiao* fills all aspects of life:
"For it is no longer *hsiao*, if one does not conduct oneself
properly, if one is not loyal to the king, if one has no
respect for officials, if one is not faithful to friends,
and if one lacks bravery in battle". (66) Wang even admitted that from a religious perspective, *hsiao* is the Chinese
religion with the parents playing the role of God.

In Wang's argument, Christianity, if properly understood,
is not against the doctrine of *hsiao*. He urged that, "We
have to understand the difference in cultural backgrounds.
In Jewish culture, religion is the center; so God is the
first premise. In Chinese culture, ethics is the center; so
parents come first. The Jews look upon God as Father; the
Chinese regard parents as God. The meaning is the same". (67)
In this way, harmony is achieved by showing our love for God
through loving our parents. Even Jesus did not allow people
to usurp the portion due to their parents by pretending that
it was to be offered to God (Mark 7:11). Therefore, there
should be no conflict between Jesus' ethics and the Confucian *hsiao*.

In discussing the doctrine of *jen* and *yi*, Wang was not
hesitant in searching for Christian analogy. He took *jen*
as equal to love-for-others and *yi* as love-for-self, which
is discussed in First Corinthians 13. (68) Mencius rejected
Mo Tzu's all-embracing love as the extreme of *jen* and Yang
Chu's self-centered interest as the extreme of *yi*. (69)

The harmony between *jen* and *yi* is clearly seen in Mencius' synthesis in teaching a love with gradation and discernment. In Christianity, the balance of love and truth is embodied in the words of Jesus: "Give to those who ask of you" and "Cast no pearl before the swine". (70)

Another leader in cultural harmonization was Fan Tzu-mei, (71) editor of the magazine *Ch'ing-nien chin-pu*. Fan's confidence in indigenization came from his belief that since Christianity was originally an Eastern religion, its oriental qualities should have favorable response from the Chinese culture. Fan, like Wang, was aware of the difference between Christianity and the religious experience of the Chinese people. In his analysis of the God-idea in Chinese tradition, Fan showed that the religious outlook of the Chinese will not easily accept the Christian concept of deity. The Chinese naturalistic view of God will reject the Christian emphasis of divine personality. Their humanism will not accommodate the mythical aspect of the Christian worship. And their polytheistic background is not congenial to Christian monotheism. (72)

Fan's indigenous program was to explore the possibilities of harmony between the pristine form of Christianity and the undistorted doctrine of the Confucian orthodoxy. (73) In this manner, the best of both could be compared.

The Christian religion and the Chinese tradition are, in Fan's view, cultures of the "weak". (73) Both exalt virtues above power and peace above violence. The history of the Chinese people is full of examples in which barbaric invaders were assimilated to the Chinese society by the "force" of her urbane culture. The Confucian teaching of *jen, yi, chung,* and *shu* lay the foundation of the peace-loving political outlook of the Chinese. Jesus' life was a similar expression of such "weak" qualities which finally overcame the "strong". During the national crisis of the time, Fan advocated the cooperation of the two peace-oriented cultures to save the world from mutual hostility and exploitation. (75)

Fan considered Confucianism as the orthodox representation of Chinese culture which is ethical in basis. Although the religious dimension of the cultural heritage have conflict with Christian monotheism, in the ethical sphere there is much agreement over the doctrine of love and service, despite the difference in expression. Confucianism teaches *chung, shu, hsiao,* and *ti*; Christianity

promotes the brotherhood of men and the Kingdom of God. And
the Christian doctrines, Fan claimed, will render the meaning of Confucian morality more "simple and intimate". (76)
Chinese ethics is humanistic in framework, and, in a deduc-
tive manner, it extends family love to friends and then to
things. Christian ethics is theistic in structure, and, in
an inclusive way, it embraces men and nature. (77) The
teaching of the brotherhood of men stems from the fatherhood of God. In the practice of love and service, little
difference is observable between the two systems. But the
metaphysical emphasis in Christianity helps clarify the
ethical obligation in human relationship. To Fan, Confucianism is more a moral philosophy than a religion, without denying the existence of God. (78)

Fan frankly admitted the cultural degeneration in Confucian tradition that called for immediate renewal. However, he was optimistic about the future of Chinese culture
because he believed in the cyclic process of human history,
a view he held entertaining a sense of determinism. The
present cultural decline in China would soon be followed by
its renovation to which Christianity could contribute. As
Fan said, Christianity would introduce "an enthusiastic
spirit that would restore to new life the ethical doctrines
which are going to wither and freeze after two thousand
years". (79)

Advocates of cultural harmonization like Wang and Fan
cannot entirely conceal their cultural predilection. In
seeking to assimilate Confucian theories and Christianity,
they are eager to show that the ancient Chinese concepts
really have something genuinely positive to be synthesized.
They cling to the best of orthodox Confucianism as a protection for the survival of the tradition. Their effort of
cultural harmonization seems to look for, in the teaching
of Jesus, Christian support for the selected portions of
Confucian thought. Thus, Christianity and Chinese culture
are not equal partners in the program. Such inequality
gives rise to their concern for the preservation of Chinese
culture with the aid of Christianity. Their indigenization
is also their attempt to maintain simultaneously the double
loyalties --to Christianity and to China. In this way, they
can profess themselves Chinese Christians.

To Fulfill, Not to Destroy

Many contemporary Christian intellectuals in the Chinese Church held a third position in viewing the relationship between Chinese culture and the Christian faith. In the example of Jesus that was before them, he came not to abrogate the Law and the Prophets but to fulfill them. They believed that Christianity would improve the traditional culture and thereby enrich it. They were willing to admit similarity, but not identity as Wu Lei-ch'uan did, between Christian doctrines and Chinese classical concepts. It did not mean that their love for the ethnic culture was less or that they wanted to adopt the path of total westernization. (80) They were interested in preserving Chinese civilization, but they went beyond seeking for points of cultural contacts. They saw the inadequacy of Chinese culture not so much because of the current anti-Confucian iconoclasm as because of having a higher theological conviction. Their confidence in indigenization was well expressed in the words of Wei Cho-min:

> Christianity has nothing to fear in her contacts with the Eastern cultures, but has everything to gain from them. Truth will triumph. We shall find much that is congenial in the Chinese culture for the presentation of the Christian message. A new emphasis of our religion may thus be brought into prominence to supplement Western Christianity and to enrich the Christian heritage by bringing into it the cultural heritage of China, which may mean the Christianization of that culture by purging from it whatever elements and features are not compatible with Christianity. In this way there may arise a Chinese theology. . . . (81)

Several premises were accepted in this way of indigenization. First, they believed that God has not left himself without witness to his activity in the Chinese society. As Ch'eng Ching-yi remarked, "By the grace of God China has been preserved for thousands of years, and her spiritual heritage has certainly played a very great part in this preservation. In seeking to utilize this God-given heritage, Christianity may itself become not a little enriched without losing in the least any part of its distinctive value". (82) Thus, Chinese culture is simultaneously the work of God and of man. Glimpses of divine revelation are perceptible in the teaching of the Chinese sages. The attitude of superiority among missionaries of the previous generation

was now replaced by that of humility. As Ch'eng continued to
say, "Christian people are beginning to see more clearly that
God has more ways than one to work in human hearts and that
the marks of his guidance in events can be traced in all
countries. This new emphasis has made Christians more willing to learn from others". (83) However, Wei Cho-min cau-
tioned against a religious eclecticism in which there was
overeagerness to search for values in other cultural faiths
that Christianity did not have. (84)

Secondly, cultural assimilation was an inevitable process.
In the high tide of nationalism many Chinese took to defend
the integrity of Chinese culture by regarding the Western
presence as culturally aggressive. But this group of Christian intellectuals were optimistic about the future of the
ethnic culture. (85) They saw culture as organic in nature,
capable of growth and modification when subjected to external
forces. Modern China was still in the making due to the
cultural synthesis she had undergone. Instead of suffering
from external threat to her national culture, China would be
enriched by Western ideology and technology. (86) They
entertained the hope of a cultural fusion between the East
and the West in which the fine components of each would be
selectively conserved. (87) "A middle course" had to be
found. (88)

Thirdly, they recognized the finality of Christianity in
one way or another. The centrality of Christ was the focus
of their Christian message. In comparing Christianity and
Confucianism, Chao Tzu-ch'en said, "The greatest contribution
that Christianity can make to Confucian culture is its experience of God as revealed in the Word Incarnate, Jesus,
the Christ". (89) And Hsieh Sung-kao (90) asserted, in his
lengthy discussion of the Confucian civilization, that the
"best religion is the Christian religion". (91) This position of Christ above Chinese culture differed from Wu Lei-
ch'uan's denial of the uniqueness of Christianity.

It was these theological convictions that motivated and
directed them to seek ways of presenting the Christian faith
to the Chinese mind. Wei Cho-min saw Christianity as constituted of two inseparable things: the Divine Life through
Jesus Christ and the human expression of it. (92) As Divine
Life, Christianity has never been indigenous in China. Yet,
there is no pure, unculturalized Christianity, for it must
be contained in a cultural context if it is to have any meaning at all. Wei believed in the ultimacy of the revealed
Truth in Jesus Christ, but the presentation of it is not final.

Therefore, there is a definite possibility for Chinese Chris-
tians to contribute to a fuller expression of the Absolute
Reality.   There is a mutual necessity in Wei's argument.
Culture needs Christianity for enlightenment; Christianity
requires cultures for a better interpretation.   This explains
Wei's interest in getting hold of the virtues in the non-
Christian religions and philosophies in China and incorpora-
ting them "into the heritage of the Ecumenical Church". (93)

A similar distinction between the nature and the expression of Christianity was made by Ch'eng Ching-yi.   To him,
the essence of Christianity remains unchanged, but "the
special form and development that organized Christianity
should take in different countries will vary with the civilization and conditions which prevail in each.   They will vary
even in the same country, owing to changing conditions". (94)
And Chao Tzu-ch'en also commented, "The religious life force
of Christianity can enter into Chinese culture to be its new
blood and life.   The spiritual heritage of Chinese culture
can contribute to Christianity by expressing itself as a
religious form of it.   When Christianity dismantles the
heavy Western bondage and clothes itself with a local expression, it will be understood and accepted by the Chinese
people". (95)

In what way could Christianity fulfill Chinese culture?
Why did Chinese culture need to be fulfilled?

Proponents of this pattern of indigenization were persistent in pointing out the humanistic basis of Chinese culture
which lacks adequate perspective to give a complete philosophy of life.   Man does not have enough data to explain
the human destiny.   This finiteness of man is coupled with
his sinfulness that neglects, if not obscures, the inner
light in human hearts.   The Chinese do not "possess a gloomy
sense of sin, as did the Hebrews of old". (96)   These limi-
tations in nature call for the work of divine grace which
does not destroy but perfects nature.

With such theological belief these Chinese intellectuals
sympathetically and critically examined their cultural inheritance.   Very often their sympathy outweighed their criticism.   They looked for areas where the Chinese sages and
Christianity could meet and pointed them to the way of
greater truth.   As Wei Cho-min said, "This method will
awaken in them through Christian experience of God's grace
the consciousness that 'in Christ are hid all the treasures

of wisdom and knowledge'. These treasures do not contradict
the best in their own traditional moral and religious teaching but surpass it by fulfilling it". . . (97)

In his analytical essay, entitled "Chi-tu-chiao yü Chung-
kuo wen-hua", Chao Tzu-ch'en listed several tendencies in
Chinese culture. Chinese thinkers, Chao said, value the
harmony between man and nature. When nature maintains internal and external equilibrium, life will prosper. (98)
The whole universe is permeated by the activity of *Tao* "as
the creative and ethical urge working towards the realization of its purpose both in nature and in human nature". (99)
The Confucian doctrine does not teach the conquest of nature
but seeks to understand its ways. (100) The Chinese mind
seldom goes beyond nature itself but stays constantly within
the sphere of human affairs. The practical emphasis of the
Chinese partially accounts for the weakness of their metaphysics and the vagueness of their religious dimension.
This psychological disposition, Chao remarked, should cau-
tion against any speculative presentation of the Christian
faith. Similarly, according to Wei Cho-min, attention
should be given to the description of God's act in history
and God's relation to men rather than to his abstract attributes. Wei said, "for this reason we may expect the theological development of Christianity in China to be along
the historical and moral rather than the speculative line".
(101) Thus, Jesus of Nazareth as the supreme expression of
the Divine Life will offer an excellent point of departure
for indigenous Christian thought.

The Chinese idea of God, whether expressed as *Shang-ti* or
T'ien, is present in the *Shu Ching* and *Shih Ching*. (102)
And Hsieh Sung-kao indicated that the existence of God was
taken for granted in China's religious history. He thought
that the idea of God in Confucianism has a personal element,
even though it does not give us distinctly a personal deity.
The term 'Shang-ti', the supreme ruler, designates a person.
And the term 'T'ien', translated as 'Heaven', has personal
attributes though it sounds impersonal. Hsieh argued that
T'ien had been substituted for *Shang-ti* in Chou times (ca.
1100 B.C.) and thereafter, because in the teaching of the
Ch'un Ch'iu (The Spring and Autumn Annals), we have to avoid
"using personal names of men of honor, elders, and men of
virtue". (103) In Hsieh's critique,

The weakness in Confucianism, so far as the
idea of God is concerned, lies not in the use of
terms, but rather in China's lack of theologians
and religious prophets. According to my judgment,
the God recognized in Confucianism is personal,
but there has been no Jesus in China to reveal
God unmistakably and distinctly. (104)

However, in Tsu Yu-yue's (105) study, God is never described as having personal relationship with men or as reveal-
ing himself to human senses. It is an ambiguous concept, not
much discussed in Confucian thought. From an historical
perspective, Tsu said, "The God-idea of the Classics, instead
of being clarified, grew dim and vague in the atmosphere of
Confucianism, and finally, in the ambiguous term, *T'ien*, it
became no more than an impersonal moral principle or law of
the universe". (106)

Chao Tzu-ch'en argued in the same vein that in Confucian
tradition there is no explicit indication of the reality of
nature or the personality of God. The development of Confucianism after Han Dynasty ceased to impart significance
to a personal deity. (107) Since the Neo-Confucianism of
Sung Dynasty, *T'ien* has completely lost its personal qualities and is identified with the principle of Nature. "Chinese thinkers", Chao said, "on one hand, felt that the
origin of ethics was contained in heaven and earth; on the
other, they regarded heaven and earth as having no personality". (108) Whether it is the lack of personality or the
absence of prophecy to describe it, the traditional view of
deity has to be strengthened by the doctrine of personal
theism that Christianity presents.

Confucian ethics mainly deals with human relationships.
The cardinal doctrine of the system is *jen* which is expressed in *chung* (loyalty) and *shu* (reciprocity). In Chao
Tzu-ch'en's word, "To realize one's self and one's ideal
through unflagging effort is loyalty, while to be sympathetic, to be able to put one's self in the place of
another, doing to the other first as he expects to be done
to, is reciprocity". (109) And Hsieh commented, "To Confucius *Jen* was the philosopher's stone and therefore it was
everything, but no one term can represent the whole of *Jen*".
(110) The entire program of Confucian education is to cultivate *jen* in the students.

As *jen* is the substance of Chinese culture, *hsiao* is the basis of *jen*. And *hsiao*, in Chao's view, is "the virtue of cultivating the good of the past in one's present life". (111) However, the teaching of *hsiao* is for men, not for God; in the world, not beyond the world. The achievement of *jen* and the practice of *hsiao* are purely human exercises. Man's nature, due to its intrinsic goodness, is capable of self-improvement without calling for assistance from super-natural intervention. In Confucian theory, man requires no other god than himself in the realization of the true, the good, and the beautiful.

However, the inadequacy of Confucian morality lies in the overconfidence in human ability and the lack of a sound metaphysics to support the ethical structure. Christianity will enable the Chinese theory to establish its foundation, beyond the maintenance of the man-nature harmony, upon the religious experience of a God-man personal relationship. Hsieh criticized that Confucian ethics is, at best, a human-istic moralism, wanting the dimension of faith and hope to complete the emphasis of love. "The lack forever places Confucius as a mere moralist. Confucius' love was the love of man, not love of God. The highest point that Confucius reached was only a beginning in Christianity. Confucius was on the right road, but he did not live long enough to see its consummation". (112)

Wei Cho-min thought that from the background of the strong family tie, the Chinese will easily understand the Christian doctrine of the Fatherhood of God and the Brotherhood of men. The Chinese interest in the horizontal relationship will gain a vertical dimension which is qualitatively different. Thus, the Christian view will enrich the Chinese concept of family, which includes the living and the dead bound together through *hsiao*, by the extended idea of a universal family. (113) Traditional submission to, and respect for, parents will enable them to appreciate the obedience to God's will. The Chinese individual is now liberated from the bondage of the traditional family to a heavenly fatherhood and a world brotherhood which is the Confucian aspiration. As Chao Tzuch'en put it, "the depth and height of human brotherhood will not be reached without the religious homogeneity of a world God-consciousness that Christianity alone can give". (114)

The Christian theory of sin will be useful to the making of a Confucian *chün tzu* (or "superior person"). The attain-ment to the status of *chün tzu* requires more than the tra-ditional adherence to the moral code of behavior and the

constant practice of self-cultivation. In Chao's understanding, as man realizes his own fallibility and infirmity, he
will ask for divine forgiveness and acceptance. The prohibition of the law is to be removed by the pardon of grace.
Freedom replaces restriction in the formation of personal
character. The life of Jesus offers the religious possibility of reconciling man to God and the moral precedent to
imitate. (115)

These Christian critics were cautious in their comments
not to curtail the positive aspects of the Confucian system.
Rather "Confucianism may find Christianity its own source of
life, and Christianity may see in Confucianism its own agent
of truth". (116)

Cultural Dualism

Standing apart from the intellectual main current of indigenous theology was a most popular preacher at Peking,
Wang Ming-tao. (117) Wang established the Christian Tabernacle in the 1930s and attracted the largest crowd of Chinese believers in the vicinity. In a time of social disorder and political instability, most of the members of
Wang's church found psychological comfort and spiritual
renewal from his conservative message. From the *Spiritual
Food*, a quarterly magazine edited by Pastor Wang himself,
flowed a series of Christian writings which attempted to
combat the contemporary liberal Protestantism in China and
to offer practical solutions to problems of life.

Wang's indigenization of Christianity was governed by his
theology of history. In his view, the world and the Church
are two competing forces, different in both nature and institution, that move the wheel of history toward a definite
end. The world is controlled under satanic authority and
dwelled in by sinners who rebel against God in their immor-
ality and impiety. (118) Such a thoroughly corrupted social
order was beyond any possibility of redemption. For Wang
said,

Since the fall of Adam, the world has been in
continuous corruption. From the human perspective,
among the nations of the world some are civilized,
others are barbarous; some wealthy and powerful,
others poor and weak; some superior in virtue,
others inferior. But in God's sight, not one of
them is not filled with brutality and sin. God

does not want to repair the depraved world but has
predetermined to destroy the nations rebellious
against God and to build up a righteous and eternal
kingdom. (119)

Therefore, the transitoriness and corruption of the world
situation largely shaped his approach to relate his theology
to cultural problems. Wang was not concerned with the preservation or reformation of cultural values, for they would
inevitably pass away. Logically, Wang did not expect any
divine activity in culture or God would have to destroy his
own work in the last day. Yet, in introducing a Christianity detached from the wicked world, Wang was aware of
the impossibility of living out of contact with culture.
After all Jesus instructed his followers that they were in
the world but not of the world.

How did Wang resolve this dilemma? Wang's solution was
founded in his hope for the Church triumphant. The Christian Church, Wang continued, is the bride of Christ purged
with his blood of sacrifice, saved by his substitutionary
death, and united to him without blemish or wrinkle. (120)
To Wang, only the redemptive history of the people of God
matters. The Church is exalted far above the community of
lost sinners though living among them daily. His eccle-
siology is strongly eschatological in outlook and other-
worldly in emphasis.

The theological dualism is extended to the status of the
individuals before God. Sonship to God is exclusively
given to believers in the Church. Non-believers in the
world are only enemies of God. (121) The cultural contact
between these two antithetical groups is evangelistic
mission. Christians in the world should not be contaminated
by sin, but they should witness to the grace of salvation in
Jesus Christ. Wang's writing on the topic of evangelism was
characterized by a militant language in which God and Satan,
light and darkness, were in constant struggle behind the
human scene. Chinese culture in its long tradition is
therefore associated with the sinful activities of man. It
is not to be harmonized with, or fulfilled by, Christianity
but to be evangelized by it. Christ is exclusive for the
Church, as the groom is for the bride, whose function is the
mission of Jeremiah, calling the people to repent their sins
and to return to God. (122) Wang's theological order was
that only changed man could change the world. He took a low
view of the effort of social reconstruction by the liberal
wing of the Chinese Church. As he said,

The Gospel of Christ is not to reform all the
evil customs of society or the various undesirable
systems. Its function is to enable a person to be
regenerated through faith to become a new creature.
This newly created person will hate sinful things
but love the holy and the good things, resembling
the way of God. After a person has undergone this
thorough change inside, all external sins and evils
will be erased completely. When society has one
more truly reborn Christian, it has actually
increased by a virtuous member. The Gospel is not
for social reform, but society will benefit because
some one has believed the Gospel. (123)

Wang's Christian Tabernacle was a successful indigenous
group in the 1930s as far as self-support, self-government,
and self-propagation were concerned. But ideologically, the
anti-cultural bias in Wang negated any attempt at indigenous
thinking, or, it can be said, his indigenization was to
introduce Christianity as a way of life distinct from
culture. (124) His theological method was to collect proof-
texts from Scripture to bear on the issues. Priority was
given to the literal sense of the text, for he firmly believed that it is the inspired revelation of God. The
authority of the Bible depends upon the infallible inspiration. And such authority qualifies the Bible as the em-
bodiment of eternal truth, applicable in any place and at
any time. In his view, the Bible sees people in two separate categories: saints and sinners, holy and profane.
Sinfulness has no cultural distinction. Sinners, whether
American or Chinese, need the same Gospel for their salvation. In this manner, the universality of the Gospel has
little difficulty in relating to the particular Chinese
culture. The question of indigenization is dealt with by
returning to the plain sense of Scripture as the timeless
and timely word of God. For the Chinese Christians in our
third pattern of indigenization (*supra*, p. 69), this universality resolves the problem of indigenization. For Wang
Ming-tao, it dissolves the problem. (125)

Interpreters of Wang's thought may easily think of him as
promoting a Christian moralism beside an other-worldly message. (126) But this view has not taken Wang's doctrine of
regeneration seriously enough. It cannot be reconciled with
Wang's appreciation of divine grace in his conversion experience and in his view of justification by faith. (127)
Nor can this interpretation explain Wang's depreciation of
the social reform program by the liberal Chinese Christians.

Wang emphasizes the visibility of genuine Christian life as
a necessary and inevitable sign of rebirth, not prior to but
subsequent to it. To him, the kingdom of God is not man's
task, but God's gift. (128)

In Wang's theology, we see the constant dichotomy between faith and reason, the Church and the world, sons of
God and enemies of God, individual Gospel and social Gospel.
This cultural dualism has naturally led to a form of monas-
tic retreat from the world in turmoil and to a breeding of
self-righteousness in social relationship. The shortcoming
of his position is that Wang had an incomplete theology of
culture and was still living in the mentality of the nineteenth century missionary. (129) Although Wang may be
strong in his doctrine of salvation, he has largely neglected
the doctrine of creation which precedes the redemptive
schedule of God.

Christianity Judges Culture

Although theologically conservative like Wang Ming-tao,
Chang I-ching was more positive in his view of Chinese
culture and more comprehensive in his apologetic effort.
(130) Unlike the liberal Chinese Christians, Chang was
more critical than sympathetic in his examination of Chinese
tradition. (131) Instead of showing areas of similarities
between Christianity and Chinese culture, Chang was ready
to point out the differences and weaknesses of Confucian
thought. This emphasis characterizes another pattern of
indigenization.

In Chang's view, Christianity judges Chinese culture and
is able to convert it to the ultimate truth in Jesus Christ.
His conservative theology did not exclude cultural interest
as Wang Ming-tao tended to do. Wang's apologetics was an
application of Scriptural literalism. But Chang, having a
sound knowledge of Chinese history and literature, was able
to enter into a cultural debate with Confucian scholars from
a theological standpoint. He single-handedly established an
evangelical line of apologetics in the *Chen-kuang tsa-chih*,
with the ambition of transforming the traditional culture.

Chang was ready to admit the presence of God's activity
in Chinese civilization. The Lordship of Christ prevails
over both the creative and the redemptive dimensions. Equal

attention should be given to both in the formulation of an
indigenous theology. The coming of sin has not entirely
vitiated the cultural work of man and God, who still bestows
sunlight and rainfall to the human world. For example,
Chang acknowledged the existence of certain truth in the
Neo-Confucianism of Chu Tzu. In Chu Tzu's theory of the
universe, *Li* (principle) was there even before the formation
of the cosmic order. Behind the pluralistic universe, there
is the Supreme Ultimate *T'ai Chi*. Chang regarded this philosophical view as pointing to the *Tao* discussed in the Gospel of St. John 1: 1-3. (132)

However, the gravity of man's sin has, according to Chang,
deeply and widely affected his cultural activity. Even the
best of Chinese culture is not exempted from the tinge of
sinfulness. Man's receiving apparatus for truth has been
distorted and his vision obscured. The sages of the Chinese
past had only glimmers of light that were to be gathered to
the True Light in Jesus Christ. By no means could these
glimmers of truth achieve any redemptive possibility in
Chinese culture without the special revelation from God.

Chang adopted a sun-moon analogy to compare Jesus with
Confucius. (133) Jesus is the Sun whose light is intrinsic
and intense. Confucius is the moon whose light is a reflection of sunlight, having no illumination of its own. Wu
Lei-ch'uan looked upon Jesus and Confucius in the same human
category. Chao Tzu-ch'en regarded Jesus as a supreme man.
Chang argued that the difference between Jesus and the Chinese sages is that between God and man. Jesus' stupendous
claims, authoritative teachings, miraculous deeds, and ful-
fillments of prophecies—are unique evidence of his divinity,
incarnate in human form. Like other sages of China's past
desirous of knowing the *Tao* of heaven, Confucius sought
after it without the aid of special revelation from God.
This explains Confucius' agnostic reserve in commenting on
the religious and supernatural realm of reality. And this
Tao is none other than Jesus Christ. (134) If Confucius was
longing to see the *Tao*, his disciples should turn to Jesus
for the *Tao* of heaven. The limitation of the Confucian wisdom is obvious. At its best, it is humanistic rationality—
the glow at full moon. At its worst, it is subject to un-
warranted speculation—the eclipse of the moon.

To Chang, the world is not the pagan sphere to shun but
the mission field where the reforming power of the Gospel is
to be made manifest. Chang's apologetics is noted for its
evangelistic enthusiasm. He encouraged the Confucianists to

believe in Christianity without abandoning their Confucian
interest and respect. For Christian belief does not suppress
other religions, as elements of truth are not totally absent
in them. To transform Chinese culture by introducing it to
Jesus is like "leading the flower lovers to the sunlight"
(135) or replacing the moonglow by sunshine. Respect for
Confucius, Lao Tzu, and Buddha are acceptable if it does not
become religious worship. (136) However, unlike Wu Lei-
ch'uan, Chang was reluctant to admit the existence of precedents of Christian teaching among the ancient sages. Similarity cannot be taken as equivalence, for they are qualitatively different in their metaphysical structure. (137)
It is wrong to identify Jesus with Chinese Mo Tzu just because both of them seemed to teach altruistic love.

Chang's reluctance was due to the difference in epistemology. The Confucian way of knowing has its starting point
in man and nature, proceeding to discover the *Tao* in heaven
above. The Christian way begins with God in his act of self-
revelation to man below. (138) Man's blind search gives
rise to religious polytheism commonly found in the religious
experience of the Chinese. Chang showed that in the Confucian document *Li Chi (The Book of Rites)* different kinds of
gods are described as roaming on earth. (139) Such polytheistic outlook should be corrected with the monotheistic doctrine in Christianity.

Chang was impatient with the teaching in the *Chung Yung*
that when man asserts himself fully, he may achieve harmony
with heaven out of which all things in nature will prosper.
(140) In his view the order in the universe and the welfare
in nature are the providential activities of God in his creation. The cosmic regulation is totally beyond the control of
man. The humanistic emphasis in Confucianism is well expressed in Ch'en Kuan-chang's speech in advocating Confucianism as the state religion. Ch'en argued that "it is the
people who prosper the *Tao*, not the *Tao* to prosper the
people". (141) Chang reversed the basis of such idea by
arguing that human achievement is made possible by the work
of *Tao* which is the Logos operating in the life of man (Gospel of St. John 1:1-3). Reward and punishment are up to the
disposal of God. (142)

Regarding the national crisis, Chang's hope was dependent
on his theology of divine grace and judgment. It is improper
to argue that Western nations are strong because of Christianity or that China should adopt the Christian religion in
order to strengthen herself. Chang felt that the core of the

issue of national reconstruction lies in the transformation
of the individual and the community together, a transformation through the grace of God. The primary reason for be-
lieving in Christianity, in Chang's view, is to resolve the
problem of sin on both personal and national levels, no
matter whether the country is strong or weak. (143) For
human effort alone is never sufficient to turn egoism to
altruism, selfishness to sacrifice, and exploitation to
service. The promotion of good and the prohibition of evil
are human possibilities realized only through divine assistance. The kingdom of God is both a task of man and a gift
of God.

THEOLOGICAL COMMON GROUND

The question of indigenization is ambiguous as well as
complex. This chapter has attempted to deal with this "enduring problem" (144) in a period in the history of Chinese
Christianity. The nature of the problem itself defies a
final solution, for an indigenous theology is a task that
involves at least three aspects of intellectual effort: the
definition of Christianity, the identification of culture,
and the expression of the former in the latter. Each of
these presupposes a context which is conditioned by both
time and space.

In the missionary activities during the nineteenth century, the problem was largely tackled by preaching a Christianity which was characterized by a Western Christ against
Chinese culture. Since the late nineteenth century, due to
the ineffectiveness of the missionary approach and the growing appreciation of the Chinese tradition, the emphasis of
the Christian message consisted in a Western Christ of Chinese culture. (145) The emergence of the Christo-centric
apologetics in the Chinese Church in the 1920s, occasioned
by the challenge of the anti-Christian movement, sought to
present a Chinese Christ of the Chinese culture. They longed
to see that the Chinese Christ would save the nation in
crisis. The numerous intellectual experiments to indigenize
the Christian faith in the decade were like the blossoming of
a hundred flowers. The five patterns discussed above represent almost the entire spectrum of positions in indigenization. They could even be treated as working models which,
with appropriate modification, may illustrate the struggle
of the Chinese Church with the "enduring problem" in a later
period of Chinese Church history. (146)

At one extreme of the spectrum, there is Wu Lei-ch'uan, anxious to show that Christianity has its classical precedents in Chinese sages. In his view, Christianity has been concealed in Chinese culture, which Wu now explicitly acknowledged. Wu employed both for the political end of national reconstruction. Slightly less radical, Wang Chih-hsin and Fan Tzu-mei attempted to preserve the Chinese inheritance with the help of Christianity by searching for areas of doctrinal harmony in both systems. To the right of the cultural line, Wang Ming-tao exalted Christianity to the exclusion of Chinese culture. His cultural dualism presented to him an irreconcilable tension which he hardly recognized. Between Wu Lei-ch'uan and Wang Ming-tao, there was the mainstream of Chinese intellectuals whose positions varied according to their consent to the extent of God's work in China. Chao Tzu-ch'en emphasized that Christianity fulfills Chinese culture. Chang I-ching insisted on the transformation of Chinese culture through evangelism.

Among these patterns of indigenous thought, we can establish three premises of durable values. First, no culture is beyond the redemptive activity of God, which is the common basis of Christian hope of all five patterns. The current situation of the nation intensified this theological expectation among the Chinese Christians. Though totally pessimistic of the world, Wang Ming-tao's enthusiasm for evangelism expressed certain belief in cultural redeemability. Fan's cyclical renewal of Chinese culture and Wu's national reconstruction were more explicit of this conviction.

Secondly, no definition of Christianity is absolute, for culture itself is relative. Any claim to a full expression of the Christian faith is simply blind dogmatism. If such claim is not possible within a culture, the possibility is even less in cross-cultural evangelism. No pattern is completely sufficient to give an indigenous theology, for indigenization is an ongoing process in which the Christian Church fulfills its *Missio Dei* in God's world. Therefore, a full identification of traditional concepts with Christian doctrines will usurp the unique value of revelation in Jesus Christ. Here, Chang I-ching's distinction between common and special revelation would help Wu Lei-ch'uan to avoid the danger of cultural idolatry. And Wu had a hard time to answer the question: Why choose Christianity if the Chinese sages already have the truth? To some extent, both Wang Chih-hsin and Fan Tzu-mei had to face the same question in their program of cultural harmonization.

Thirdly, no culture is exempted from divine judgment although every culture has traces of God's activity. Chang was right to urge for cultural repentance of all nations. And Chao Tzu-ch'en's argument that Confucian sages were agents of truth is also well taken. Any cultural recognition of truth, good, and beauty assumes the existence of the absolute, which may not be visible in the ambiguity of life. And it is this absolute reality that judges all cultural decisions made in existential contexts.

We have now seen how Chinese Christians sought to present Christ to modern China when she was searching for her cultural identity. During the twenties nationalism was the chief stimulant to Chinese thinkers to examine the traditional heritage in the light of the Christian faith. It is natural to expect that the Chinese Church had much to say on the issue of nationalism itself.

4

Nationalism:
Impact of the
Anti-Christian Movement

Prior to the present century, China esteemed herself as the
Middle Kingdom, *Chung-kuo*, a world self-sufficient and self-
contained. In a keen sense of ethnocentrism China saw her
own civilization as orthodox and superior. She took little
interest in having commercial and cultural exchanges with
outsiders whom the Chinese despised as barbaric. However,
the image of cultural supremacy, as implicit in the title
Chung-kuo, was questioned in the mind of the Chinese intellectual in late nineteenth century. After China opened her
door to the West through the unequal treaties, there were
increasing contacts with foreign ideology and technology.
In the adversity of the Sino-foreign relationship and the
growing awareness of the country's internal weakness, the
challenge of Western alternatives to the Confucian tradition
became more strongly felt by the Chinese. They realized
that China could no longer hold the time-honored title of
Chung-Kuo. She was only one of the nations, a *Chung-kuo*
among many *kuo*. And *Chung-kuo* needed to be strengthened
through modernization. (1)

The first period of modernization took place around the
middle of the nineteenth century. This stage was generally
represented by the phrase: Chinese learning for substance
(*t'i*) and Western learning for application (*yung*). The
Chinese scholar-officials were impressed by the scientific
and military power of the Westerners. They thought that
China could be strengthened by imitating them in terms of
technological construction in the country. However, they
remained certain of the superiority of the spiritual values

of Chinese culture over those of the West. Reformer Chang
Chih-tung (1837-1909) championed this eclectic approach to
introduce Western technology to fortify the Confucian
structure.

The humiliating defeat of China in the Sino-Japanese War
in 1895 brought new realization to the Chinese. Merely
military and scientific equipments could not help China
stand against the aggressive foreigners. The previous *t'i-
yung* method of modernization was not adequate. Reconstruction of the country must be conducted on a deeper level in
both ideology and institution. Western models of government
and political theories were then introduced. And they were
getting popular through the translation of Yen Fu (1853-
1921) and Lin Shu (1852-1924). (2)

Unfortunately, the reform movement ushered by K'ang Yu-
wei and Liang Ch'i-ch'ao ended in the disaster of the *coup
d'etat* in 1898. Many Confucian conservatives, supported by
the Manchu government, attempted to resist the intrusion of
alien values into the traditional society. And the enthusiasm to protect the ancient heritage formed the basis of
many antiforeign outbreaks, instigated by the local gentry
and literati. The tragedy of the Boxer Uprising in 1900 was
the climactic manifestation of the long-incubated sentiment
of xenophobia. To the informed Chinese, it seemed that
nothing less than a radical change of the government system
could save China in the time of national agony. While re-
formers like K'ang Yu-wei searched for means of making a
transition to a constitutional monarchy, the radicals directed their energy to bring about revolution. The collapse
of the Manchu dynasty and the establishment of the Republic
in 1912 appeared to promise a new day for the nation.

But the Chinese were soon disillusioned by both internal
dissension and external invasion. The new government failed
to unite the country, and its existence was largely dependent on the whimsical intent of the powerful warlords.
Before the Republic could stand on its feet, in 1916 Yüan
Shih-kai restored the monarchy. That threatened to throw
the nation into chaos. In 1915, Japan, seeking to fulfill
her pan-Asian expansionist ambition, presented to China the
notorious Twenty-one Demands. Chinese intellectuals, caught
in the confusion of the time, had to face the urgent problem
of national salvation. The May Fourth Demonstration in 1919
fully expressed Chinese patriotism in response to the problem of the Shantung privilege at the Versailles Peace Conference. Entering the 1920s, China was exclusively engaged

in the task of redefining her identity in the modern world.
The anti-Christian movement that occurred in the decade has
to be viewed in the context of growing nationalism, a
nationalism whose form and content were in the process of
formation.

ANTI-CHRISTIAN ACTIVITIES
IN 1922 AND 1924

The outbreak of the anti-Christian movement in 1922 was
a reaction to the international meeting in April at Tsing
Hua University near Peking, sponsored by the World's Student
Christian Federation (WSCF). To prepare and publicize this
Conference several popular Christian magazines devoted
special issues to introduce the WSCF. The *Ch'ing-nien chin-
pu (Association Progress)*, published by the Chinese Young
Men's Christian Association, and the *Sheng-ming yüeh-k'an
(The Life Monthly)* of the Peking Apologetic Group cordially
welcomed this worldwide fellowship to take place in China.
(3) The organ of the WSCF, *The Student World*, had a January
issue containing articles written by Chinese Christians,
evaluative of the ministry of the Chinese Church and the
mission schools. All these propaganda immediately aroused
the response of the Shanghai students, apparently communist
in orientation, who organized the *Fei chi-tu-chiao hsüeh-
sheng t'ung-meng* (Anti-Christian Student Federation). On
March 9, 1922, they sent out a manifesto, flagrantly attacking the WSCF in strong Marxist-Leninist language. It began
with these words:

> We oppose the World's Student Christian Feder-
> ation because we decide to protect the welfare
> and happiness of humanity. We now wish to proclaim
> our real attitude so that the public may know it.
> We understand that Christianity and the Christian
> Church have created many evils and have committed
> many crimes. (4)

The next day a telegram was addressed to the students of
Tsing Hua University and the whole nation, protesting the
WSCF Conference to be held in a national college. It insisted on the independence of both politics and education from
religion. (5) At the same time, a booklet was distributed,
entitled "Why we oppose the World's Student Christian
Federation". (6)

The movement then spread to Peking and took the name *Fei tsung-chiao ta-t'ung-meng* (Great Anti-Religion Federation). A declaration came out on March 21 in the name of the Federation, condemning the evil of religion as worse than that of "floods and ferocious beasts". In human society, it said, "religion and mankind cannot exist together". (7) This declaration was signed by over seventy people among whom were leaders of various intellectual camps, all committed to opposing religion. The previous communist tone was totally absent. Their sole purpose seemed to oppose religion on the grounds of science and humanity.

As scheduled, the World's Student Christian Federation held its conference at Tsing Hua University from April 4-9, 1922. This meeting betokened a spiritual solidarity among Christian students of different nationalities since the conclusion of the First World War. Its significance was recognized by the reception given by President Hsü Shih-chang of the Republic and the Ex-President Li Yüan-hung. The commotion of the anti-Christians hardly made "a ripple within the Conference". (8) The delegates represented five races and thirty-two countries: 129 from outside and 635 from China. Both the Roman Catholic Church and the Greek Orthodox Church sent their delegates.

The theme of the Conference was "Christ and Reconstruction". As Dr. John R. Mott, a founder of the WSCF, said, the purpose of the Conference was "to demonstrate and emphasize the spiritual solidarity of Christians throughout the world and to show that the forces which brought the delegates together is greater than the dissipating forces now operating throughout the world". (9)

The two subjects most discussed and interesting were the relation of Christianity to capitalism and to war. The majority of delegates saw that capitalism bred social evils and had to be changed. Western churches were criticized for having acquiesced in the errors of such system. But the representatives disagreed whether or not capitalism could be Christianized. The question of war was debated in all its moral and religious complexity. The Conference was the first time that international Christians participated in studying the problem. In their resolution, they accepted the fundamental equality of all races and nations, and regarded it their duty "to fight the cause leading to war, and war itself, as a means of settling international disputes". (10) A. A. Paul, General Secretary of the Student Christian Association of India, Burma, and Ceylon commented, "We were under the

impression that western nations are bent on exploitation and
thus on war and are satisfied that there is no hope of getting rid of war. This Conference has given us the conviction that this is not so. Christians everywhere are suffering on account of this question. They loathe war. They are
struggling for a better way". (11)

On the last day of the WSCF Conference, the Great Anti-
Religion Federation gathered over a thousand students at
Peking University. Li Shih-tseng, professor of the University, criticized religion as useless in the modern world.
Ts'ai Yüan-p'ei's speech was read, condemning the failures
of religion and advocating the independence of education
from religion. (12)

Anti-Christian activities in South China was focused in
Canton and headed by Wang Ching-wei. In response to the
appeal of the Anti-Christian Student Federation and the
Great Anti-Religion Federation, Wang issued a telegram to
the Canton Educational Association, declaring his support
to "sweep the poison of religion out of Canton and make the
first contribution to the movement". (13) He held that the
Christian religion is nothing but bigotry and prejudice and
that its absurdities must be exposed. It will be a stumbling block to modern education and to national reconstruction. (14)

Despite all the clamor of the anti-Christians, the movement did not maintain its intensity. By the end of 1922,
the Great Anti-Religion Federation was in demise while the
Anti-Christian Student Federation continued its existence
in a passive way.

The anti-Christian movement was a student movement of
pre-calculated emotion. The instigators of the movement
capitalized on the nationalistic fervor of the students and
channelled it to form an anti-Christian force. The tactic
and strategy they employed resembled those of the May Fourth
Movement. All were aimed at condemning Christianity as denationalizing. Telegrams, proclamations, speeches and pamphlets were used to arouse emotion rather than to encourage
better understanding of the "Christian enemy" before taking
action. An important change of emphasis took place when
the movement came to Peking. The anti-capitalistic criticism by the Anti-Christian Student Federation became the
anti-scientific and anti-democratic argument of the Great
Anti-Religion Federation. The base was widened, and more
thought was given to their antagonism. The emotional inten-

sity began to show decline. Second thought sent the students to evaluate the validity and usefulness of all these
commotions. The movement then entered a conceptual stage
when more anti-Christians expressed their feeling in words.
As early as in July, Jacob G. Schurman, the American Minister in China, reported that the "movement no longer appears
to be interesting to the public". (15)

However, two years later we see the re-emergence of the
Anti-Christian Federation amidst political manoeuvres. In
the early twenties, the possibility of national salvation
was frustrated by the ambitions of the warlords. In the
north Li Yüan-hung became president again after the defeat,
in the summer of 1922, of Chang Tso-lin, the Feng-t'ien warlord. Yet, the presidency fell into the hands of Ts'ao
K'un after a year, and Ts'ao was later removed from his
position in the second Feng-t'ien-Chihli war in 1924. Tuan
Ch'i-jui returned in November to Peking as the Provisional
Chief Executive.

In the South, Sun Yat-sen was troubled by the insubordi-
nation of Ch'en Chiung-ming and the military governors. In
February 1923, the military government was re-established
at Canton, and Sun took the title of Grand Marshall. The
failure of the Paris Peace Conference to give a fair settlement of the Shantung problem and the lack of enforcement of
the Treaties at the Washington Conference (16) had impressed
Sun of the insincerity of the Western Powers. Sun's attention was turned to the Soviet's success in the Bolshevik
Revolution and her friendly offer in the abolition of the
unequal treaties. With the aid of Soviet advisors, the
Nationalist Party was reorganized, admitting the Chinese
communists as individual members. The policy of "alliance
with the Soviets, accommodation of the Communists" (Lien-O
yung-kung) was adapted in the First National Congress of the
Kuomintang held in Canton in January 1924. (17) The political objectives of the revitalized Kuomintang were to deal
with the foes of imperialism and warlordism in the country.
(18)

The Chinese Communist Party was formed in July 1921 under
the leadership of Ch'en Tu-hsiu in the south and Li Ta-chao
in the north (Nan-Ch'en pei-Li). The introduction of
Marxist socialism and Lenin's theory of imperialism was
appealing to the Chinese radicals who wanted to shake off
both the obsolete Chinese tradition and foreign domination.
Ch'en had confidence in the workers to take part in the role
of revolution. Li devoted himself to the mobilization of

peasantry. (19)   Despite the ideological differences between
Ch'en and Li regarding the implementation of Communist politics, their firm stand against imperialism and warlordism
became the common ground for temporary cooperation with the
Kuomintang, though not without the pressure from the Soviet
agents.   A situation was created in which a communist bloc
was inside the Nationalist Party.   And the influence of the
Communist was easily recognizable in Kuomintang's program to
combat imperialism. (20)

In Sun's effort to establish a new revolutionary army to
save the nation, the Whampao Military Academy was founded
and was given the responsibility of the political mission.
Chiang Kai-shek was the superintendent of the Academy; Wang
Ching-wei and Hu Han-min were among the political instruc-
tors.   The Deputy Head of the Political Education Department
was Chou En-lai, and the director of the Propaganda Department was Tai Chi-t'ao.   The training of the army cadets
included a thorough indoctrination program in which they
were exposed to various kinds of literature. *San Min Chu I,*
the theory of class struggle, imperialism, and Christianity
were some of the topics.   Most of them appeared in the
Party's newspaper *Min-kuo jih-pao (Republic Daily)* published
in Shanghai and Canton.   Its supplement *Chüeh-wu (Awakening)*
was a most vocal organ in opposing Christianity.   The
Communist weekly *Hsiang-tao (Guide)* was edited by Ch'en Tu-
hsiu and Ts'ai Ho-shen, adopting a similar platform of anti-
imperialism and anti-militarism. (21)   The propaganda in
these channels were contributive to the founding of the Great
Anti-Imperialism Federation in Canton and Peking by the
Nationalist Party in 1924. (22)

During the intensive campaign against warlords and imperialists, the Anti-Christian Federation was revitalized in
the summer of 1924 under the sponsorship of some Kuomintang
leaders.   In a meeting in Shanghai on August 13, Wu Chih-hui
of the Central Control Committee of the Kuomintang wrote its
constitution and gave a speech, criticizing the future of
Christianity to be similar to "a bow bent to its extremity".
(23)   Christianity was summarily declared as the "vanguard
of imperialism".   The return of the Anti-Christian Federation was directly related to the activity of the Great Anti-
Imperialism Federation founded a month before. (24)

Anti-Christian activities in 1924 came to a summit during
the Christmas week when the Anti-Christian Federation scheduled a large-scale demonstration throughout the country.
Big cities like Canton, Changsha, Hankow, were greatly dis-

turbed. Christianity was placated as the "running dog" and
the "cultural arm" of imperialism; mission schools were regarded as producing "slaves of the foreigners". The nature
of the propaganda was well expressed in the words of a
circular:

> The Movement attacking Christianity is the
> most important movement under the canopy of the
> sky. We all know clearly that Christianity is
> a religion of superstition and vagueness which
> makes people more ignorant than they are. More
> than that, it is our duty to fight against this
> religion of imperialist civilization. (25)

THE CHARGE OF IMPERIALISM

The protest of the anti-Christians with respect to the
WSCF was an eruption of long-latent nationalistic sentiment.
The representative anti-Christian publication in 1922 was
the special issue on Anti-Christian Student Federation in
Hsien-chü (Vanguard) which consisted of several provocative
essays in addition to the manifesto, the telegram, and the
Constitution of the Federation. This bi-weekly magazine
took a communist position in criticizing Christianity. (26)

From the manifesto of the Anti-Christian Student Federation, the primary thesis of attack dealt with the capitalistic structure of modern society, adopting the Marxist
analysis of class distinction. As it said:

> We know that the organization of modern society
> is that of capitalism. In such capitalistic social
> structure, there are on the one hand the class of
> property-holders which eats without working; and
> on the other, the class of proletariat which works
> without getting the means to eat. In other words,
> there is, on the one hand, the exploiting and op-
> pressing class and, on the other, the exploited
> and oppressed class. (27)

According to the manifesto, the reason why the class of
property-holders can exploit the proletariat is that they
own the means of production. The purpose of class struggle
is to seize it back from the property-holders. (28) And
class struggle is the only way to overthrow the corrupted
capitalistic society and reform the present world order.
Toward this goal, the proletarians of all nations should
unite and cooperate. (29)

In the argument of the manifesto, world capitalism has matured and has begun to degenerate. Capitalists of every nation--whether in Britian, America, Japan, and France--have become panicked about their future and have sought all possible ways of survival. Consequently, they crowd into China one after another and practice their economic invasion. The struggle for foreign market and colonial expansion are signs of imminent collapse of capitalism. World War I is regarded as the result of international competition for market and industrial resources, which is approved by the Christian churches of the West. (30)

Christianity is then linked with capitalism. Slanderous slogans are heaped upon the Christian faith and the Christian Church. They are taken as the means employed by capitalists to achieve their purposes. As one writer commented, "Not one of the foreign missionaries is not supported and fed by the capitalists or government so that they can be the pioneers of their invading army". (31) In Ch'en Tuhsiu's words, "many pastors are unproductive idlers", and "not a single national church is not begging importunately from the capitalists everyday". (32) Christian pastors are also accused of deceiving the peasants and workers for their livelihood. Consequently where capitalism flourishes, Christianity prospers, for the Christian Church conforms itself to the wishes of the capitalists. The YMCA is considered as the "faithful running dog of capitalists" and the WSCF as the effort "to sustain world capitalism in China". (33) The economic power of the Church in its ownership of banks, industries, and educational institutions is becoming an exploiting force.

In the telegram, Christianity is charged of having been used by foreign diplomats and merchants as the herald of colonization: "The Four Gospels came to the soil of the Orient through the force of wealth (gold) and power (iron). Gold and iron enslaves with material means; the Gospel enslaves our spirit". (34) As Lu Shu said in his article: "If we want to oppose capitalism, we cannot but oppose Christianity. If we want to overthrow the capitalists, we cannot but overthrow the society of Christians first, especially to oppose the clamorous World's Student Christian Federation". (35)

Another popular line of antagonism against the Christian religion was to point out the blunders of the Christian Church in history. According to their criticism, Christianity has been in the hands of the oppressor class to advo-

cate injustice, exploitation, and slavery. This situation
has not changed today. The Christian Church has been ob-
sequious to the privileged and powerful class, as in the
early Roman and Medieval feudal society. In the modern
world, Christianity becomes the "ghost of capitalism" and
the "sound-recorder of the capitalistic class". (36) Negative remarks of this kind were intended to undermine the
historical validity of the Christian religion so that the
Marxist theory of historical materialism would serve as a
substitute. In Ch'i Yüan's words, "The principle of social
progress has already been satisfactorily affirmed by the
theory of historical materialism invented by our founding
teachers Marx and Engels". (37) At this junction the redemptive history of Christianity seemed to be challenged by
the communist promise of world salvation.

The most common accusation was that religion is the
opiate of the people. It is "a bondage to man's spirit, a
barrier to human thought, and a means of protecting capitalism". (38) Its languishing effect on human soul and body
would result in a reversal of social progress. China was
in a critical movement of her national destiny. The first
step toward national reform, in Ch'ih Kuang's view, is the
complete overthrow of the Christian religion with all its
deceptions to the people. (39) In order to seek the greatest benefit for the majority, the struggle with the obsolete
Christian society is inevitable and communism must be promoted.

These arguments appeared, in a more measured language
with no less abusiveness, in the anti-Christian propaganda
two years later. The former emotional appeal was reduced
or substituted by more historical evidence to back up their
charge. The most significant anti-Christian publication at
this time was a booklet, entitled *Fan-tui chi-tu-chiao yün-
tung (The Anti-Christian Movement)*, consisting of four defamatory essays. (40) The shift from the anti-capitalist
argument in 1922 to the anti-imperialist one in 1924 was
perceptible when the anti-Christian writings were compared.
The word 'imperialism' was not mentioned in the 1922 manifesto, but it came out repeatedly in the documents in 1924.
This was evidently due to the increasing popularity of
communist doctrines, especially Lenin's theory of imperialism. The activities of the Great Anti-Imperialism Federation provided a clue to the ideological change of emphasis.

The aim of the Federation was twofold: to abrogate all unequal treaties previously signed with foreign powers and to
join with all oppressed nations of the world to oppose
imperialism. (41) This motive was explicitly reflected in
the writings of the Anti-Christian Federation.

In the new manifesto of the Anti-Christian Federation in
1924, Christianity was regarded, like other religions of
the world, as preaching a "false concept of pacifism", an
"unrealistic theory of happiness", and an "impractical view
of theistic determinism." (42) It was said that "the same
evils are taught by various religions. But Christianity has
a stronger organization and a deeper and more harmful effect.
Therefore, we should especially oppose Christianity". (43)
As capitalism succeeds feudalism in society, the manifesto
continued, Christianity is retained and employed as a device
for deceiving the workers to accept their poverty and the
farmers to view exploitation by the wealthy class as a divine
arrangement. The perpetuation of such mentality will suppress the national consciousness of the people. In the
colonization of China, the capitalists have used Christianity to persuade the Chinese that "the coming of gunboats
and armies are to bring the gift of the Gospel of God as
well as education and civilization, but not to loot money,
so that the conquered people will be permanently grateful
for their mercy and goodness without thinking of rebellion".
(44) This religious concealment is said to be the main
target of opposition by the Anti-Christian Federation.

To this charge many anti-Christian leaders attempted to
find supporting evidence in the recent history of Sino-
foreign relation. In Wu Chih-hui's speech, (45) he predicted the imminent disintegration of the Christian religion.
In his view, as Christianity suffers from demise in the
West, it looks for possibility of survival overseas. Wu
repudiated the allegiance of missionaries with capitalists
in their activities, manipulating the Chinese to deal with
the Chinese. Their hypocrisy and deception must be exposed.
Wu said, "Our society today needs people of industry and
ability. If we allow these mediocre and illusioned people
to increase, how can our society hope for progress and
advancement. How can China be strengthened one day"? (46)

In discussing the history of mission, Li Ch'un-fan sought
to show the close cooperation between missionaries and invaders to China. For example, using the advantage of the
murder of two German missionaries in Shantung, Germany
seized Tsingtau and imposed a ninety-nine year lease of

Kiaochow and the exclusive railway and mining concessions in
Shantung. Similar missionary incidents *(chiao-an)* were in-
curred in which missionaries interfered with the internal
politics of the local government to protect Chinese rascals
of unruly behaviors. The Boxer Uprising, Li remarked, was
the expression of antiforeignism which unfortunately resulted in disgrace and heavy indemnity. How could the
Christians insist that mission and imperialism are separate
and "unrelated like wind, horse, and cow"? (47)

    In his essay on "Christianity and China", Mei Tien-lung
accused Christianity of cultural and economic aggression,
which is based on Mei's observation that the failures in
China's foreign diplomacy are directly proportional to the
growth rate of Christianity in the last century. (48) Yet
before the nineteenth century, such a situation was totally
absent. If Christianity was not supported by imperialism,
the progress of the Christian occupation in China would
never have occurred. In Mei's view, the formation of the
unequal treaties is another evidence of the "inseparable
marriage between invasion and Christianity". (49) The
imperialists were anxious to obtain the assurance from the
Chinese government for the protection and freedom of their
missionaries. In the Sino-French Treaty in 1858, it was
provided that the missionaries working inland should enjoy
entire security of their persons, properties, and free
exercise of their religion. And any Chinese believer should
have the right to embrace the Catholic faith. (50)

    Thus, an unholy alliance was established between the
Christian movement and imperialism in China. Our analysis
of the anti-Christian antagonism has revealed the major
lines of argument which were found in most of the anti-
Christian writings in the decade. The charge of imperialism
was most audible during the May Thirtieth Affair.

THE MAY THIRTIETH AFFAIR IN 1925

    The "May Thirtieth Atrocious Incident" *(Wu-san ts'an-an)*
headed the list of nationalistic outbreaks that had occurred
since the May Fourth Demonstration in 1919. It was "a
tremendous surge of mass energies" (51) as seen in the
nationwide strikes, protests, and boycotts by students,
workers, and merchants. Earlier in February of that year,
Chinese workers of a Japanese cotton-mill in Shanghai protested the low wages and did not receive any satisfactory
settlement. In the middle of May, they arranged a second
strike and sent representatives to pursue the matter. The

negotiation ended in conflict which resulted in one dead and
several wounded. The Shanghai Municipal Council did not
arrest the Japanese killers but imprisoned some Chinese
workers for defying regulations against demonstrations in
the International Settlement. On May 22, a memorial service
was held for the murdered and the arrested, but many students and workers were seized by the foreign police. To
protest against all these treatments, the students staged a
massive demonstration on May 30 and marched into the Louza
district of the International Settlement. Unable to control
the situation, a British inspector Edward Everson gave order
to shoot, killing at least twelve Chinese and injuring
dozens. (52)

The May 30th Incident triggered a series of anti-foreign
agitation in different parts of the country. In Hankow,
Nanking, Chungking, Amoy, and Ningpo, similar incidents
happened. The most tragic of the subsequent clashes with
the highest death toll was the shooting at Shaki-Shameen in
Canton. The Communists interpreted the movement as the
people's struggle for liberation. And the nationalists regarded it as a good opportunity of denouncing the brutality
of the imperialists, especially the Japanese and the
British. (53) In the lamentation of a Christian leader,
"the thundering noise of the cannons of imperialism has not
been able to drown these increasingly louder and louder
cries. . . . In our present world tendency the covetousness
of theft, the might of threat, the methods of oppression and
the policies of encroachment have only numbered days left to
them". (54)

The May 30th Affair dramatized the continual struggle
between nationalism and imperialism. The loss of tariff
autonomy, the practice of extraterritoriality, and the presence of foreign concessions constantly reminded the Chinese
that their national sovereignty had been violated. Many
asked, Is China a nation or not? If other nations had the
full right of self-determination, why is it absent in China?
In Hu Shih's observation, the May 30th Incident was an occa-
sion that provoked the eruption of nationalistic sentiment.
The root cause of the problem lay in the unequal treaties in
the past eighty years. (55)

The Shanghai Affair led to immediate reactions from certain Christian bodies which saw in it a close relationship
to the task of mission. A number of manifestoes were issued,
stating their positions regarding the Incident. They included the National Christian Council, the Yenching Univer-

sity, National YMCA, the YWCA at Peking, the Chinese Christian Association at Peking, the Chinese Christian Association
at Nanking, the Chinese Christian Association at Shanghai,
the YMCA at Nanchang, the Teacher Association at Soochow
University, and the Kung Li Hui at Peking. Various patriotic societies were established to deal with the consequence
of the Incident. Temporary federations of Chinese Christians were organized at Peking, Shanghai, Soochow, Hangchow,
Changsha, Ningpo, and other places in order to take a bold
stand against injustice and to redress the situation. Christians at Nanking founded the Society to Promote the Abrogation of Unequal Treaties. It appealed to Christians else-
where to form similar societies. (56) Some local Christians
deliberately separated themselves from their mother churches
to establish independent groups; for example, the Chinese
Christian of the China Inland Mission at Shanghai and the
Shen Tao Hui at Wenchow. (57) Nearly all Christian schools
in the country called off their classes. Students demonstrated in the street and distributed pamphlets.

These responses were motivated by a sense of Christian
obligation for political involvement. As Wang Chih-hsin
commented, "Chinese Christians are also Chinese citizens
. . . We Chinese Christians should unite in a movement to
save China by direct means. We should exert ourselves to
the utmost to fulfill our heaven-bestowed responsibility,
and at least make clear our Christian attitude". (58) Chinese Christians wanted to disclaim the unholy alliance with
imperialism or, at least, to reduce it. Many were afraid
that the May 30th Affair would harm the future of evangelism
in China. As it was said in one manifesto, "In the eyes of
the Chinese people Christianity is identified with the dominant nations of the West and any action on the part of their
representative in China which seems to contradict and dis-
credit its exalted ethical teachings can do incalculable in-
jury to the Christian cause in China". (59) It was expected
that Christian involvement could minimize the antagonism of
the anti-Christians or drew some of their sympathy.

Manifestoes and telegrams by Chinese Christians expressed
deep regret and outrage at the conduct of the foreign police
on Nanking Road. Words of condemnation were found in some
declarations, calling the affair "an insult to national
sovereignty", "a burial of heavenly justice", and "an assault
to humanity". They argued that the demonstration by the
students was purely an act of patriotism, a form of student
movement acceptable in modern society. The question was
raised whether the treatment of fatal hostility they received

was justified. (60) The Municipal Council replied that
shooting was apparently the only alternative open to the
police, after warning the students, to control the confusion.
But this explanation was totally denounced by the indignant
Chinese. Some argued that the murderers must be prosecuted
and their sinister acts publicly confessed.

In an atmosphere so impregnated with unrestrained emotion,
certain calm voices were heard asking for a "prompt, thorough
and impartial investigation of the incident and of events
leading up to it and growing out of it". (61) The necessity
of accurate evaluation of the incident, followed by an un-
ambiguous report to the Chinese public, was felt in several
manifestoes. Such investigation, they pointed out, should
be carried out by a commission of inquiry, formed by both
Chinese and foreigners, that would command the confidence of
the people.

To avoid future occurrence of similar tragedy, Yü Jih-
chang (62) suggested the change of composition of the Municipal Council by admitting Chinese membership. The Chinese
had not hitherto been accorded the right to express their
opinion or vote over matters of taxation, although they contributed the main part of the Municipal revenue. A similar
request was made by a group of Chinese statesmen, including
Liang Ch'i-ch'ao, Chu Chi-chien, Fan Yüan-lien, Ting Wen-
chiang and others, that foreign nations should "seek to
understand the viewpoint of the Chinese people and at least
in some measure to consult their interests in matters vitally
affecting them,. . . " (63)

Christian organizations which had strong Sino-Western
connections were more cautious in commenting on the Shanghai
Affair. While indigenous groups were unreserved in their
rebuke, they were concerned with the harmonious relations
between the Chinese and the foreign communities in China.
Regarding the controversial situation, the Faculty of the
Yenching University suggested:

It should be their object to remove this by
means of a more sympathetic press in closer touch
with the movements of Chinese life, by readiness
to revise treaties, which have long been out of
date, and by actively working to put Chinese
foreign relations on a basis of mutual good will

rather than on the forcible retention of resented
privileges. We would appeal to all sections of
the foreign community in China to cooperate for
the attainment of these objects. (64)

Chinese Christians were quite unanimous in their demand
for the revision of unequal treaties. The thorn in the
Chinese flesh had been painful for eighty years and it must
be removed. In Hu Shih's view, these unilateral treaties
were originally formulated by the force of foreign invasion
and they should have defined a period of validity. (65)
Chinese Christians condemned the treaties on several grounds.
Their existence was looked upon as usurpation of the basic
sovereignty of China and a threat to national solidarity.
The Society to Promote the Abrogation of Unequal Treaties
argued that the Christian principle of equality has no room
for these treaties. The Chinese found themselves treated
as inferiors. As the Peking Manifesto criticized, "The
Foreign Powers in their dealings with us have not exhibited
the spirit of the Golden Rule, the fundamental law of humanity, which says, we should do unto others what we would have
them do unto us". (66)

In the shadow of these treaties, the Gospel was not
preached in the spirit of genuine friendliness but under the
protection of armed forces. The Great Commission of Jesus
Christ, as Chang I-ching pointed out, has no element of
treaty in it. (67) In the criticism of Ch'eng Hsiang-fan,
Associate General Secretary of the China Christian Educational Association, "If reliance be placed on the terrifying
power of guns and men-of-war, if a weak country is to be
kept in check by treaty bands, if China's relations with
other countries are to be founded on treaties which have no
moral sanction, how can the great Gospel of salvation be
effectively preached?" (68) Although the treaties were
helpful to some extent to early missionaries, they had done
much greater harm than good. Many *chiao-an* could have been
avoided if the treaties were not there. (69)

Lo Yün-yen ascribed the primary reason for the ascendancy
of the anti-Christian movement to the historical connection
between Christianity and the unequal treaties. (70) As the
Chinese Church was in the process of indigenization, the
previous charge of having alliance with imperialism should
be eliminated. The Chinese Church had to extricate itself

from the rebuke of anti-Christians by requesting the abolition of missionary privileges in the treaties. As long as
the treaties were unrevised, the stigma would remain in the
path of Christian mission. (71)

Some Chinese Christians regarded the Shanghai Incident
as a testing stone for the missionary whether he gave
priority to Christianity or to his country. In Chien Yu-
wen's view, the unholy alliance could be partially disentangled if missionaries were willing to give up the protection by their government. Foreign missionaries should
state their positions, individually or collectively, concerning the Shanghai Affair. They should report to their
home churches and government the inhumanity of the Incident.
(72) Wu Lei-ch'uan warned that if foreign powers continued
high-handedly to seek protection for their missionaries,
then "the time of suicide of the Christian Church in China
will have come". (73) Wu anticipated that if the unequal
treaties were abandoned and missionaries were replaced by
local workers, there would be no more pretext for anti-
Christians to stigmatize Christianity as imperialistic. The
Shanghai massacre was a catalyst to the indigenous church
movement which the Chinese Christians viewed as a practical
and urgent remedy to the anti-Christian antagonism.

A number of missionary organizations spoke out immediately after the May 30th affair, for they knew that
silence would be guilty. Some British missionaries in Peking
openly admitted "a large share of blame in the tragedy and
remarked that the incident was largely due to underlying
racial animosities . . . It is the duty of Britons overseas
to seek sincerely the friendship of the people in whose
land they dwell, and whose guests they are. Mutual understanding between individuals is a powerful healing influence in international relationships". (74) Liu T'ing-fang
commented that it was the first time that British missionaries honestly and publicly spoke to the Chinese from their
conscience on diplomatic affairs. (75)

The Shanghai Missionary Association in a letter to the
Chinese Christian Union said, "We are confident that all
good citizens of Shanghai, whether Chinese or foreign,
deeply deplore the events of May 30th". (76) The Mukden
Missionaries' Statement confessed,

As Christians pledged to strive for the accomp-
lishment of the Christian ideal of brotherhood and
peace among all men, we affirm that our purpose is

to put Christ first and nationality second; and we
would call on Christians of every nationality, and
on all men of good-will everywhere, to use their
utmost influence to prevent further violence and to
secure the cessation of words and actions that
arose suspicion and hatred. . . . We feel that we
foreigners should be prepared--even at considerable
personal sacrifice--to surrender privileges which
are found to be a just cause of offense to those
in whose land we dwell. (77)

Similar remarks of regret and apology were made by different missionary bodies over the country. Yet, many were
hesitant and reserved in their response to the Incident.
How were these statements received by the Chinese was another problem. Some frowned upon them; others regarded
them as "sounding brass" and "tinkling cymbals". Many
missionaries consented to the patriotic expression of the
Chinese on behalf of the May 30th Affair. Their double
identity as foreigner and Christian preacher placed them
in a most embarrassed position. They had mixed feelings for
the misdeeds of their predecessors in entering, and of their
contemporaries in occupying, the territories of another
country by force. And their very presence in China owed to
the privilege granted in the unequal treaties. But their
Christian conscience reminded them that the treaty system
violated the principle of equality in the Gospel they were
preaching. The missionary enterprise in China contradicted
the theory of separation between church and state which
they espoused at home. Their question was: How can their
religious conviction in coming to China be politically justified? The May 30th Incident brought this historical question into sharp focus. (78)

Despite the effort of missionaries and Chinese Christians
to extricate themselves from the charge of imperialism, the
anti-Christians did not give them a chance. The anti-Christian movement, as has been mentioned, had regained its momentum in the revival of the Anti-Christian Federation in
the year before. It identified itself with the national
campaign to oppose foreign aggression and accused the Church
of its allegiance with it. There was an explicit change of
attitude toward Christianity from indifference before the
May 30th Incident to involvement after it. (79) The intensity of the movement was succinctly reflected in an important resolution of the National Student Union in July 1925.
Part of it went as follows,

The anti-Christian movement publicly undertaken
the fight against imperialism. We the National
Student Union, being one of the powerful organizations opposed to Christianity and to Christian
education have adopted the following concrete
methods:

1. We decided that Christmas day, December 25th,
and the week, December 22nd to 28th, should be observed as anti-Christian week. During this week when
the Christians are trying to recruit followers, every
student union should stir up the mass of people to
carry on all sorts of activities against Christianity.
We must make the anti-Christian movement everywhere
work toward anti-imperialism. Most important of all,
Student Unions everywhere should collect facts and
material regarding Christianity and imperialism in
connection with the massacres which happened in
Shanghai, Hankow and other places. . . .

2. Student unions everywhere should continuously
inform the public of the evils of the Christian church
and of Christian education and show that they are not
filling the needs of China. We should also explain
to the public the insiduous plan of cultural invasion
employed by the imperialists. (80)

A new line of policy was formulated in the resolution
that during summer and winter vacations, students were urged
to return to rural and industrial areas to inform the people
of the evils of Christianity. In a report of the anti-
Christian activities in Changsha at the end of the year,
Christianity was looked upon as a greater evil than imperialism:

Laborers, farmers, students, merchants and all
who are oppressed! We do not fear the imperialism
shown in machine guns, in the customs conference
held by the allied powers, in the unequal treaties.
What we do fear is the subtle, invisible, cultural
invasion of Christianity, because it brings with it
the deceptive instruments of tenderness and phi-
lanthropy. It is these activities that destroy
our nation, weaken our place among peoples, make
us insensitive, so that we think "even the thief
is our father". A hundred thousand foreign sol-

diers in Shanghai cannot kill our patriotism,
the murdering of men at Shameen cannot destroy
our purpose to save China. But this subtle
Christianity! (81)

The May 30th Affair gave momentum to another significant
national movement in the decade which frustrated the Christian enterprise in China. This had to do with the educational rights in mission schools.

CHRISTIAN EDUCATION--THE
DENATIONALIZING AGENT?

Before educational prerogative became an issue in the
1920s, mission schools had been a separate educational community in China. The Chinese Government disliked the foreign nature of these schools and was suspicious of their
goal and function. After the abandonment of the Civil
Service Examinations in 1905, Chinese students could still
enter government service if they possessed proper creden-
tials under the new school system. Returned students to
China were asked to take examinations if they desired government appointments. But these privileges were not granted to
graduates from mission schools whose status was not recognized by the government. Missionary educators did not want
their Chinese converts to attend government schools where
Confucian ceremonies were observed. And they were impatient
to see their school graduates unable to get equal access to
career opportunities.

As early as 1905, some missionaries attempted, through
diplomatic means, to seek from the National Board of Education the benefits accorded to students of government institutions. They were willing to subscribe to government
regulations in order to acquire recognition of the Christian
schools. In 1907, the Board announced that mission schools
were not required to be registered lest foreign interference
of national education would hinder the abrogation of extraterritoriality. However, no uniform policy was enforced and
quasi-recognition was given in some places. (82) Other
missionaries were hesitant to approach the government, for
they thought that external control would affect the evangelical activities in the campus. Generally speaking,
missionaries considered government recognition as advisable,
a position expressed in the Conference of the China Continuation Committee in 1913. (83) Since the question was not
urgent, no further action was taken by Western or Chinese
educators.

During the decade after 1905, the Chinese education system was only in the elementary stage, having little concern
to oppose the more developed foreign schools. In early
twenties, the growing nationalistic sentiment among students
apparently brought the potential issue to the surface. No
longer could a separate education scheme outside the government jurisdiction be tolerated.

The Christian movement became a sizable force whose
statistical expansion caused alarm to the patriotic Chinese.
The infamous volume, *The Christian Occupation of China*,
published by the China Continuation Committee, fed the
imagination of many who had been suspicious of the missionary enterprise in the country. This survey reported the
numerical strength and the geographical distribution of
Christian activities in China. It recorded about 7600 students in 265 mission middle schools scattered over nineteen
provinces and 2000 in mission colleges with sixty-six percent professing Christians. From 1907 to 1920, the student
population in mission schools increased by over 300 percent. (84) Over 130 denominations were present in China,
and in Kwangtung province alone forty-three protestant
mission societies were stationed. The terrific growth
caused discomfort to those who regarded the Christian
occupation as "spreading infection of religious poison".
(85) Even some local Christians asked the question, "With
this partition of China, can China be made Christian this
way"? (86)

Another significant factor that provoked animosity
against Christian schools was the Burton Commission Study of
the education situation in China in 1922. The Report
asserted that Christian education was vital to the progress
of the Christian movement in China. It said,

If Christian education fails, the growing stream
of non-Christian education and of anti-Christian influence will submerge the Christian movement, or
reduce it to a place of minor importance. . . . If
the present hour of opportunity is vigorously and
wisely seized, if unimportant differences are for-
gotten and all our efforts are united to build up a
system of education, sound, vigorous, progressive,
and fundamentally Christian, which shall in turn
create a strong Christian community expressing in

its life the spirit and principles of Christianity,
we may look with hope to the time when the religion
of Jesus will be the religion of China. (87)

According to the Report, Christian education is meant for
both Christians and non-believers in order to develop a
Christian community to reform society. And this education
is to be permeated by the spirit of Christianity through
strengthening the religious program in school. Closer
supervision and efficient coordination are proposed so as to
improve the quality of the facilities and personnel. It
urges that mission schools should seize the opportunity "to
strengthen the Christian schools of China that from them
shall come the men and women who will make China a Christian
nation". (88) Many of the remarks were disturbing to anti-
Christians and were later quoted at length to oppose Christianity. Instead of reconciling the educational objectives
of the state school and mission school, the survey widened
the gulf between the two systems.

The aim, the policy, and the curriculum of the Christian
schools were hardly acceptable to the government. Evangelical priority was kept by emphasizing compulsory worship
service and Bible courses. Many non-Christian students regarded them as a coercive device of religious proselytiza-
tion. Chinese studies occupied only a small section of the
schedule. Long hours were spent in teaching English, which
was often the medium of instruction. (89) As a result, the
curriculum was regarded as inadequate in fostering national
consciousness and cultural characteristics among the students. Among the objectionable things was the autonomy of
Christian education under foreign auspices. How could the
mission schools produce good Chinese citizenship to aid the
task of national salvation? (90)

The beginning of the Movement could be traced back to
Ts'ai Yüan-p'ei's essay, entitled "Independence of Education", in which he argued for the separation of education
from religion. Education is to help young people develop
their ability and cultivate their personalities. (91) It
should not be used as a tool for any particular purpose and
should be free from politics and religion. In Ts'ai's view,
if educational rights are given to the Church, it will
violate the principle of religious liberty as stated in the
Provisional Constitution of the Republic. He proposed three
methods to deal with religious schools:

1. There is no need to put theological subjects
in a university curruculum. In the department of
Philosophy it can include History of Religion and
Comparative Religion.

2. No school curriculum should contain the teaching of religious doctrines or prayer.

3. Professional Christian workers should not
participate in educational ministry.

Many Chinese educators followed the trend. In the July
Conference of the National Association for the Advancement
of Education at Tsinan in 1922, Hu Shih, T'ao Meng-ho, and
Ting Wen-chiang recommended the elimination of all religious education in both theory and ceremony from elementary
schools where the children were not mature enough to form
their own judgment. (92)

Among advocates of the Movement were nationalists of the
Young China Association. The essay that laid the foundation
of the Movement was written by Yü Chia-chü, called "Chiao-
hui chiao-yü wen-t'i" (The Problem of Christian Education).
In Yü's view, Christian education is the most perilous to
the future of the nation. It is shameful that China has
allowed foreigners to seize national rights for religious
propagation, as if China had "no civilization of her own"
and "no men of learning". (93) The Christian religion is
exclusive in nature and does not tolerate the presence of
other faiths, like Confucianism and Buddhism. Yü was dis-
turbed by the Burton Report, which promoted the formation
of a strong Christian community for efficient social reform.
This, according to Yü, will create religious classes in the
Chinese society. As Christian schools develop their influence, religious exclusiveness will be harmful to the cultivation of national consciousness. If all religions in China
persist in a similar way of education to establish their own
ideologies and kindred communities, China can never be
united. Religion and education should be separate, or education will lose its proper function. Education, as Yü continued, is a social responsibility as it preserves national
heritage and stimulates cultural creativity. It is an office of the state. (94)

Yü and Li Huang, both members of the Association, published a volume, entitled *Kuo-chia chu-i ti chiao-yü* (Nationalistic Education), denouncing the merits of mission
education. In October 1923 the Association held a confer-

ence at Soochow, resolving that "racial education should be
promoted in order to cultivate the spirit of patriotism and
national defense. . . . We oppose Christian education which
destroys our racial character and adopts a cultural policy
close to exploitation". (95)

The campaign against Christian education gained prominence in 1924, taking the form of student revolt *(hsüeh-
ch'ao)*. Serious cases occurred in the Holy Trinity College
at Canton and in Yale-in-China at Changsha. (96) In July,
the National Association for the Advancement of Education
at its third annual conference in Nanking passed the resolution to insist on the registration of foreign schools and
colleges and to give recognition only if religious courses
be eliminated from the curriculum. (97) During the tenth
annual meeting of the National Federation of Provincial
Educational Association, held at Kaifeng in October, it was
recommended that foreigners should be forbidden to rule
educational enterprises in China and that no religious
activities be allowed in schools. (98) It urged immediate
registration and suggested discrimination against students
in unregistered schools after a certain date.

During this hour, several important writings to support
the Movement appeared in *Chung-hua chiao-yü-chieh*, edited
by Ch'en Ch'i-t'ien, an ardent nationalist. In his view,
education should not be independent of politics, as some
educators suggested. Rather, the students must be informed
of the indignity China has suffered in recent political
history. (99) It is not internationalism, but nationalism,
that China needs most. Accordingly, Ch'en advised that
more nationalistic material be included in student text-
books. His magazine devoted a special number on "The Movement for Restoring Educational Rights" in February 1925.

In a provocative essay, (100) Ch'en argued that education
is the sovereign right of the state and thus serves its
purpose. The government has authority to abrogate and
supervise all forms of education inside its territory.
National education should aim at producing a patriotic
citizenship. But Christian education, according to the
Report of the China Educational Commission, seeks to build
up a religious community through the promotion of Christian
spirit and doctrine. (101) Therefore, Christian education,
in Ch'en's view, "conflicts with the aims of national education", "reduces its educational efficiency", and "under-
mines its very foundation". (102)

Furthermore, as Ch'en saw it, Christian education has
violated the constitution of religious liberty in using
education to propagate religion. Coercive devices of chapel service and Bible class are employed to enforce religious acceptance. What the Republic's Constitution guaran-
tees is absolute freedom in religious belief but not in
religious propagation. For "if religious propagation is
given full freedom, then religious belief will lose its
fullness of freedom". (103) Judging from the effect of
education, Ch'en argued that mission school curriculum will
produce students uninformed of Chinese civilization and
unmindful of national consciousness. China has no use of
this kind of education at all.

After the Movement had established its feet in early
1925, Chinese Christians were convinced that immediate
steps must be taken to face the issue of registration which
could jeopardize the future of the Christian ministry.
They saw the necessity of having representative organs to
express their viewpoints to the anti-Christian challenge.
In March, the *Chung-hua chi-tu-chiao chiao-yü chi-k'an*
(China Christian Educational Quarterly) was started under
the editorship of Ch'eng Hsiang-fan, Associate General
Secretary of the China Christian Educational Association.
The goals were:

1. to perpetuate the indigenization of Christian
   education in China;

2. to express the real spirit of Christian education;

3. to discuss the various educational methods on
   the basis of science; and

4. to exchange viewpoints between Eastern and
   Western education. (104)

At the Shanghai meeting of the China Christian Educational Association in April 1925, the resolution was passed:
"Christian schools should immediately register with the
local or federal government, without, however, the special
function of Christianity restricted by the registration".
(105) A statement of educational principles in both English
and Chinese was prepared so as to clarify the widespread
misconception of the purpose of Christian education. (106)
This statement was most representative of Christian educators in expressing a united standpoint to the anti-Christian
critics.

The explosion of nationalistic sentiment regarding the
May 30th Incident intensified the Educational Rights Movement. (107) The National Student Union of China at the
Seventh Congress in Shanghai in July reiterated its opposition to mission school, appealing to the Ministry of Education to confiscate foreign school properties. They urged
students in Christian institutions to demand their schools
to conform to government regulation or to transfer to other
registered schools. Christian schools were condemned as
imparting "a slave education" to the Chinese people. The
Student Union decided the following policies:

   a. We should petition the Ministry of Education
   to adopt concrete methods of abolishing mission
   schools.

   b. Student Unions everywhere should organize
   committees to speed up the restoration of educational rights. Before educational rights are
   returned, we should on the one hand urge students
   not to enter mission schools and on the other
   hand to help those who are in them to leave these
   schools.

   c. To those students who receive pecuniary aid
   from the church and who are willing to leave the
   mission schools we should extend suitable economic help so as to help them go to other schools. (108)

It also encouraged that "student unions everywhere, in
carrying out the anti-Christian program, should cooperate
with the Anti-Christian Federation closely wherever there is
one". (109) And this appeal was favorably responded to by
the Anti-Christian Federation in declaring, in November
1925, its cooperation with the National Student Union in the
common struggle against Christianity and in demanding the
return of educational rights. (110)

The rampant criticism and hostility launched against
Christian schools embarrassed both students and teachers.
Many were persuaded that the government would soon take over
control of the mission institutions. A number of Christian
schools felt threatened and found it difficult to continue
their classes. School was closed before the end of the
semester. Some were uncertain if they could re-open after
summer. The frustration to the morale of Christian education was even more serious than suspension of classes or

cessation of examinations. The question in the minds of the
Christian educators was: Is there a place for Christian
education in the intellectual life of the nation?

However, it was surprising to see the positive atmosphere
of many Christian schools in the fall term of 1925. Students came back, more enthusiastic about their studies.
Teachers became more cautious of their responsibility. It
was a time of expectancy, though not entirely optimistic of
what would happen next. The year of turmoil eventually
closed with the New Education Regulation issued on November
16, 1925, by the Ministry of Education in Peking for the
recognition of foreign-sponsored schools. (111)

The moderate requirements of the New Regulation were
"unexpectedly generous" to many Christian educators. (112)
The Ministry of Education was fully aware of the chaotic
situation in the country especially after the May 30th
Affair. Any harsh measure taken against mission schools, as
demanded by the radical anti-Christian critics, would mean
deterioration. (113) The scarcity of educational opportunities made it unwise to ignore the availability of the
facilities in the numerous mission institutions. The
Ministry did not concede to the extreme nationalists in
total repudiation of the usefulness of Christian education.
Nor did it endorse coercive religious programs in it. The
Ministry cautiously dealt with both the foreign and religious character of mission education from the standpoint of
national administration. The New Regulation was a government determination to bring Christian schools under control
through registration. During the hour of boiling nationalism it could hardly allow the mission schools to continue
its autonomous enterprise. As E. W. Wallace, Associate
General Secretary of the China Christian Educational Association, said: "It is undoubted that the most general cause
for suspicion and opposition was the feeling that government
educational authorities can exercise no oversight or control
over the Christian schools, and that this is not right". (114)
Frank W. Lee, a Chinese educator, also commented that when
"the Christian schools are managed and controlled by Chinese,
much of the present opposition to them will be modified".
(115) The New Regulation was intended to calm political
activism as well as to bring Christian education closer to
the aims of nationalism.

However, the New Regulation received violent opposition
from the anti-Christian critics. They complained in writing
to the Board of Education and gathered for demonstration at

Peking. The Anti-Christian Federation held a meeting at
Peking University a week after the New Regulation was
announced. A manifesto was issued attacking the right of
Christian schools to register with the government and demanding the cancellation of the New Regulation. In their view,
the Regulation would place Christian schools on an equal
footing with public schools, thus allowing them to extend
their religious influence. As Ch'en Ch'i-t'ien said,
"Although the standards decided by the Board of Education
are close to the two major points we have asserted in the
last two years, they are still too loose and flexible and
should be subject to careful supplementation". (116) Plans
were made for further anti-Christian demonstration at
Christmas time. These expressions gave evidence to the
basic motive of the anti-Christian education movement that
they simply wanted Christianity out of the way. Education
must be completely secularized and monopolized by the State.
The Ministry of Education was caught in a difficult situation. It could not possibly abolish the New Regulation due
to the pressure from private groups. However, the significance of such demands was appreciated. In early 1926, the
Ministry announced another order requiring schools to register or to close down. But this order was not enforced
because of the unstable political situation of the time.(117)

UNDER THE BANNER OF KUOMINTANG

The long-desired Northern Expedition of the Kuomintang,
finally started in July 1926, aroused high expectation among
the people. The goal of the revolution was laid down some
years previously by Dr. Sun Yat-Sen: to abolish unequal
treaties and to unify China under a national government.
Aided by Soviet supplies and by the cooperation with the
Chinese Communist Party, General Chiang Kai-shek's army
moved in great strides from Canton to central China. City
after city were captured: Wuhan in September, Nanchang in
November, Foochow in December, and Shanghai and Nanking in
March 1927. By that time, territories south of Yangtze had
been brought under control. (118)

The spectacular success of the Nationalist Revolution was
due to several reasons: the defection from other warlord
camps, the efficiency of the Whampao Army, and the widespread propaganda. A chief factor was the force of public
opinion of the people. (119) No Longer could they tolerate
the dissension of warlordism and the oppression of imperialism. They wanted to see China united and duly respected in
the family of nations. Students threw away their books and

joined the glorious campaign. Many of them were engaged in spreading nationalist propaganda which preceded and followed the military movement. Workers and peasants were organized into unions and were mobilized to support the new regime mainly under the direction of the Communist cadres. The Revolution was regarded as the liberation of the people, and the Kuomintang banner was hoisted as a symbol of salvation that promised a new future for the country. It seemed "to give an assurance that at last the Republic would become something more than a name and the regime of the Tuchuns come to an end". (120)

The chaos provided good opportunities for anti-Christian activities under the pretext of antiforeignism. In areas occupied by the nationalist soldiers, there was a large-scale release of destructive energy. Soldiers, students, workers, and farmers were all involved, in one case or another, in the rampant disorder. Foreigners were publicly humiliated and persecuted. Unruly elements in the National-ist army confiscated and plundered missionary properties in explicit defiance of Party instructions. (121) The xeno-phobic sentiment was more extensive and intensive than that in the Boxer Uprising.

The most graphic incident was the Nanking episode in March 1927, when nationalist troops entered the city. Three Western consulates were attacked and foreigners treated with cruelty. John Williams, Vice-President of Nanking Univer-sity, was shot to death as he tried to hold back a gold watch. Only under shelter of gunfire were the foreigners able to escape. Most of them evacuated the city and sought refuge at Shanghai. (122) The Incident persuaded the missionaries of the advisability of a temporary, if not total, exodus from the China field. Only about 500 out of 8,000 protestant missionaries chose to remain at their own risk. (123) As H. T. Hodgkin, Secretary of the National Christian Council, said, "The Incident proved to be a very serious setback to the sympathy which had been developing in many quarters in Europe and America for the nationalist cause". (124)

Numerous *hsüeh-ch'ao* (student movement) broke out during the Northern Expedition. In Jessie Lutz's comment, "the timing and locale of the *hsüeh-ch'ao* in the Christian colleges correlated with the movement of the southern troops; there was also correlation with the left wing influence". (125) At Yale-in-China, students forwarded many petitions to the administration including the reduction of school

fees, the right to dismiss faculty members by a two-third
vote, and student representation on the board of governors.
They demanded the reorganization of the school by staging
protests and strikes. School discontinued and the president resigned. In Lingnan University, classes were dis-
rupted and the administration was publicly slandered. The
supply of food and water were cut off after a workmen's
strike in November. Similar outbreaks of different intensity took place in Hua Chung College in Wuchang, Fukien
University in Foochow, St. John University in Shanghai, and
Hangchow Christian College in Hangchow. In a report containing 51 missionary cases, Frank P. Lockhart, Consul-
General at Hankow, said,

> The plan of occupation was so systematized and so
> widespread that one cannot escape the conclusion
> that it was a fixed policy of the Nationalist
> Government, inspired no doubt by Bolshevik influ-
> ence, to make use of foreign missionary property
> as occasion might require. It might even safely
> be said that the radical faction of the Govern-
> ment had pursued this policy with the double pur-
> pose of utilizing the property for military pur-
> poses, and at the same time permanently driving
> the missionary from the field, or at least curb-
> ing his influence, if such could be done. (126)

Local evacuation of missionaries began during 1926 as a
result of the northbound movement of the nationalist armies.
From the beginning of 1927, large numbers retreated from
Kwangtung, Fukien, and Hunan. (127) In F. Rawlinson's
observation, "Widespread evacuation took place primarily in
connection with the Communist attack upon foreigners in
Nanking and was due either to expediency, diplomatic pressure or Chinese Christian advice. It was not due to un-
friendly feeling towards them on the part of Chinese Christians or a nationwide desire to be rid of them". (128)
Amidst many setbacks suffered by missionaries, some perplex-
ing questions kept coming back to them: If the Chinese do
not want them, shall they stay? What is the role of a
missionary today?

Most missionaries did not take a public stand with respect
to domestic politics in China. However, they hoped the
Nationalist Government would succeed. When compared with
the Communists, the Kuomintang was "the lesser of the two
evils" that could possibly tolerate Christianity in China.
(129) The presence of Christians in key positions in the

Kuomintang also imparted to missionaries and local Christians certain confidence in the goodwill of the Party regime. Frequent appeals to the government for protection against anti-Christian hostility received positive official response. For example, General Chiang issued orders in Nanking that all troops should leave occupied educational institutions by June 16, 1927, and that Christian properties should not be pillaged. (130) Some missionaries even identified Chiang Kai-shek as the Protector of the Christian faith. (131) However, the weakness of the Kuomintang were easily noticeable including the narrow political base, the power of the local warlords, the administrative inefficiency, the dependence upon Russian cooperation, and the lack of inner cohesion.

The Nationalist Revolution was a time of crisis for the Chinese Church. In Wei Cho-min's warning, "the Christian movement will stand or fall in accordance with its attitude toward the revolutionary movement". (132) Most Chinese Christians sided with the cause of the Nationalists in spite of the accompanying anti-Christian disturbance. It would be "fair to say that the general tendency among Christian Chinese in north and south alike was favorable to the nationalist movement in a general way although not to be counted on as behind any particular political group". (133) Most Christian spokesmen who commented on the Revolution were pro-revolution. In their analysis, the charge that Christianity is anti-revolution is due to the purported association of Christianity with the imperialist West. It is also influenced by the concept of political non-resistance. They knew that the time in China was such that any separation of Christianity from politics would immediately render it irrelevant.

The split between the Kuomintang and the Chinese Communist Party brought a new direction to Chinese politics. In April 1927, General Chiang ordered to dissolve the political department of the Revolutionary Army and to obliterate the Communists who were condemned as "traitors of the Revolution" and "running dogs of Russia". Students' political activism was arrested; rule and order were emphasized. Student unions were deprived of political function, and only individual membership for students was allowed in the Party. (134) Official decrees were dispatched, calling for the protection of foreigners and the return of occupied churches, schools, and hospitals. On May 13, 1927, the Shanghai Provincial Branch of the Central Political Conference urged the Government "to instruct the people that they

must not misinterpret the slogan 'Down with Imperialism'
and must not, on the basis of antiforeign and antireligious
intentions, use any influence to oppose or violate the
religious freedom of either Chinese or foreign citizens".
(135) Destructive activities in the name of "Restoring
Educational Rights" were officially prohibited by the
Central Educational Commission in July 1927. It said,

> This Commission has recently determined that
> all private schools, including mission schools and
> foreign-supported schools, shall be allowed to
> register in accordance with the official regula-
> tions and to continue to be maintained. People of
> all classes and students of private schools may,
> on no account, deliberately try to destroy a
> private institution by means of the slogan 'Regain
> Educational Rights'. (136)

The situation became relatively stable until the invasion
of Manchuria by Japan in 1931. The climax of the anti-
Christian movement in the 1920s came to a pause, at least
temporary, at this point.

However, the question of religious liberty once again
came forth for discussion among certain leaders of the
Kuomintang. In the 128th meeting of the Central Political
Conference, Generals Chang Chih-chiang and Niu Yung-chien
submitted a proposal, asking for the abolition of the slogan "Down with Religion". (137) In their argument, religious liberty is not only stated in the Provisional Constitution but is a common universal practice in different
countries of the world. China should not be an exception.
The antireligious slogan is a Communist invention to create
confusion in government policy and should be abrogated
immediately. They asserted that Christianity has revolutionary significance, and confessed that their service in
the Party had received motivation from it. That Christianity is imperialistic was a false accusation.

The reply of the Central Executive Committee to Niu-
Chang proposal was favorable and reaffirmed the resolution
passed in May 13, 1927, concerning the protection of religion against antiforeign and antireligious manoeuvres. (138)
It said that the practice of religious freedom by abolishing anti-Christian and antireligious slogans was already
embodied in that resolution. However, the appeal of Niu-
Chang led to a debate on the pages of *Min-kuo jih-pao*,
Chüeh-wu, and *Wen-she yüeh-k'an*. Although the scope of the

debate was not as sizable as that in 1923 over science and philosophy of life, the issue raised was no less significant. It dealt with the existence of Christianity under the banner of Kuomintang. Much anti-Christian criticism in the debate had already appeared earlier in the decade. For example, Christianity is imperialistic, primitive, denationalizing, and unproductive. The central issue lay in the relationship of Christianity with the Nationalist Party.

After the Niu-Chang proposal came out in February 1928, several essays in *Chüeh-wu* attacked their position. In an article, entitled "The Religious Problem: A Discussion with Mr. Chang and Mr. Niu", (139) the author, Yeh Sheng, requested the government to confiscate all religious properties in the country and to send the monks and priests back to productive labors in society. In his argument, there is no need even to oppose Christianity, for in the future it will inevitably decline as it cannot stand the test of intellectual and social progress. In another essay called "Discussing the Abolition of the Slogan 'Down with Religion'", (140) Yüan Yeh-yü suggested that all Kuomintang members should subscribe to the *San Min Chu I* as a substitute for religion. Both Yeh and Yüan charged Christianity of having been used as a tool of imperialism, which fully justified its abrogation. Much evidence, they said, testifies to this historical fact. (141)

Some Party members gave sole consideration to Party interest. Chang Chen-chen noted that all kinds of benefits produced by religion have been otherwise available through the Party. Party members were too busy to have religion, and there should not be organized religion in it. (142) All forms of activities, inclusive of the religious, should be subjugated to the direction of the Party. In his view, the sole leader of the Party is Dr. Sun, who surpasses both Jesus and Moses in greatness and learning. And his *San Min Chu I* is more practical and relevant to modern China than Christianity. The tendency to exalt Sun Yat-sen to a personal cult and to make the Party rule absolute caused alarm to Chinese Christians.

As a natural corollary to the consolidation of the one-Party rule, the Kuomintang introduced its Party Education. In May 1928, Ts'ai Yüan-p'ei, President of the University Council, convened the first national education conference at Nanking when official regulations were declared requiring

all schools, both private and government, to teach Party
principles in their curriculum. In the view of Kuomintang
leaders, this seemed to follow the expectation of Dr. Sun
as he said in the preface to the *San Min Chu I*:

> I hope that all our comrades will take the book
> as a basis or as a stimulus, expand and correct it,
> supply omissions, improve the arrangement and make
> it a perfect text for propaganda purposes. (143)

The goal of the Party, as stated in the Resolution on
Educational Reconstruction passed by the joint meeting of
the University Council and the Political Educational Commission in February 1928, was to "reconstruct the country by
the Party and to educate the people to conform to *San Min
Chu I*". (144) Educators under the new scheme were to promote among students the spirit of cooperation and cultural
self-consciousness in order to establish a modern republican government in China. In the same Resolution, the
name *'Tang Hua chiao-yü'* (Education Transformed by the Party)
is said to have no definite context and explicit origin and
is to be replaced by "*San Min Chu I chiao-yü*". (145) The
theory that education is a function of the State, formerly
asserted in the educational rights movement, was now practiced in the program of political instruction.

In following the movement of anti-Christian activities
throughout the decade, we observe that nationalism was the
constant ideological factor underlying the various forms of
anti-Christian expressions. As the country was suffering
from internal division and external aggression, the highest
hope of the people was to see it united and defended.
During the anti-Christian outbreak in 1922, Christianity
was opposed in a strong communist language and was regarded
as the instrument of Western capitalism. Marxist-Leninist
theory gained popularity among the Chinese radicals who
sought to manipulate the anti-Christian campaigns for their
own ends. As the movement was extended to attack religion
in general, Christianity was accused of being unscientific
and unsocial that would hinder the progress of national
reconstruction. Whereas the Christians argued that Christianity was the religion that China needed most for her
future, their critics simply denied the necessity of religion. To the Chinese intellectual, Christianity was alien
and had no Chinese root at all. For this reason, it could
not help establish China's national identity which required
an element of the past for its formation.

Missions were associated with foreign political manoeuvres. And the charge of imperialism was the dominant theme
in the anti-Christian writings. The Treaty System reminded
the Chinese of the historical alliance of Christianity with
the West. Their frustration over this issue was dramati-
cally ventilated in the aftermath of the May 30th Incident.
The demand for revision of these treaties became desperate
and justified. Foreign presence was severely protested
against by the Chinese nationalists. The numerous mission
schools over the country were criticized as imperialist
agents which sought to dull the national consciousness of
the Chinese youths. To many nationalists, Christian education should have no place in the national system of education.

All in all, nationalism had become the criterion of value
judgment in the era. Theories and actions of all kinds were
to be evaluated in terms of their possible contribution to
the task of national regeneration. To a large extent, the
anti-Christian movement was the effort to replace Christianity by the political religion of nationalism. Its religious dimension was especially recognizable in the development of the so-called "cult of Sun Yat-sen" during the Kuomintang regime. How did the Chinese Christians cope with
the challenge of this religious rival?

5

Nationalism:
Response of the
Chinese Church

Nationalism is a modern phenomenon in politics and has its
origin in Europe. It penetrated the civilization of the
West during the last century and was brought into China
through various cultural contacts. In its essentials,
nationalism has two basic constituents: a consciousness of
nationality which is a composite of the common linguistic,
cultural, and historical inheritance, and a loving commitment to it. In Carlton J. H. Hayes' definition, it is "a
condition of mind in which loyalty to the ideal or fact of
one's national state is superior to all other loyalties and
of which pride in one's nationality and belief in its intrinsic excellence and its 'mission' are an integral
part". (1)

For centuries, the Chinese have been proud of the Confucian culture, especially in comparison with what they
considered to be the "barbarism" of their neighbours.
Although the dynasties rose and fell, the superior civilization remained undisturbed. The Chinese commitment and
loyalty to the idea of a political state came after the
establishment of the Republic in 1912. In traditional
China, the central unit of society was the family which had
almost exclusive claim on its members. The exaltation of
the family's role had largely usurped the people's devotion
to national affairs. The Confucian doctrine of filial piety
(hsiao) permeated all aspects of social life. The *Classic
of Filial Piety (Hsiao Ch'ing)* has put it: *"Hsiao* is the
unchanging truth of Heaven, the unfailing equity of Earth,

the (universal) practice of man". (2) As Wu Lei-ch'uan commented, in Chinese tradition the people only knew the family
(chia) but not the country *(kuo)*. (3)

    In a similar vein, dedication to parents actually took
priority over that of the emperor. As Mencius taught, "Of
services, which is the greatest? Service toward parents
is the greatest. . . ." (4) Hsien-feng, the Ch'ing emperor
from 1859-1861, complained that many officials resigned to
care for family affairs during the T'ai P'ing Rebellion. (5)
Even among the gentry and literati, the so-called Chinese
patriotism was identified with loyalty to the emperor who
claimed to rule under a heavenly decree. The concept of a
nation was vague and undeveloped as long as the pattern of
social structure remained intact. However, in the later
years of the nineteenth century, this age-long Confucian
worldview was shaken at its foundation due to the impact of
the West. China's cultural heritage was found inadequate
by many Chinese intellectuals as seen in the anti-Confucian
movement in the early years of the Republic. In Joseph R.
Levenson's analysis, nationalism has substituted cultural-
ism. Levenson said:

    . . . when, for one reason and another, modern
    Chinese turned to foreign ways for China, the
    exaltation of nation over culture, of *kuo-chia*
    over *t'ien-hsia* was one of their manoeuvres.
    Culture should be changed, they said, if the
    change would serve the nation. Such a criterion
    was intellectually and emotionally helpful. Using
    it, one could feel both justified in calling for
    a break with tradition and soothed while contem-
    plating the tradition's decay. (6)

    Chinese nationalism at this time was ambiguous in shape.
This is easy to understand from our definition of nationalism. If nationalism is basically consciousness of the
cultural identity of the country, Chinese nationalism was
just right at a cross-roads, for its traditional identity
was being challenged. Many Chinese showed little or half-
hearted interest in the China of the past. They were
ambitious for Western alternatives; others were reluctant
to accept the West as both teacher and betrayer at the same
time. The lack of cultural reference explained the ideological openness to political novelties.

Despite this ambiguity, it is possible to trace the profile of Chinese nationalism. It was self-defensive rather than aggressive. The political tradition of China has been assimilative with regard to other peoples. As Bishop Stephen Neill, in *Colonialism and Christian Missions,* says:

> The Chinese have not been an imperialistic people in the sense of wishing to subject foreigners to their yoke. But over the centuries they have mani- fested an unwearied power of expansion and assimi- lation. Moving slowly but irresistibly forward into the forbidding ways of Central Asia, crossing the frontiers into what are now Vietnam and Thai- land, establishing and maintaining for centuries suzerainty over Korea, the Chinese people extended continually the sphere of Chinese culture, and thus brought some among the barbarians out of darkness into the clear light of day. (7)

China has been relatively free from international competitions that spotted the European continent. The emergency of nation-states in Europe and their mutual struggle for establishment and expansion were foreign to Chinese politics. Therefore, Chinese patriotism lacked, or had not yet developed, the aggressiveness, if not oppressiveness, of her Western neighbors. (8) Subsequent to the series of political setbacks--the unequal treaties, the territorial concessions, the Boxer indemnity, the Twenty-one Demands, the Versailles betrayal, and the Washington Conference--, the Chinese could no longer yield to the West in international negotiations. She had to defend her territorial integrity and national privileges. The upsurge of nationalism was a strong reaction to external pressure. While Western nations had already organized internally and some became an imperialistic force, Chinese nationalism was in the elementary stage of development. Whether it would follow the imperialistic path of the West was to be seen. Many westerners were worried about that possibility. But some Chinese Christians expressed confi- dence that traditional virtues of the Chinese people would prevent that from happening. Their desire for peace and willingness to forgive would cultivate a self-contained nationalism, free from aggressive ambition. (9)

Before Liang Ch'i-ch'ao published his *Ou-yu hsin-ying lu (Impressions of My European Travels)*, a single trend stood out in the various phases of modernization--the imitation

of the West. Science and democracy became the orthodox
principles. However, the adoption of the Western way could
not conceal the psychological tension in the thought of the
Chinese intellectuals that their teachers were also their
exploitors. Their dissatisfaction gave rise to the expectation to seek parity with the West and even to surpass it.
     The socialist appeal from Soviet Russia was therefore
attractive as it seemed to offer such possibility. And
Lenin's theory of imperialism gave his Chinese disciples
the belief in China's role in world revolution. But in
pre-Leninist Marxism, it was the standpoint of Continental
Marxists that the West was to impart guidance in the progress of revolution. Though willing to accept Soviet aid,
Dr. Sun Yat-sen was unwilling to substitute Marxist
Communism for his Three People's Principles, which he
recognized as the political solution for New China. Sun did
not formally oppose imperialism until his lectures on *San
Min Chu I* in 1924 after he had allied with the Communists.
It was possible that Communist influence had to some extent
affected his view of the aggressive West. Before this time,
Sun conceived of imperialism as territorial expansion
rather than political threat to China's national integrity.
(10) Nevertheless, Sun's understanding of imperialism was
not in economic terms as Lenin's last stage of capitalism.
Sun's goal was to abolish the unequal treaties and to unite
the country, which had been the hope of the people ever
since the establishment of the Republic.

     The two political forces that undergirded the anti-
Christian movement in the decade were communism (11) and
nationalism. Although the Communist movement was not yet
powerful in the early twenties, it was nonetheless a sus-
taining arm to the anti-Christian propaganda and hostilities. Nationalistic sentiment was the constant motivation
throughout the entire anti-Christian movement, and it
became dominant in the later twenties when the Kuomintang
consolidated its power. In the defense against the charge
of imperialism Chinese Christians attempted to confront
these two constituent forces in their apologetics.

RESPONSE TO THE COMMUNIST

     Among the political ideologies that captured the atten-
tion of the Chinese intellectuals during the May Fourth
Movement was socialism in its various forms. The word
'socialism' was a common slogan among the students. Ideas
of socialism (12) became a popular alternative to the
political ideologies imported from Western Europe and

America. Marxism, Bolshevism, and anarchism were hot topics of discussion in contemporary journals, such as *Min-kuo jih-pao, Hsin ch'ao, Hsin Ch'ing-nien, Chieh-fang, Shao-nien Chung-kuo.* Through the writings of Li Ta-chao, Ch'en Tu-hsiu, Chang Tung-sun, Bertrand Russell, Li Shih-tseng and Wu Chih-hui, various schools of socialistic thought were introduced.

Whether socialism was practicable in China was a controversial issue of the time. Liang Ch'i-ch'ao pointed out that "the socialist movement has to depend upon the emergence of the capitalist class and then the establishment of the labor class in China". (13) But Ch'en Tu-hsiu argued that the reconstruction and existence of China depend on the cooperation of the international socialist movement. The capitalist class of China is still immature, but everyone knows the oppression of foreign capitalism. Therefore, the Chinese should develop the concept of class struggle. (14) However, Lenin's theory of imperialism affirmed the possibility of revolution in non-industrialized countries like China and predicted the inevitable disintegration of Western capitalist nations. It offered to China a definite role in world revolution.

The coalition government of the Kuomintang and the Chinese Communist Party embodied different political views of socialistic revolution. Li Ta-chao was concerned with the transformation of Marxist ideas in the context of the Chinese peasantry. Sun Yat-sen, impressed by the Soviet example in the recent revolution and unable to elicit financial support from the West, began to lean to the left. Many Party leaders in Kuomintang, such as Tai Chi-tao, Hu Han-min, and Liao Chung-k'ai accepted part of Marxism from a nationalistic standpoint. (15)

Capitalism Evaluated

Many Chinese Christians were ready to agree with the socialists in condemning capitalism. To Chang I-ching "the capitalist system should not exist". (16) In Liang Chün-mo's view, "capitalism is the arch-enemy of Christianity. And in order to preserve itself, Christianity can only refute, without any reason for supporting, capitalism". (17) Chang Shih-chang, Secretary of National YMCA, similarly argued, "Christianity and socialsim teach that all kinds of property are entrusted by society and should be subject to the public use of it. Therefore, we consent to 'communism' and oppose 'capitalism'". (18)

Capitalism, as Liang Chün-mo defined it, designates the
private ownership by a social minority of the means of production and the production itself. In his critique, Liang
retreated to the historical Jesus, saying that he was an
excellent example in history who practiced anti-capitalism.
(19) Since Christ opposed capitalism, about eighty percent
of his disciples in history were proletarians. And many
have lost their Christian qualifications because of their
greed for wealth. In the Christian concept of stewardship,
all human beings are theoretically proletarians, for all
properties belong to God.

Chang I-ching contrasted the vulnerability and tran-
siency of earthly possession with the durability and perma-
nence of the heavenly riches. (20) Chang presented the
kingdom of God and its ministry as an alternative to the
acquisition of wealth and power. As Jesus taught, "No one
can serve two masters; for either he will hate the one and
love the other, or he will be devoted to the one and despise
the other. You cannot serve God and Mammon". (Matthew
6:24) (21) Jesus' life style repudiates any form of
capitalistic ownership. Although foxes and birds had their
resting places, the Son of Man had nowhere to lay his head.
Instead of explaining why capitalism is evil and should be
rejected in the Chinese society, many Chinese Christians
gave a theological condemnation of it. Their rationale
went like this: Since Jesus was not rich and since it is
difficult, if not impossible, for the rich to enter the
kingdom, to be rich is not necessarily good.

In South China, the influences of the Communist Party
were so prevalent among the students and so hostile against
the Christian Church that Chang I-ching and Liang Chün-mo
seemed to be anxious to seek common ground for dialogue
with them without unnecessarily disparaging their viewpoints. (22) Their attack on capitalism was intended to
undermine the anti-Christian indentification of Christianity
with capitalism. They hoped to show that the abuses of the
anti-Christians were not justified according to the Christian belief.

A moderate position, however, was adopted by other Christian spokesmen like Mi Hsing-ju of Nanking Theological
Seminary. Their attitude was reformative, not antagonistic,
seeking to understand the nature of capitalism and its
operation before exposing its weakness. As Mi Hsing-ju
said, "We are not like the anarchists, trying to overthrow
all existing institutions, nor the communists advocating

public ownership of all property". (23) He admitted the corruption and evil of the existing capitalist structure, but he found it difficult to get a substitute for it. Private ownership, in Mi's view, is not intrinsically evil, but the misuse of it is. Therefore, whether it should be abandoned or not is closely related to human decision regarding its disposal. In this way Mi is putting private ownership back into the hands of the individual, a reversal of the socialist argument. Private ownership has its indestructible social value in establishing the spirit of independence and in stabilizing one's enterprise, which will promote social progress. (24) However, Mi distinguished between the "property for use" and the "property for power". And it is the latter that Mi rejected, for it could be easily used as a means of oppression. The problem of the present social order stems from turning the "property for use" into the "property for power", resulting in the total control of wealth by a social minority.

The Christian responsibility, Mi continued, is to restore the system of "property for use". He was fully aware of the dangers of the capitalistic system which could easily give rise to the loss of the workers' freedom due to the control of capital, the inequitable treatment of laborers, and the absence of motivation of service in society. And it is the Christian obligation to live within the system and to improve it on both individual and communal level.

Mission and Imperialism

How did the Christians answer to the accusation that Christianity is the "running dog" of imperialism? In *Hsin wen-hua tz'u-shu (Dictionary of the New Culture)*, which was consulted by contemporary Chinese scholars, it said:

> As a person's right is jeopardized by others one can seek protection from the government and society. . . . But when one's right is jeopardized and can find no place for appeal, the citizen takes up defense in his own hands. As a result, if the highest authority to protect people's rights is absent, there is no other way of protecting the people and their properties apart from the use of soldiery. This is the teaching of imperialism. Imperialism carries the meaning of invasion. . . . Moreover, imperialism is conservative not defensive. As the British people say, we do not want to expand our territory but only hope to conserve what we

already have. However, in order to conserve our
existing territory, we may, if the need arises,
advance to invade our neighboring areas. (25)

This doctrine of invasion, as most Chinese Christians
commented, contradicts the Christian ethics of sacrifice,
service, and love. In Ch'en Li-t'ing's (26) view, there is
another dimension in the doctrine. Imperialism is a form
of individualism which exalts oneself and despises others
to the extent that any opposite form of authority and ideology must be suppressed. This undoubtedly is part of the
whole imperialistic mentality. (27)

In Lenin's theory, imperialism is the highest stage of
capitalism when the industrial powers compete with each
other to seek overseas markets for their products. By
exploiting the colonial peoples, the capitalists will create
a new proletariat which includes the toiling mass of the
backward countries, dividing the world into the exploiting
and the exploited. The struggle for revolution now involves
the cooperation of the oppressed people of all nations.
Anti-imperialism becomes an integral part of the communist
program to foster class consciousness of the proletariat
among the backward people in colonial and semi-colonial
countries.

What is the relation between Christian missions and this
form of foreign invasion. Nearly all Christian writers
denounced imperialism and denied their alliance with it.
They set up Jesus as an anti-imperialistic model who com-
bated the Roman imperialism of his time. He refused to be
crowned king by his own kinsmen in order not to assert a
form of Jewish imperialism against the local government. (28)
His anti-imperialism resulted in his crucifixion, which was
a clear witness to his devotion to the struggle with the
existing oppressive system.

Ch'en Li-t'ing analyzed the relation between imperialism
and mission into two aspects: 1. Had imperialism high-
handedly used religion for its purpose? 2. Was Christianity willing to be the running dog of imperialism? (29)
Ch'en argued that if Christianity was manipulated by
imperialists, it should not be its fault but that of the
manipulators. Previously, Bismarck of Germany attempted to
employ Darwin's theory of the survival of the fittest to
justify his blood-and-iron politics. But the theory of

evolution was not, according to Ch'en, to be held responsible for the criminality of the German invasion. Christian missions should not be identified with any political
or economic exploiters.

The two notorious missionary incidents often referred to
by anti-Christians as historical warrant of the imperialist
behavior of Christianity were the German occupation in
Shangtung and the Boxer indemnities. In Ch'en's explanation,
the murder of the two German Roman Catholic missionaries
just happened to be the opportunity to fulfill their ambition of establishing a base for their East Asian development. Many *chiao-an* (missionary cases) were due to the
undesirable elements of society seeking religious protection for their anti-social practices. It had nothing to do
with the Christian faith.

The criticism of Christian missions as cultural invasion
was hardly acceptable to the Christians. They argued that
this kind of invasion is culturally non-existent. In the
history of Chinese civilization, the mingling of two cultures has given forth a higher product, assimilating the
best of each. (30) The neo-Confucian scholarship in the
Sung Dynasty was a synthesis of traditional Confucianism
and imported Buddhism. Chinese leaders, like Chao Tzu-
ch'en, Wei Cho-min, and Ch'en Li-t'ing, were optimistic
about the cultural outcome when Christianity came into contact with Chinese civilization. For example, the Christian
concept of the Fatherhood of God is an extended family
ideal which harmonizes with the family-oriented Chinese
society. (31)

From the standpoint of anti-Christians the allegiance
between Christian missions and imperialism was due to
several reasons:

1. The coming of Christianity during the nineteenth century was under the protection of the gunboats and the Unequal Treaties.

2. Western capitalistic countries were also the
'Christian' nations.

3. Numerous missionary incidents had been used
by the Western Powers to elicit territorial concessions and indemnities from the Chinese Government.

4. Christianity taught a theory of determinism
which easily fooled the Chinese people into accepting as divine arrangement oppression and corruption
without resistance, thus minimizing the possibility
of revolutionary reform most needed by the country.

These four reasons seem to be well supported by evidence
from the history of modern Sino-foreign relations. The
difference between the accuser and the defender of Christianity is the interpretation of historical data. Whereas
anti-Christians associated evangelism with imperialism,
Christian apologists maintained that the connection was not
casual and that other factors should be considered to give
an adequate historical picture. Often these other factors
were not easily appreciated by people outside the Church.
How could they sympathize with the religious enthusiasm of
the missionaries in coming to 'heathen' China to save
'sinners'? How could they not suspect the motives of the
missionaries in scattering to different parts of China as
closely related to political intrigue? How could they
understand the separation between church and state in the
West when they saw the missionary and diplomat coming
together in the same ship?

These questions undoubtedly created intellectual gaps in
the minds of the Chinese, widened by the misdemeanor of the
Christian Church and the scandalous propaganda of the anti-
Christian movements, which made it difficult for any Christian apologetics to gain a hearing. For the anti-Christians
the 'unholy alliance' remained profane despite the amount of
holy water sprinkled over it. However, some Chinese Christians shared the conviction of Hsü Pao-ch'ien that "among
the intellectual class in China, at least there is a section that will admit that although Christianity actually has
been willfully connected in history with imperialism or has
been used by it, opposite evidences are however not lacking.
Therefore, Christianity and imperialism could, in some way,
be disentangled from each other". (32)

What, then, is the role of the Christian Church in
society? Some Christian apologists affirmed the similarity
of purpose between the socialist movement and the Christian
movement. Both want to create a new world. They feel that
the present social order is too corrupt and evil, but they
trust that reform is possible. In a comparative study of
Christianity and socialism, Chang Shih-chang argued that
both of them are working for the happiness of the individual
and the community. (33) Despite their common goal, Chris-

tianity and socialism adopt different methods. In Christianity, the Church is the agent of the ameliorative function in restricting evil and promoting good. But the
socialists would employ governmental sanction to institute
legal procedures to control life and property. (34) The
Christian program is slow and progressive; the socialist,
drastic and revolutionary. The Christian reform usually
starts with the individual and ends with society. But the
socialist will first deal with the social structure before
the social individual.

In the understanding of many Christian writers, Christianity is not unfamiliar with socialism, for a form of
communism was practiced in the early church. The passage in
The Book of Acts was often quoted.

> And all who believed were together and had all
> things in common; and they sold their possessions
> and goods and distributed them to all, as any had
> need. (2:44-45, RSV) (35)

The spirit of communism is, in Liang Chün-mo's view, not
lacking at all in the early church at Jerusalem. "Christianity teaches the liberation of the spirit and affirms the
inborn equality of all human beings". (36) If man's conscience still operates in him, he will not endorse any class
distinction. Liang held that Christianity can be regarded
as a source of communist ideology, though different from
modern communism which is established on the basis of
economics.

There are, however, as many differences as similarities
between early Christian communism and modern communism. As
Chan Wei of the University of Shanghai pointed out, Christian
communism was not a necessary condition for membership in
the early church. The sharing of property was an act of
free will and did not exclude private property. (37) Early
Christians were led by their conscience to help the needy,
and there was no collective coercion to bind on them. The
spirit of mutual aid prevailed in those days, out of the
recognition that they all belonged to the same Body of Christ.
But such voluntariness and religious consciousness are not
present in modern communism.

Possible Coexistence

Can Christianity and Communism exist together in China?
This was not a question at all for the Communist proponents
who right away denied the possibility. Some argued that in
both theory and practice Communism and Christianity cannot
be mentioned together. A Christian communist or a communist
Christian is a contradiction in terms. Li Huang studied the
problem and affirmed the humanistic origin of socialism. In
his essay on "Socialism and Religion", Li argued that the
emergence of socialism in the eighteenth century was due to
the intellectual struggle against religious dominance. (38)
The advent of science, in his view, has given adequate
indication that the universe does not come from creation but
from evolution. Man is able to build a society of freedom
and equality without any reliance on deity. "Therefore",
Li said, "from the eighteenth century until now, the
Europeans have been engaged in the task of creativity,
dependent on their own strength. With the principle of
equality, freedom, and mutual assistance of the human race,
they have developed socialism". (39) Li Huang admitted
certain similarities in the practice of Christianity and
socialism, but in spirit the two worlds are miles apart. To
him, any religious talk was regarded as harmful to the exer-
tion of human effort in working for a better future. For
"the spirit of socialism is entirely in this world but the
spirit of religion is in heaven. Socialism does not create
a speculative world, beyond the present one, that controls
individual thought and behavior. . . . Simply speaking,
socialism is rational not superstitious, scientific not
mystical". (40)

The viewpoints of Chinese Christians regarding the question of coexistence of Communism and Christianity were
divided. In an analysis of the reform movements in China,
Chan Wei took a depreciative attitude toward Chinese communism, affirming that it was not suitable for China. (41) In
Chan's argument, China is not yet a country in which
capitalism has matured. There is still much possibility for
economic development, and the social structure has not
reached a point of collapse. A socio-economic revolution is
not needed, as suggested by the Communists. What China
urgently wants, according to Chan Wei, is enough capital to
develop the rich untapped resources in the country.

It is true, Chan Wei continued, that capitalism in
Western nations has its shortcomings, but China can select
what is beneficial and avoid the harmful. Workers can

organize cooperative guilds, accumulating their properties
to start other factories in competition with the capitalists.
The greatest difficulty of the nation is not the inequitable
distribution of properties but the inadequate development of
her potential. Chan warned that if communism is practiced
in China, the existing capitalists will transfer their money
to the International Settlement or overseas, aggravating the
internal situation of poverty. And it is under the capitalistic system that China will expect production of higher
quality and quantity.

In a communist regime, in Chan's opinion, private enterprises will be totally discouraged. As testified by the
progress of Western industrial nations, private business
often stimulate creativity and initiative which will be
absent in the communist system. When distribution of wealth
is according to necessity instead of according to perform-
ance, many people will become idle and the national efficiency of production will be lowered. (42) As the government becomes the owner of all enterprises, its officials
will be given too much authority to control the people's
welfare. The corruption of the warlords is already a warning to such situations. Though capitalism has its weakness,
it is, in Chan Wei's conclusion, a better alternative to
communism in reconstructing the economic life of China.
And Christianity is believed to be able to improve capitalism and make it practicable.

Between the positions of a total rejection of Christianity
and an unsympathetic criticism of Marxist socialism, there
were Chinese Christians interested in showing the similarities, rather than in illustrating the differences, between
the two faiths. Their interest largely stemmed from their
concern for reconciling the mutual antagonism. They were
optimistic about the possible cooperation between the two
movements. It is easy to note a psychology of compromise
which existed among the Christian apologists as they took
issue with the anti-Christian movement which was strongly
sponsored by the Communists.

Chang Shih-chang and Liang Chün-mo were advocates of
socialism in China. They maintained that Christianity and
socialism concur in their major premises and differ only in
minor points. Chang saw the necessity of practicing some
form of socialism in China due to the uneven economic situation. Many Western socialists, such as Fourier, St. Simon,
and John Spargo have belief in the Christian religion. (43)
The Christian and the socialist will agree to affirm the

intrinsic value of the person, the responsibility of the
individual to the community, the sharing of property, and
equal opportunity of development for all. In Hsü Pao-
ch'ien's comment;

> . . . in communism there are certain points in
> agreement with the spirit of Christianity. First,
> both seek to liberate the oppressed nations of the
> world; secondly, to unite with the oppressed of
> the world to resist the oppressors. In other words,
> both communism and Christianity are international
> in character. (44)

Some Christian leaders pointed out the weakness of the
socialist view in having a materialistic interpretation of
life. Liang Chün-mo acknowledged the importance of the
spiritual dimension as complementary to the material life.
Religion is a kind of spiritual belief, internal and
personal. Communism emphasizes the material way of life,
external and social. In Liang's opinion, they are not
mutually exclusive. He predicted that "if communism is to
be practised in the future, Christianity will be even more
prosperous. At that time, the present hardships of material
life are removed, more attention will be given to spiritual
devotion. Religion will then be inevitable". (45) And
"The communist movement cannot be successful without the
spirit of religion". (46)

In seeking cooperation between Christianity and socialism,
some Christians were worried about the radicalism of the
socialist approach. In an attempt to overthrow all existing systems, it may not be able to construct better ones
afterwards. (47) They hoped that in the future "these two
powerful forces will be able to rebuild a new society.
However, socialism should need Christianity for its modification in order to contain its radicalism for achieving the
intended purpose". (48) The fear that class struggle could
happen in China was shared by the Chinese Christians, for
Marxism considered it an indispensable step to revolution.
The use of violence contradicts the Christian principle of
forgiveness and altruism. It was suggested that Marxist
socialism can be tempered by the Christian pacifism of
Rauschenbusch and Harry Ward. (49) The movement of Christian socialism in the West was regarded as a successful
example of non-violent reform. Most Christian leaders saw
the contemporary situation as an opportunity that Christianity could not afford to lose in joining hands with
socialism to reconstruct the nation.

RESPONSE TO THE NATIONALIST

Political Involvement

In the era of unrestrained nationalism, the question of
politics provoked various reactions among the Chinese
Christians. The majority were indifferent to the issue.
(50) Conservative Chinese Christians believed in withdrawal
from politics, for it was "dirty" and "secular". Many
centered their Christianity on the pre-millennial return of
Christ, an outlook of otherworldliness. (51) In their view,
the Church and the world are opposite in value, and any
political matter involves compromise of Christianity. The
duty of the Christian is to keep himself uncontaminated
with the corruption of the secular order. Some Christians
were afraid that mutual interference between church and
state would be harmful to the promotion of both good
citizenship and spiritual life. The Church would easily
lose sight of its mission of evangelism if it was entangled
with matters of secondary importance.

On the other side, there were those who took a political
interpretation of their faith. Since the early twenties,
Hsü Ch'ien, (52) a close colleague of Dr. Sun in the
Kuomintang, had been advocating national salvation through
Christianity. He held that Christianity should be the
basis for the Chinese Republic. Under his leadership the
Christian National Salvation Association was organized,
admitting into membership both Christians and non-believers
who would subscribe to the goal of the Association. (53)
In an anti-Christian gathering at Wuchang in 1927, Hsü
explained the position of the Kuomintang and urged Chinese
Christians to join the nationalist revolution. (54) From
the inspiration of the Lord's Prayer, Hsü established a
form of Christian anarchism in a theocratic structure. In
his view, all hypocritical systems of monarchy and constitutional democracy will vanish when the people are subjected to the reign of God. It is superstitious to believe
that the present world is too evil to be improved. We
should reform our world before the coming of the heavenly
kingdom. Hsü attempted to render Christianity politically
useful to the nation before the challenge of anti-Christians
and nationalists. He emphasized that "unless the nation is
saved, man and the world will never be saved". He asked,
"How can those who have lost their nation be permitted to
enter the kingdom of God"? (55) As the former conservative
group was skeptical about the virtues of politics, Hsü and

his followers were convinced of the merits of a politicized
Christianity. Hsü felt that his mission was to preach
revolution to the Christians and Christianity to the
revolutionists.

The political thought of Wu Lei-ch'uan bore similarity
to Hsü Ch'ien's radicalism. Wu's effort was to relate
Christianity, divested of traditional irrelevance and
Western elements, to the task of national reconstruction.
In his view, political actions were part of social reform,
leading to the formation of the ideal society, the promised kingdom of God. He struck an optimistic note about
the impact of the May 30th Incident on the Church. For the
first time, Wu observed, Chinese Christians were so concerned with national affairs that they joined the mass
movement to protest against racial injustice. (56) From
Jesus' parable of the talents in Matthew 25, Wu argued that
in matters of political reform, God will help those who
help themselves. In order to save his nation, Jesus devoted
himself to revolutionize religion which was the center of
Jewish politics and tradition. His disciples should apply
the spirit of Jesus in the struggle for the nation's
future. (57) Although Wu saw Christianity and revolution
fully compatible with each other for China's salvation, he
was critical of the government of Chiang Kai-shek. To him
the policy of the Nanking regime would destroy the confidence of the people and suppress intellectual activities.
(58)

Some Christian officials in the Kuomintang sought to
integrate Christianity into the program of revolution by
having religion serve the purpose of politics. Sun Fo,
the son of Dr. Sun Yat-sen, persuaded the Christians to
join the Kuomintang. He said, "Although Christianity and
Kuomintang have different tasks, their goals are the same.
Therefore, we look forward to their cooperation in the
future in building a powerful Republic of China". (59) The
purpose of the Kuomintang was purely political, but its
membership was open to all Chinese, regardless of their
religious backgrounds. Chang chih-chiang, Chief-of-Staff of
the Revolutionary Army, set revolution to be the criterion
for genuine Christianity. Chang stressed the political
aspect of Jesus' life and took him as a leader of the
proletarian revolution. In his view, Jesus' model of altruism and service should form the basis of a revolutionary
ethics for the Chinese people. A real follower of Jesus
will make a faithful member of the Revolutionary Party. He
can never be anti-revolutionary. (60)

Between the view of total separation and total involvement, there was a middle party which promoted a politics of calculated participation. They acknowledged the danger in going either direction, and they did not overlook the political dimension of the Christian Gospel. As Hung Wei-lien, dean of Yenching University from 1924-27, said: "On the one hand, we do no longer desire to maintain an attitude of other-worldly disinterestedness, or a policy of exclusive evangelical individualism. On the other hand, we want to avoid the danger of church-state and the temptation of ultra-secularism". (61) In Yü Jih-chang's opinion, the Christian Church in modern China could not be exempted from reproach, for it had sought political protection and had allowed foreign governments to use it to realize their ambitions. The Church should not meddle with government policies. But if politics transgressed the basic Christian principles of peace and freedom, Yü asked, could the Church remain passive? From the Confucian doctrine of the mean *(chung yung)*, Yü suggested a political *via media* for the Chinese Church, which was "not only to avoid extremities, but to follow the path discovered after careful investigation of the situation, seeking the greatest benefit for the whole community". (62) Yü's purpose was not to politicize Christianity but to Christianize politics. For all spheres of human life, in Yü's view, are under the providential concern of God, and Christianity does not preach a compartmentalized life with the false division between the spiritual and the secular. If we see politics as part of man's search for purpose and meaning in his historical existence, God will definitely have a part in it.

The question of Christianity and politics became more acute when the Nationalist Government commenced its Northern Expedition in the summer of 1926. Should the Christian Church as a religious body participate in it or stay away from it? Chao Tzu-ch'en was politically conservative in reaction to this question. In his view, church and state should organically separate and functionally cooperate. The Church is primarily a community of believers seeking to cultivate their relationship to God. The state maintains order and conserves progress. Due to the difference in nature, the Christian Church should not conform itself to any political ideology or join any political party. (63) Chao said, "The Church transcends parties and organizations, for its voice is a judgment of right and wrong, advocating righteousness and opposing wickedness. If the government is corrupt with evil, the Church condemns it without excuse. If the government does good in political action, the Church

should commend it and ask God to bless it". (64) And under
whatever political circumstances, the Church should never
fail to practice Jesus'principle of sacrifice and altruism.
Chao's political conservatism gave him unresolved conflict
when confronted with the revolutionary atmosphere of the
hour. He tried hard to maintain a middle path between
"total revolution and total compassion". He commented that
"I have decided to be revolutionary in spirit and adopt a
gradual course of action". (65)

Morality in Politics

    Chinese Christians in favor of political participation
as part of the Christian civil responsibility welcomed the
rising tide of nationalism. They thought that Christianity
is not incompatible with its growth. If the Chinese are to
practice a sane nationalism, the best way is to promote the
spirit of Christianity and to imitate the reform of Jesus
in the early church. As the ardent nationalists were concerned with the achievement of political ends, Chinese
Christians gave attention to the morality of the means.

    Theoretically, two kinds of nationalism were disting-
uished. "Narrow nationalism" is another term for antiforeignism that seeks to establish one's power and wealth
at the expense of other nations. This form of nationalism
easily extends itself beyond the national boundary to
imperialistic exploitation. (66) "Broad nationalism" is
loyalty to the welfare of one's country and commitment to
develop its resources and tradition for the benefit of all.
It does not neglect the interest of other nations and hopes
to maintain harmony in international relationship. Chinese
Christians believed that "broad nationalism" does not
violate the principles of the Christian faith and is suitable for China's future. (67)

    However, in Hsü Pao-ch'ien's observation, "the movement,
though called nationalistic, is really blown about by the
winds of current fashions and is nothing more than copying
the out-worn wisdom of Europe and America". (68) Since
Chinese nationalism practically followed the tendency of
narrow nationalism, conflict with Christianity seemed inevitable. As Lucius Porter, professor at Yenching University,
put it, it was a conflict of priorities. Porter said, "The
problem is one that every Christian must face for himself
since the majority of his countrymen will put national
loyalty first and personal conviction second". (69) And
Chinese Christians had a hard time to explain to anti-

Christians why they espoused a higher loyalty to other than
their nation and, at the same time, claimed to be patriotic.
They consented to the goal of the nationalist movement to
defeat imperialism, to abolish unequal treaties, and to seek
self-determination. But a constant Christian challenge to
the nationalist revolution was directed to the morality of
its politics. As Hsü Pao-ch'ien criticized, "this movement,
at the most, only urges a strong China, but does not ask
about the standard by which the desired strength shall be
measured". (70) Although the primary goal of the Church is
not political and the Church is not to join any political
party, it, however, plays the role of a political critic.
In Hung Wei-lien's remark, "While we as ministers and
missionaries must not, as our Lord did not, participate in
political activities, we ought to study and understand the
political movements of our day. We ought to have our convictions of their rights or wrongs. We need not refrain
from expressing our judgment, if our judgment has any influence to make things better". (71)

In emphasizing "judgment" and "standard" for political
actions, the Christian leaders attempted to bring morality
to politics. As Yü Jih-chang said, "Our effort is to raise
our (political) thought to a higher spiritual level". (72)
What is the Christian basis in moralizing politics
among non-believers? Some Chinese Christians faced this
question by appealing to the moral unity of the human race
which allows both Christians and non-Christians to cooperate
for a common political goal. In Lo Yün-yen's view, a political spirit of right and wrong lies in man's heart, and it
can be cultivated through the function of religion. (73)
The belief in this inborn capacity encouraged Chinese Christians to advocate broad nationalism to substitute for narrow
nationalism. The principles of justice, equality, freedom,
and fraternity constitute the criteria for political participation. While the nationalists placed the interest of the
nation before everything else, the end before the means, the
Christians followed moral principles and were confident that
they would better serve the nation's interest in the long
run. The priority of interest became a major cause of anti-
Christian opposition from the standpoint of nationalism.

Chinese Christians found support for their position in the
life of Jesus. His patriotism was seen in his mission and
compassion for his Jewish kinsmen. "Jews first, then
Gentiles", defined his evangelistic order. (74) That Jesus
wept for Jerusalem was repeatedly quoted to show the intensity of his national sympathy (Luke 13:19). The use of

violence to achieve political aims was hardly taught. Moreover, national authority and racial privilege never had any
absolute claim in Jesus. His view of nationalism was balanced by redemptive individualism and cooperative internationalism. (75) Many believed that the doctrine of universal solidarity of mankind would be the Christian remedy
to the possible peril of narrow nationalism in China.

National egoism is contrary to the political heritage of
the Chinese people, many Chinese Christians argued. One
said: "It is to be feared that such nationalism is not sufficient to manifest, either the inner spirit of China's
traditional culture, or to offer to the world China's real
message and contribution". (76) In Fan Tzu-mei's analysis
of the Confucian political theory, the political vision of
the Chinese sage went beyond national boundaries. World
politics would move toward the ultimate phase of the Great
Peace *(T'ai P'ing)*. (77) In practical politics, two kinds
of approach were distinguished. The government of *wang*
(sage king) is conducted through moral education but that of
pa (warlord) through compulsion. In Fan's view, the Confucian *wang-tao* should be the political solution for the
chaotic decades after the establishment of the Chinese Republic. Along a similar line of seeking classical defense
against the current narrow nationalism, Hu I-ku urged that
the moral virtues in Chinese political tradition had to be
preserved. The way of *Chung Shu* and the willingness to
overcome evil with good, which had sustained the political
relationship with foreigners for many centuries, would be
appropriate in modern China. (78)

In order to temper the intensity of Chinese patriotism
and to channel it to a constructive direction, Chinese
Christians emphasized internationalism. They thought that
nationalism and internationalism are complementary to each
other. According to Yü Jih-chang, internationalism simply
means universal friendship in the family of nations. In a
family, each member will not lose its identity but contri-
butes to, and receives benefit from, the common welfare.
The same thing should happen in the international family
where no one can exist without depending on others. Internationalism, in Yü's view, is not only compatible with the
highest patriotism but is helpful to its development. (79)
Frank Lee also commented, "The Christian basis for international cooperation does not preclude China from becoming
a strong nation; for it will make China internally strong
and exalt her among the nations". (80) This conviction had
led the Christian community to appeal to foreign countries

for sympathy and support after the May 30th Affair. The
practice of internationalism was prevalent in the modern
world in the area of literature, commerce, industry, science
and arts. It was not a dream but already a reality. However, for the Chinese people to accept such a view in the
hour of political disparity, an "international psychology"
had first to be cultivated. (81) And Christianity was most
suited to this task, for the Christian spirit was a spirit
of internationalism. The religious basis of such cosmo-
politan outlook, built upon Jesus' doctrine of the universal
kingdom, should help realize an ecumenical politics. "Only
a true nationalist can be a true internationalist, and, on
the other hand, only a true internationalist can make a true
nationalist". (82) Nationalism, according to the Christian
apologists, is a necessary stage to internationalism, and
internationalism is the completion of nationalism.

However, this ecumenical politics was hardly welcomed by
the nationalists. In their minds, nationalism and internationalism are opposite terms. Anti-Christians regarded
the Christian view of internationalism as a disguised form
of denationalization. During the critical time when China
was struggling against foreign aggression, this theory, they
argued, would undermine the fighting spirit of the Chinese
people. The preaching of internationalism would only betray
the future of the nation. Mindful of the severe opposition
to the Christian proposal of internationalism, some Christian leaders found a way out by emphasizing the order of
approach in the task of national construction. They consented to Dr. Sun Yat-sen's view in his lecture on People's
Nationalism by putting nationalism before internationalism.
Dr. Sun compared internationalism to the lottery ticket and
nationalism to the coolie's bamboo pole. In his excitement,
the coolie threw away the bamboo pole in which he had put
the winning lottery ticket. He lost both of them. If the
Chinese forgot nationalism, in Dr. Sun's view, they would
"face the possibility of a lost nation and a vanishing
race". (83) Sun argued, "We must espouse nationalism and in
the first instance attain our own unity, then we can consider
others and help the weaker, small peoples to unite in a
common struggle. . . . Together we shall use right to fight
might, and when might is overthrown and the selfishly ambitious have disappeared, then we may talk about cosmopoli-
tanism". (84)

Employing Dr. Sun's viewpoint, Chao Kuan-hai, an articulate Christian spokesman, insisted that it would be advisable to delay internationalism until the nation itself was

put in order. (85) Even Jesus' mission began with the Jewish race. While nationalists gave exclusive priority to
nationalism, Chinese Christians considered its precedence
to internationalism. According to Wu Lei-ch'uan, both
nationalism and internationalism are found in Christianity,
like the practice of Great Vehicle and Small Vehicle in
Buddhism. The Buddhist believer cannot ignore the discipline of Small Vehicle in his admiration of the perfection
of the Greater Vehicle. As far as national boundary remains,
Wu commented, we should first be concerned with national
construction before international harmony. (86) In his view,
both Jesus and Confucius taught the theory of world peace,
but religious patriotism and political patriotism are in
some measure different. Whereas, a political movement resolves a temporary problem, religion deals with a life-long
issue. (87) Christian patriotism will cultivate useful
citizenship that survives the nationalist revolution. Yet
weak China should first be strengthened, and the attainment
of peaceful coexistence among the nations is to be accomplished on the basis of balanced strength.

Christian Education for Moral Cultivation

The Christian emphasis on morality in politics was consistent with the popular theory of national salvation
through character *(jen-ko chiu-kuo)*. It is on this basis
that Christian apologists faced the challenge of the anti-
Christian educational movement.

As it has been shown in the previous chapter, anti-Christians did not want the presence of Christian education in
the national system. Chinese educators insisted on the
separation of education from religion in order to protect
the religious liberty of the students and to preserve the
principles of education. Nationalists argued that foreign
control must be returned to the Chinese and that mission
schools must be purged of any "stink of religion". Communists accused Christian education of being a form of cultural invasion harmful to the national character. The most
audible voice was that Christian education does not cohere
with the purpose of national education and has no place in
it.

Christian educators had been persistent in defending the
usefulness of Christian education in China. In the Report
of the China Education Commission in 1922, it was affirmed
that Christian education is indispensable to the Christian
movement. Its goal is to establish the Christian community,

which is the *raison d'etre* of its existence. Education and
evangelism are the dual aspects of the process. The Report
regarded Christianity as an "educative force" in character
formation. As E. W. Wallace said, "It is here that emphasis
must be laid in the future, if our education is to be of
lasting value to China or to the Christian community". (88)
In Ch'eng Hsiang-fan's view, the present social disorder is
due to the lack of religious and moral training of the
people. Such training given in Christian schools would
enable students to cultivate a Christ-like spirit of dedication, uprightness, and loyalty, which is necessary to
national reconstruction. This extra dimension marks the
difference between Christian education and public education.
(89)

The unique place of Christian education in China was well
expressed in the Statement of Educational Principles prepared by the China Christian Education Association. It
said,

> The primary purpose of all education is the
> development of personality and of moral character,
> and it is in this sphere that Christian people
> believe that they have a special contribution to
> make to the life of China. (90)

According to the Statement, the existence of private
schools coheres with the spirit of democracy and offers a
diversity of education which will enrich, rather than
hinders, the national system. The China Christian Educational Association affirmed its readiness to integrate
Christian schools into the government scheme by seeking
registration and accepting academic supervision. This
answered the anti-Christian charge that Christian education
was autonomous and outside state control. Another important
thesis dealt with indigenization of administration. It
said,

> It is their ideal, which is being increasingly
> realized, that Christian education should become
> Chinese in spirit, in content, in support and in
> control. This is the expressed purpose not only
> of Chinese and western Christian educators, but
> also of the mission bodies which have in the past,
> supported the Christian schools, and of the Chris-
> tian community which is gradually taking over their
> support and control. (91)

The demand for transfer of leadership to Chinese hands
was fully met. In the interpretation of the constitution
of religious liberty, the Statement was cautious not to
mention the propagation of religion save the provision of
religious training for "children of the members of the Christian community and for others who desire to avail themselves
of private schools of that type". (92) This was the "special
function" of the Christian schools that they were eager to
defend, the only condition they did not surrender for the
sake of registration. There was no mention of the debate
over the advisability of voluntary religious activities, for
it was absorbed in their willingness to gain recognition
with the local or central government. (93) The position of
the Statement was similar to the declaration of the *Chung-
hua chi-tu-chiao chiao-yü chi-k'an (China Christian Educational Quarterly)* which affirmed the principles that Christian education should be democratized and indigenized. (94)

The general tendency of Christian education during the
Kuomintang regime was the reorganization of the school from
the foreign to Chinese basis. The obligation of Party
Education was one step forward in the nationalistic direction to place education on the Party line. This was part
of the policy of the Kuomintang to "govern the nation by the
Party". Christian educators were afraid that Christian
education would, under the pressure of the time, be subjugated to the whims of the Party or lost its distinctiveness.
By now, the problem of registration was largely settled.
But the question about the role of Christian education continued to be discussed.

Some included Party education in Christian education,
convinced that the evangelistic program of Christian missions would be preserved without neglecting its responsibility to the Party. This view still kept a religious
priority and regarded education as a tool of religion.
Others denied any independent purpose, religious or not, of
Christian education. Christian education was not to hoist
another flag in competition with Party education or to consider it secondary. It should serve the Party, and in doing
so, it would preserve its uniqueness and achieve its goal.

In spite of the diversity of viewpoints, the persistent
argument was that Christian education helped character
formation which was important to Party construction. According to Hsieh Fu-ya, (95) professor of Lingnan University,
"Christian education will cultivate benevolent, courageous,
pure, and unselfish men for our Party. They will undertake

the task of the Party and accomplish its mission. . . . In order to revivify the Kuomintang the Christian party members should make their utmost contribution in support of the party. In order to expand and stabilize the party, Christian education should occupy a permanent and supreme place in the plans of the party". (96) Various steps were taken by Christian schools to achieve such aim, for example, recruiting teachers of real Christian character, increasing Christian student body to cultivate a Christian atmosphere in campus, and strengthening the relationship between students and teachers, between church and school. (97)

The emphasis of character training was a search for common ground between Christian education and Party education. Christianity had to combat the accusation that it was useless to China in the upsurge of nationalism. As *jen-ko chiu-kuo* had been a prevailing slogan in the decade to awaken Chinese youths to the task of national reconstruction, *jen-ko chiu-tang* continued the theory, applied more specifically to reviving the Party. It formed a sound basis of argument for a place, perhaps a permanent place, for Christian education. As one educator said, "If we can give to China a large number of absolutely honest and truly unselfish men and women . . . there will be no question of the place of our Christian schools". (98) This conviction stemmed from, and was consistent with, the theological motif of the contemporary apologetics. Changed individuals would change society. The example and spirit of Jesus offered both the pattern and the power to the moral cultivation of the Chinese people. Loyalty to this conviction kept missionaries and Chinese educators in their ministries in spite of the vicissitudes in the political and social scene.

Party and Christianity

The main problem that confronted the Chinese Church under the Kuomintang government dealt with its relation to the Party. Could the separation of church and state be practiced in China in the present political milieu? If not, to what extent should they cooperate? And how was such cooperation to be justified in the light of the Christian faith?

In the observation of some Chinese Christians, the Kuomintang has become a religious organization with its dogmas and rituals. (99) The religious dimension was seen in the memorial service of Dr. Sun, the bowing before his portrait, the Three Minutes' Silence, the public reading of his will, the celebration of his birthday, and the taking of oath

before his tablet. And his *Chien-kuo fang-lüeh, Chien-kuo
ta-kang,* the Manifesto of the First National Congress of
the Party and, above all, the *San Min Chu I*--became the
canon of the Party 'religion'. In the hearts of the people
the spirit of the great Leader reigned. As E. R. Hughes
said, "It is the Nationalist Party itself which has nailed
its color to the mast, their watchword obedience to Sun
Chung Shan (Sun Yat-sen) and his principles, he, being dead,
alive in their midst, vitalizing the Party and stirring life
in the breasts of the common people everywhere". (100)

Ever since the reorganization of the Kuomintang in 1923,
there had been a strong tendency in Dr. Sun's strategy to
put the Party above the State during the period of revolution. His position was made explicit at the beginning of
1924 when Sun adopted one-Party rule, following the effective Soviet principle. (101) When Chiang Kai-shek took
over leadership, he applied Sun's doctrine and continued
the one-Party reign. In the opinion of many Chinese Christians, it was a matter of political expediency for them to
accept the new government. But its 'religious' activities
made them uncomfortable.

While anti-Christian Party members saw religion and the
Party as mutually competitive, Christian apologists regarded
them cooperative. In explaining the ground for such
cooperation, Chang Shih-chang stressed that it does not mean
the subordination of one to the other. (102) Religion and
politics have a division of labor according to their respective nature. The Party will be inspired by the spirit of
religion without adopting its ceremonies. And religion will
be protected by the Party from the dogmatism of state
religion. In this way, Chang was willing to accept the
one-Party rule over the State. But he objected to the uni-
fication of the Party and religion which, in his view, would
easily lead to the subjugation of religion to the Party.
The inevitable result will be the swallowing up of religion
by the Party. If, as some Kuomintang members demanded,
religious doctrines become part of the Party ideology, the
distinctiveness of religion will soon be lost. And the
Kuomintang will become a religious state. History has
many examples of state religions deteriorating into inflex-
ibility and corruption. A religious war may even occur in
China.

Some Chinese Christians not only believed in the possibility of cooperation between the Kuomintang and Christianity, but they also suggested that Christianity will help

the Party achieve its end. Hsieh Fu-ya asserted that "The
personality of Christ does not conflict with the Kuomintang,
but will serve as the foundation upon which the success of
the Kuomintang depends". (103) In his view, the Christian
faith is a moral transforming force that will save the Party
members from corruption and dissension. Hsieh said,

> If each Party member could imbibe the supremely
> benevolent and courageous spirit of Christ then the
> Party would instantly be illuminated with endless
> rays of hope; the Nationalist revolution would suc-
> ceed at once, and the Chinese nation would obtain
> liberty and equality. (104)

Hsieh's view represented a kind of political optimism
among Christian educators who expressed confidence in the
new government. His view was agreed to by Frank W. Price of
Nanking Theological Seminary that "Christianity is in full
sympathy with the three principles of nationalism, democracy
and social welfare. Christianity can help to purify them
of wrong associations and methods and fill them with richer
meaning". (105)

The view of cooperation, according to these Christian
apologists, was compatible with the doctrines of Dr. Sun in
San Min Chu I, which was a series of lectures delivered in
Canton in 1924, presenting Sun's view in the reconstruction
of New China. In the interpretation of Chu Ching-nung, (106)
the concept of equality is the central premise in Sun's
thought. The Three Principles are constructive propositions
set forth to attain international equality by the Chinese
nation, equality in government, and economic equality in
people's livelihood. (107) Chu noted the eclecticism of
Sun in choosing the best from the West to supply what China
lacks. In his view, Dr. Sun intends to establish his
revolutionary program on the ethical basis of Chinese
traditional values. Sun emphasizes the restoration of
ancient virtues in cultivating the people's nationalistic
fervor. These include loyalty and filial piety, humanity
and love, sincerity and righteousness, peace and humility.
Similarly, Wang Chih-hsin pointed out the intellectual
continuity with traditional Chinese philosophy in Dr. Sun's
theory. For example, the Principle of People's Sovereignty
is not alien to Confucian thought but present in Mencius'
teaching that the people are more important than the ruler.
(108) Their understanding of Dr. Sun was in line with Tai
Chi-t'ao's commentary on Sun's doctrine in the *Philosophical
Foundation of Sun Yat-senism*, published in May 1925.

Beside the traditional line of interpretation, Wang
emphasized the Christian impact on Sun's doctrine. In his
comparison of *San Min Chu I* and Jesusism *(Yeh-su chu-i)*,
Wang was ready to present Sun as a Christian hero in China.
He said, "The Three Principles of the People form the core
of Sun's doctrine, founded on liberty, equality, and universal love. The first advocate of these three principles
was Jesus, so that Sun's principles are also Jesus' principles. They both applied these principles to the task of
national and international salvation". (109) Wang compared
Sun's forty years of revolutionary labor to Jesus' death on
the Cross for the purpose of building a new order. The
same spirit of liberty was present in both. While Jesus
worked for the spiritual liberty of mankind; Sun strove to
secure political and economic liberty for the Chinese. The
spirit of equality in Jesus' teaching, according to Wang, is
contained in the ideal of human brotherhood in relation to
one heavenly Father. This forms the basis of solidarity and
community among all people. Sun's principle of People's
Sovereignty is the application of Jesus' view of brotherhood
to the Chinese government. (110) In Wang's opinion, although
the Principle of People's Livelihood deals with the economic
problem of wealth distribution, its motive lies in the
spirit of universal love. This spirit comes entirely from
Jesus. Dr. Sun may be called a second Martin Luther and
deserves to be regarded as a true disciple of Jesus Christ.
Wang even took the symbol of the Lord's Supper to be the
objective of People's Livelihood.

San Min Chu I reflects a sensitive mind seeking a political solution for China's crisis. The influence of Chinese
tradition on Sun is easily recognizable, but not to the
extent claimed by the interpreters along the traditional
line. It is true that Sun's education and long contact with
the West had inclined him to look to the West for guidance.
San Min Chu I absorbs different socialist theories and in-
corporates modern democratic models of government in Sweden
and America. But it does not mean a blind adherence to the
Western way. Sun's originality in synthesizing ideas and in
working out a Chinese solution for the Chinese problem should
not be neglected. It is fair to say that Christianity has
influenced his career and his thought. As he said in 1912,

> Several years ago I advocated revolution and had
> consistently worked for it. But it is mostly from
> the church that I learned the truth of revolution.
> The establishment of the Republic today is due, not
> to my efforts, but to the service of the church. (111)

But whether Dr. Sun had received so much inspiration from Christianity, especially from the historical figure of Jesus, as suggested by Wang Chih-hsin is questionable. No doubt, Sun regarded the Christian missions as an effective mediator of Western civilization to the Chinese. However, judging from his political writings, one will find it difficult to trace direct Christian sources, apart from a few references. The whole treatise of *San Min Chu I* has not mentioned much about religion. Jesus is spoken of as a religious revolutionist. (112) The moral teaching of Jesus on "universal love" appears once in comparison with Mo Tzu's "love without discrimination". The conspicuous absence of religion in the document will challenge any over-assertion of Christian influence on the Leader's doctrine. But the enthusiasm of Chinese Christians is easy to appreciate, for if they could get Sun to their side, they would establish a strong apologetics for their Christian claims. Sun Yat-sen was a professing Christian, and the *San Min Chu I* contains no anti-religious statements. The priority of his political career was to redefine China's identity, a task which crossed religious boundaries.

To many Chinese Christians who saw the necessity of Christian involvement in politics, loyalty to the Party and to their religion were not in conflict. There was no discontinuity between Christianity and patriotism. In their view, Dr. Sun acknowledged the merits of the Christian labor in China and recognized religion as a shaping force to establish the nation. And the *San Min Chu I* "not only seeks to improve the material lives of the people but also aims at cultivating their spiritual lives. To that effect, religion helps". (113) They found strong support for the integration of Christianity and the Party in the Christian baptism of General Chiang Kai-shek in October 1930. As the sole leader of Kuomintang, Chiang was the orthodox interpretation of the *San Min Chu I*. As a Christian convert, he seemed to give sanction to the continuation of the Christian efforts in the years of turmoil to come.

POSSIBILITY OF RECONCILIATION

Chinese nationalism in the 1920s was characterized by the slogan "Remove the nation's robbers internally, resist the foreign Powers externally". The May 30th Affair and other similar incidents were eruptions of the Chinese outrage against imperialistic exploitation. Although Chinese

nationalism had not become an imperialistic force, its
development in both scope and intensity could hardly be contained. How can we interpret this release of tremendous
national energy in the historical context?

To a large extent, the history of Republican China had
not yet begun *de facto*. The presence of foreigners reminded
China of her semi-colonial status among the nations. The
internal disintegration due to warlordism indicated that
China was not a united nation. The existence of the treaty
system aggravated the agony of the people whose political
consciousness was now awakened by the numerous outbursts of
nationalistic sentiment. China was aware that she was not
yet the subject of her own history with the full right to
determine her course in the modern world. The struggle for
inalienable national identity was most poignant for a people
who used to think of themselves the center of world history
for centuries. The fervent nationalism during the decade
will be better appreciated if the legitimate ambition of the
Chinese to write their own history is taken into consideration.

The confrontation between Christianity and nationalism
is a "religious" conflict in which each side sees the other
as a religious rival. Liu T'ing-fang aptly commented,
"Nationalism has become a passion and almost has become a
religion, replacing time-honored system of ethics and religious faiths. It commands the whole activity and becomes
the center of the absorbing attention of the younger generation". (114) Nationalism undoubtedly has its religious
dimension. If religion is defined as the crystallization
of emotion, as Liang Ch'i-ch'ao saw it, nationalism certainly
offers opportunities for emotional commitment. If religion
is regarded, in Liang Sou-ming's opinion, as an attempt to
transcend the present human environment for comfort and
encouragement, then nationalism in a quasi-manner does provide the vision of a better future for China. (115) To save
the nation has become a religious call that demands thought
and action of the contemporary Chinese intellectuals. The
religious consciousness of Chinese nationalism has its doctrine, ritualism, and obligation. As seen in the Kuomintang
regime, the religious commitment to national salvation
turned *San Min Chu I* into a Chinese Bible and Dr. Sun Yat-
sen into the superior authority. The emergence of such political religion is comprehensible in the aftermath of the New
Culture Movement when the Chinese intellectuals were groping
for a new faith, subsequent to the decline of Confucian tradition, that offered hope to the nation in confusion.

In the early years of the 1920s, nationalism was more popular than communism for several reasons. When compared to Marxist Communism, nationalism is more personal and has a "warmth and a pietistic character which communism lacks". (116) When communism promises freedom, nationalism also gives individuality as well. Communism is an imported ideology, but nationalism, despite its Western origin, takes on indigenous color more readily. It does not appeal to only one section of the population but to all classes in the country. As a "religion of modern secularism", (117) nationalism claimed the absolute dedication of the Chinese, especially at the crucial hour when their consciousness of nationality was in full expression. The conviction, "my country, right or wrong", could not accommodate any equal devotion to other faiths.

To the Chinese nationalist, Christianity is a political idolatry that profanes the sanctity of the national temple. The Christian proposal of internationalism as a viable way to contain nationalism and to avoid undersirable excess is regarded as an unacceptable alternative. To some Chinese Christians, nationalism becomes a religious idolatry if it goes against Christian principles. It is not right to obey man but God. However, to others the area of conflict is reduced in their concern for seeking cooperation with the existing government.

In response to the anti-Christian opposition from the standpoint of Marxism and Leninism, the Chinese Church sought to present a cooperative apologetics. They knew that the concept of historical materialism, economic determinism, and class struggle were alien to the Christian philosophy of life and history. But the external pressure due to the growing Communist Party made it dangerous and unwise to take a bold anti-Communist stand. The Christian majority entertained the hope for the coexistence of the two faiths. And Christianity serves to modify, improve, and complement the Communist program. For Christianity does not dictate any particular political structure as sacrosanct. It is primarily a religion spelled out in certain doctrines, rituals, and community activities. With its claim of universality, Christianity is believed to be able to exist within any socio-political system. It does not completely conform to, or contradict, such system. This was a common theological

conviction of the contemporary Chinese Christians in seeking
to relate their faith to the rising Communist movement.
They believed that Christianity can include the ultimate
significance of communism, which will enable Communism to
become a great force in the modern world.

What enables Christianity to be accepted in the contemporary political and social order is a set of moral and
spiritual principles. Justice, service, and sacrifice are
given a status of value unrestricted by any temporal and
spatial system. These principles are exemplified in the
life and teaching of Jesus of Nazareth. And Jesus is portrayed as the first perfect anti-imperialist whom the
Chinese Christians are supposed to imitate. This personality argument forms the theological core of the Christian
apologetics in the decade. The overall picture they give
to the challenge of nationalism is positive and optimistic.

Conclusion

The confession of Christ in China during the 1920s was a
difficult theological task for the young Chinese Church.
The diversity and complexity of the social and political
situation seemed to be too excessive for the Chinese Christians to work out a theology that might gain the hearing of
the non-Christian world. Not much help was available from
the missionary message inculcated in a foreign thought pattern and cultural tradition. An enlightened section of the
Chinese Christians realized that it was primarily their
responsibility to re-examine and re-define the Christian
faith in the immediate context. Any delay on their part
would turn out to be a stumbling block to the cause of
Christian missions. Thanks to their efforts, whether
successful or not, we see the shape of the Christian apologetics during the decade of the anti-Christian movement.
Similar in some ways to the theology of the early church,
the Chinese theology of this time was constructed mainly as
a response to the external ideological and circumstantial
pressure. Added to this factor was the traditional dislike
for the foreign religion.

Although the religious controversy in the early twenties
had not conclusively proclaimed the futility of religion,
Chinese Christians were aware that the path before them was
going to be rough. The impact of the New Culture Movement,
characterized by the scientific and democratic outlook,
caused them to re-think the nature of religion itself. In
their view, the kind of religion that Young China needed
should take into serious consideration the society and the

individual, the present and the future, the material and the
spiritual. It should deal with human life in the complexity
of its existence. In the argument of the Christian apologists, Christianity in the modern version, divested of its
dogmatism, ritualism, and credalism, was the religion for
China. Such assertion and conviction inevitably led them to
a diligent search for a preachable message. It is true that
many familiar themes in Western Christian thought appeared
in the discussion, but they took on a new, local significance. They found a theological reality in Christ, not so
much his transcendence as his immanence in the mundane realm
of human activities. This was consistent with the quest for
relevance in contemporary Chinese theology and compatible
with the Confucian emphasis on human relationships in the
cosmic order.

Radical thinkers, like Wu Lei-ch'uan, stressed the historical Jesus whose revolutionary experience became norma-
tive for the Chinese Christians in their own struggle.
Others like Chao Tzu-ch'en, acknowledged the transforming
power of the Christ of faith, but to them Jesus was categorically human. Among conservative Christians, Chang I-
ching and Liang Chün-mo gave credence to both the divine and
the human dimension of Jesus' life. The human Christ offered a pattern of moral living, and the divine Christ imparted
a dynamic to sustain it. Their ontological interpretations
of Christ varied according to their theological presuppositions, but their functional views of Christ were similar.
And it is this functional Christology that provided a common
basis for the Christo-centric apologetics.

In Christ, they found a key to resolve the controversy,
imported from the Western Church, between the fundamentalists and the modernists. In Christ, they obtained a synthesis of both particularity and catholicity. For the universal principles of justice, equity, and service, as embodied in his life, were now applicable to the existential
situation in China. In Christ, the foreignness of the
westernized Gospel was dismantled. Christ became the
hermeneutical principle to relate the Christian faith to the
contemporary Chinese experience. This theological retreat
to Christ as an attempt to interpret Christianity in minimal
and essential terms. But they were not fully aware that
when they affirmed religion in terms of life and presented
Christ as the core of Christianity, their Christology indeed
was inclusive. Such a Chinese Christology had to deal with

the cultural heritage and the problem of nationalism. The anti-Christian movement brought both issues into focus, presenting an overwhelming intellectual challenge to the Chinese Church.

During the 1920s, China was caught in a tremendous cultural crisis. The China of old was being consigned to the past, and the new China was not yet born. In this phase of transition from the old to the new, a cultural gap was created in the mind of the Chinese intellectual. The search for cultural identity had inevitably affected the Chinese Christians who wanted to relate the Christian faith to the Chinese ethos. Like many contemporary Chinese thinkers, they had a hard time to make up their minds. They did not like to adopt the line of "total westernization" which would easily imply the abandonment of the Chinese tradition. They were worried that, under the pressure of nationalism, such a step would perpetuate the impression that Christianity was aligned with the aggressive West. Nor could they return to find cultural security in the Confucian past, for the Confucian past was no longer secure in the wave of anti-traditional iconoclasm. Most of them took the path similar to that of Liang Ch'i-ch'ao and Ts'ai Yüan-p'ei, practicing a form of cultural selectivity. In this manner, they retained certain intimacy with that which made them Chinese and, at the same time, felt justified to consider Western values.

In the effort to indigenize the Christian faith, Chinese Christians looked for "classical sanctions", "harmonization", "cultural fulfillment", and "value judgment". (1) These were the various emphases to present Christ to culture based on a similar cultural presupposition and theological methodology. Their approaches to the problem of cultural relevance of Christianity conditioned the effectiveness of their Christian apologetics. Cautious and critical as they were, the intellectual accommodation of the past ran counter to the ethos of the time which was marked by the future-oriented outlook and the quest for modernity. In seeking common ground for dialogue between Christianity and Confucianism, they had assumed that the traditional thought form and content were still applicable to the present age. This partly explained the fact that the iconoclastic accusations of Confucianism were also used in the anti-Christian criticism. Christianity was called "outdated", "unscientific", and "superstitious". They could not entirely be blamed for

their ineffective approach because there seemed to be no
better way available that would lead to a more viable
theology of culture.

The most pressing theological theme in the decade was how
to apply the Christian faith to the task of national reconstruction. Chinese nationalism of the twenties reflected
the express will of the people to create a political reality
for themselves. Due to the double threat of imperialism and
warlordism, the future of the nation was in limbo. The upsurge of nationalism stemmed from the determination of the
people to be the subject of their own political destiny,
instead of being subjugated to others. Such courage to
assert the people's will was supported by most Chinese
Christians, as seen in their spontaneous reaction to the
May 30th Incident. In their inclusive Christology, they
stretched the political dimension of the Gospel by emphasizing the revolutionary life of Jesus in his time.

Some held the continuity between the church and the state
through theologizing their political experience. In their
view, no conflict should be there in a Christian communist
or Christian nationalist. God's will was to be expressed
in the political struggle of New China. Others played the
role of a political critic by bringing religious criteria
to it. The double loyalties to the ruling Party and to
Christianity were reconciled through cooperation. In both
Sun Yat-sen and Chiang Kai-shek they founded supporting
evidence to such practice. The Christo-centric principle
was again at work in constructing the Christian view of
communism and nationalism. To the communist, Jesus was
portrayed as the first proletarian who despised wealth and
power. The Gospel of liberation was to be preached to the
poor and the oppressed. To the nationalist, Jesus was a
patriot whose cry for Jerusalem and whose evangelistic
concern for the Jews bore witness to his nationalism. Such
argument gave political flexibility to the Christian faith
to exist under whatever regime that happened to reign in
the country. Their response to the challenge of nationalism
was governed by a theological tactic of survival. As the
anti-Christian movement attempted to replace Christianity
by the political religion of nationalism, Chinese Christians
were eager to show that there was no rivalry between them.
In their drive toward cooperation for the sake of political
expediency, many Chinese Christians unconsciously jeopar-
dized the role of Christian mission by neglecting the judg-
mental side of it. They turned Christ into a versatile
figure who passed approval to whatever direction the wind of
politics might blow.

A strong eschatological urge was also found in their apologetics. For in bringing Christ to the task of national reconstruction, the ideal of the kingdom of God became a present possibility to be realized here and now in China. This gave optimism to their theologizing effort, despite the circumstantial adversity. To imitate Jesus was the Christian way to support the campaign of national salvation through character *(Jen-ko chiu-kuo)*. The same theological motif undergirded the argument of Christian educators that Christian education was useful to the nation, for Christ would make the Chinese a better people. From Christ's doctrine of the universal Fatherhood of God, Chinese Christians believed that internationalism was the remedy to narrow nationalism. It enabled New China to relocate herself in the family of nations. This theistic insight, though hardly accepted by Chinese nationalists, offered a solution to international conflicts. It introduced a teleology to the political ordering of national priorities.

The Christian apologetics in the twenties was not a rewriting of Western theology but the beginning of a new trend of theological independence. It reflected the variety and vitality of indigenous thought by an informed group of Chinese Christians. As they defined religion as a life movement in terms of Jesus Christ, their theology went beyond mere theoretical interests to practical utilities. It was mainly a theology of the present, anticipating future possibilities. This 'contextual theology' began with particular events and specific problems of the time. There was no systematic theology or metaphysical scheme, for the Chinese experience was chaotic and unsystematic. Rather, it was a living theology forged on the anvil of fear and hope, frustration and promise. Its fragmentary character was due to the fact that it was developed out of the consciousness of the demands and opportunities of the situation.

However, the effectiveness of this apologetics was hard to measure. The anti-Christian movement did not reduce its intensity and few anti-Christians were converted, as a result of these arguments. Ideologically the Chinese Christians had done their best to speak theologically to the national crisis. They offered an alternative solution on a religious basis to the Chinese who were culturally dislocated and politically bewildered. But the anti-religious mentality of the agnostic and anti-foreign Chinese mind, coupled with the modern democratic and scientific attitude, had little room for a religious solution. To the anti-Christians, the "scandal of the Cross" was an offensive

message, and the request to follow the historical figure of
Jesus Christ was retrospective and irrelevant. In the final
analysis, the confrontation between Christians and anti-
Christians was a question of intellectual choice for or
against the Chinese Christ. The goal of the Christian apologetics was to bring the thinking Chinese to such a decision.

Appendix I

A STATEMENT OF EDUCATIONAL PRINCIPLES PREPARED
BY THE GENERAL BOARD OF THE CHINA CHRISTIAN
EDUCATIONAL ASSOCIATION, APRIL 2, 1925

1. The Function of Christian Schools

The special function of Christian schools, and the main
justification for their maintenance supplementary to the
public schools of China, is that they provide an education
Christian in character for the children of the members of
the Christian community and for others who desire to avail
themselves of private schools of that type.

2. Private Schools in a Democracy

It is in accordance with the spirit of democracy and with
the practice in all democratic nations of the modern world
that permission should be granted to individuals or to
social groups, who so desire, to establish and maintain
private educational institutions, in addition to the public
system of education maintained by the state. This right is
granted on condition that these private schools maintain the
minimum standards legitimately imposed by the state upon all
schools, both public and private, and that they do not conflict with the interests of the nation and of society as a
whole.

3. Private Schools and Progress

It is generally agreed that progress in education is
dependent upon the existence of diverse types of school and
the largest possible freedom of variation. To deny the
right of variation, and to insist that all schools follow

the same uniform procedure, would be contrary to the educational interests of the state. Provided that private
schools meet the essential requirements of all schools, the
greater the freedom of variation allowed, the better for
education, and for the state.

4. Private Schools and Religious Freedom

The maintenance of private schools in which religion
forms an integral part of the educational process, is in
accordance with the principle of religious freedom, which
has been accepted in the constitution of the Chinese Republic, and with the practice in other democratic nations.
Religious freedom includes not only the right of the individual to follow his own conscience in matters of personal
religious belief, but also to provide training in religion
for his children. This principle applies equally to the
adherents of any religious faith.

5. Christian Schools and the National Programme of Education

It seems advisable that private schools in China should
come under the cognizance of the public educational authorities and form part of the national programme of education.
Such a relationship would naturally take the form of registration of the schools, the adoption of the essentials
required for all schools, the attainment of recognized
standards of efficiency, and a system of visitation to
insure the maintenance of these standards. Beyond this
there should be freedom. Christian educators welcome such
a relationship with the public educational authorities.
Such supervisory control of these schools as is maintained
by Christian agencies is solely for the purpose of promoting
efficiency and is meant to supplement, not to take the place
of, the general supervisory relation of the public educational authorities.

6. Ethical and Religious Teaching in Christian Schools

The primary purpose of all education is the development
of personality and of moral character, and it is in this
sphere that Christian people believe that they have a
special contribution to make to the life of China. The
insistence by the educational authorities upon conditions of
registration that imposed restrictions upon the ethical and
religious teaching and life of the Christian schools, would
not only be inconsistent with the principles of educational

and religious freedom, but would prevent these schools from
achieving the purpose for which they have been founded, and
from making their distinctive contribution to the educational needs of China.

7. Christian Schools and Patriotism

The Christian spirit naturally expresses itself in an
enlightened patriotism. Christian schools aim to develop
in their students the love of country; if they fail to do
so, they are to that extent untrue to their purpose. The
idea of "denationalizing" students, or of using the Christian schools as the agencies of a "foreign imperialism" is
abhorrent to the leaders in Christian education, both Chinese
and westerners.

8. Christian Education Becoming Indigenous

While Christian schools in China were originally established and are still largely maintained by foreign missionaries and their supporters in the west, their purpose has
been to serve the best interests of the Chinese people. It
is their ideal, which is being increasingly realized, that
Christian education should become Chinese in spirit, in
content, in support and in control. This is the expressed
purpose not only of Chinese and western Christian educators,
but also of the mission bodies which have in the past
supported the Christian schools, and of the Chinese Christian community which is gradually taking over their support
and control.

9. The Permanent Foundation of Christian Education

The permanent maintenance of Christian education depends
upon securing the whole-hearted support of the Christian
community and of enlightened Chinese public opinion in
general, not upon treaties between China and other nations.

Appendix II

The unofficial translation of the New Education Regulation made by the China Christian Educational Association read as follows:

1. Any institution of whatever grade established by funds contributed from foreigners, if it carries on its work according to the regulations governing various grades of institutions as promulgated by the Ministry of Education, will be allowed to make application for recognition at the office of the proper educational authorities of the government according to the regulations as promulgated by the Ministry of Education concerning the recognition on the part of all educational institutions.

2. Such an institution should prefix to its official name the term 'szu lih' (privately established).

3. The president or principal of such an institution should be a Chinese. If such president or principal has hitherto been a foreigner, then there must be a Chinese vice-president who shall represent the institution in applying for recognition.

4. If the institution has a board of managers, more than half of the board must be Chinese.

5. The institution shall not have as its purpose the propagation of religion.

6. The curriculum of such an institution should conform to the standards set by the Ministry of Education. It shall not include religious courses among the required subjects.

(Taken from *China Christian Year Book 1926*, pp. 227-28).

Notes

Introduction

[1]For example, Kiang Wen-han, *The Chinese Student Movement* (New York: King's Crown Press, 1948), pp. 60-68, 87-95; Tatsuro & Sumiko Yamamoto, "The Anti-Christian Movement in China, 1922-1927," *Far Eastern Quarterly*)February 1953): 133-47; Chow Tse-tsung, *The May Fourth Movement* (Cambridge: Harvard University Press, 1960), pp. 314-27; Paul A. Cohen, "The Anti-Christian Tradition in China," *Journal of Asian Studies* 20.2 (February 1961): 169-81; Joseph R. Levenson, *Confucian China and Its Modern Fate: A Trilogy* (Berkeley & Los Angeles: University of California Press, 1968), pp. 117-24; and Yip Ka-che, "The Anti Christian Movement in China, 1922-1927, with Special Reference to the Experience of Protestant Missions" (Ph.D. dissertation, Columbia University, 1970).

Chapter 1

[1]
The New Culture Movement is variously called the May Fourth Movement, the New Thought Movement, the New Thought Tide or the Chinese Renaissance. It was a time of intellectual revolution in modern China that began roughly in 1917 and continued into the next decade. During this period, the Confucian tradition was criticized, Western thoughts were introduced, and the vernacular language became popular. See Chow Tse-tsung, *The May Fourth Movement* and Hu Shih, *The Chinese Renaissance* (Chicago, 1934; 2nd ed., New York: Paragon Book Reprint Corporation, 1963).

[2]
Wing-tsit Chan, *Religious Trends in Modern China* (New York: Columbia University Press, 1953), pp. 218-19.

[3]
Chow Tse-tsung, "The Anti-Confucian Movement in Early Republican China", *The Confucian Persuasion*, ed. A. F. Wright (Stanford: Stanford University Press, 1960), pp. 288-92; also Hsiao Kung-ch'üan, *A Modern China and a New World: K'ang Yu-wei, Reformer and Utopian, 1858-1927* (Tokyo: University to Tokyo Press, 1975).

4
Ch'en Tu-hsiu, "Po K'ang Yu-wei chih tsung-t'ung tsung-li shu" (Refuting K'ang Yu-wei's message to the President and the Prime Minister), *Hsin Ch'ing-nien* 2.2 (October 1916); hereinafter referred to as *HCN*. Translated by Kiang Wen-han, *The Chinese Student Movement*, p. 53.

5
Ibid.

6
Neander C. S. Chang (Chang Ch'in-shih), ed., *Kuo-nei chin shih-nien lai chih tsung-chiao ssu-ch'ao* (Religious Thought Movements in China During the Last Decade) (Peking: Yenching School of Chinese Studies, 1927), p. 183. Chang's volume is hereinafter cited as *KNCS*.

7
T'ien Han, "Shao-nien chung-kuo yü tsung-chiao wen-t'i" (Young China and the problem of religion), in *KNCS*, pp. 51-58.

8
KNCS, pp. 147-48, concerning Li Huang's correspondence with French scholars.

9
Ibid., pp. 148-54.

10
Liang Ch'i-ch'ao (1873-1929), a disciple of K'ang Yu-wei, was a scholar-politician in modern China. His earlier idea of national reform was reflected in his edited magazines *Shih-wu-pao* and *Ch'ing-i pao*. During the turn of the century, Liang, influenced by the Western theory of liberty, equality, and fraternity, began to advocate the ideal of a new people for the salvation of China. With the establishment of the Chinese Republic in 1912, Liang terminated his political cooperation with K'ang Yu-wei and organized the *Chin-pu-tang*. After a series of political involvements, Liang felt that the chaotic situation was adverse to the task of national regeneration. He started the *Hsin-hsüeh-hui* to promote intellectual and cultural reform in China. Liang was a neo-traditionalist, seeking to preserve the best portion of the Confucian heritage in cultural cooperation with the West. See Howard Boorman, ed., *Biographical Dictionary of Republican China*, 4 vols. (New York: Columbia University Press, 1967-71), 2:346-51.

11

Liang Ch'i-ch'ao, "P'ing fei tsung-chiao t'ung-meng" (A critique of the Anti-Religion Federation) in *P'i-p'ing fei chi-tu-chiao yen-lun hui-k'an ch'üan-pien* (Answering Attacks Upon Christianity), ed. Chang I-ching (Shanghai: China Baptist Publication Society, 1927), p. 252; hereinafter referred to as *PFCTC*.

12

Ibid., p. 253.

13

Ibid., p. 257.

14

Liang Ch'i-ch'ao, "Lun tsung-chiao-chia yü che-hsüeh-chia chih ch'ang-tuan te-shih" (A comparison between the religionist and the philosopher) in *Yin-pin-shih ho-chi, wen-chi* (Collected works from the Ice-drinker's Studio, collected essays) (Reprint ed., Taiwan, n.d.), ts'e 4, 9:44-50.

Liang had a strong interest in Buddhism, for he thought its spirit and doctrine were suitable for the morality of the Chinese people. Although he was impressed by the achievements of Christian missionaries in China, he adopted the role of a neutral critic of Christianity. See "Lun Fo-chiao yü ch'un-chih chih kuan-hsi" (Discussion of the relationship between Buddhism and public uplifting), ibid., 10:45-52.

15

Ts'ai Yüan-p'ei (1868-1940) was a *han-lin* scholar who later received Western education in Europe. In 1915, Ts'ai and others organized the *Societe Franco-Chinois d'Education* at Paris and sponsored a work-study program for Chinese students. He was appointed Minister of Education in Sun Yat-sen's cabinet, but resigned during the presidency of Yüan Shih-kai. A leading voice in the New Thought Movement, Ts'ai was the chancellor of Peking University from 1916-26, a most critical period in modern Chinese history character-ized by the spirit of national and social reform. Under his leadership, Peking University became the cradle of the New Culture Movement. In 1927, he was appointed president of the *Ta-hsüeh-yüan* which replaced the former Ministry of Education. In the early twenties, Ts'ai advocated the separation of education and religion.

16
   Ts'ai Yüan-p'ei, "Li-hsin yü mi-hsin" (Reasonable belief
and superstitious belief), in *Fei tsung-chiao lun* (Discussion
on Anti-Religion) ed. Anti-Religion Federation (Peking:
Hsin-chih shu-she, 1922), pp. 14-15.

17
   Ts'ai Yüan-p'ei, "I mei-yü tai tsung-chiao" (Substitut-
ing religion with aesthetic education), *HCN* 3.6 (August 1,
1917). Also reproduced in *KNCS*, pp. 1-9.

18
   Ts'ai, "I mei-yü tai tsung-chiao", pp. 5-8.

19
   Wing-tsit Chan, *Religious Trends in Modern China*, p. 222.

20
   Liu Po-ming, "Tsung-chiao wen-t'i chih-wu" (The Problem
of Religion, V), *KNCS*, pp. 136-46; first appeared in *Shao-
nien Chung-kuo* 2.11 (May 1921).

21
   Liang Sou-ming was a lecturer on Buddhist and Indian
philosophies at Peking University (1917-24). His representative work *Tung-hsi wen-hua chi ch'i che-hsüeh*, published
in 1922, went through eight editions in one decade. Liang
discarded the idea of cultural synthesis and anticipated
that the future culture of the world would be a renaissance
of Chinese civilization. He sought to reformulate Confucianism and to apply its relevance to contemporary Chinese
problems. He thought that Christianity was in decline in
the West for its supernaturalism was not rationally acceptable. The philosophies of Comte, Haeckel, and Eucken were,
in his comment, showing signs of deterioration. See *Tung-
hsi wen-hua chi ch'i che-hsüeh* (The Cultures of East and
West and Their Philosophies) (Shanghai, 1922; reprint ed.,
Shanghai, 1934), pp. 79-80, 108-9, 125-45. From 1927-37,
Liang was a leader in the rural reconstruction movement.
See Guy Alitto, *Chinese Cultural Conservatism and Rural
Reconstruction* (Berkeley: University of California Press,
1977).

22
   Liang Sou-ming, "Tsung-chiao wen-t'i chih'ssu" (The
Problem of Religion, IV), *KNCS*, pp. 110-12; taken from
Shao-nien Chung-kuo 2.8 (February 1921).

23

Liang, *Tung-hsi wen-hua*, pp. 90-110.

24

T'u Hsiao-shih (1893-1932) was a well-known educator and his lecture in the religious debate, sponsored by the Young China Association in 1921, was in favor of religion. T'u was not a believer of any religion but was an objective voice in the anti-Christian movement. See T'u Hsiao-shih, "Tsung-chiao wen-t'i chih-san" (The Problem of Religion III), in *KNCS*, pp. 92-100; taken from *Shao-nien Chung-kuo* 2.8 (February 1921).

25

Ibid., pp. 95-97.

26

T'u Hsiao-shih, "K'e-hsüeh yü tsung-chiao kuo-chen pu-neng liang-li ma"? (Are science and religion really not able to exist together?), *Sheng-ming yüen-k'an* 3.1 (September 1922): 1-11; hereinafter cited as *SM*.

27

Hu Shih (1891-1962) was best known in our period of study as the leading advocate of the literary revolution. From 1917 to 1927, he was professor of philosophy and later chairman of the Department of English Literature at Peking University. From 1930 to 1937, Hu became dean of the School of Letters. He introduced Western philosophical terminology and methodology in Chinese classical studies. In his view, China should follow the Western way to modernize herself, and he believed in the gradualism of social reform rather than the communistic radicalism. He appreciated the appeal of Christian morality to the Chinese, but disliked its theological construction and superstition. See Hu Shih, "Chi-tu-chiao yü Chung-kuo" (Christianity and China), *SM* 2.7 (March 1922). For a good treatment of Hu's life and contribution from 1917-37, see Jerome B. Grieder, *Hu Shih and the Chinese Renaissance* (Cambridge: Harvard University Press, 1970).

28

Hu Shih, "K'e-hsüeh yü jen-sheng-kuan hsü" (Preface to Science and Philosophy of Life) in Wang Meng-tsou ed., *K'e Hsüeh yü jen-sheng-kuan chih lun-chan* (Debate over science and philosophy of life) (Shanghai, 1923; reprint ed., Hong Kong: Chinese University of Hong Kong, 1973), pp. 2-3.

29
   Hu Shih, "Wo-men tui-yü Hsi-yang chin-tai wen-ming ti
t'ai-t'u"(Our attitude toward the modern civilization of the
West) *Tung-fang tsa-chih* 23.17 (1916):73-82; translation by
D. W. Y. Kwok, *Scientism in Chinese Thought, 1900-1950* (New
Haven and London: Yale University Press, 1965), pp. 96.

30
   Wang Hsing-kung was born in Anhwei, 1889. During his
studies in England from 1908-17, Wang obtained the A.R.C.
Sc. (Associate of Royal College of Science of London) in
Chemistry and the D.I.C. (Diploma of Imperial College,
London). He was professor at Peita from 1917-26. Wang
became professor of Science at the National Central University, Nanking, and Head of the National Wuhan University
in 1927. *Discussion of Scientific Method* and *Introduction
to Science* were his representative writings.

31
   Wang Hsing-kung, "Tsung-chiao wen-t'i chih-i" (The
Problem of Religion, I"), *KNCS*, pp. 59-68. Also see Wang,
K'e-hsüeh fang-fa lun (Discussion of Scientific Method)
(Peking, 1920; reprint ed., Taiwan: Shiu Niu Press, 1966),
pp. 141-54.

32
   Ch'en Tu-hsiu (1879-1942) received education in Japan
and France and was deeply influenced by French thought and
civilization. A representative of the New Thought Movement,
Ch'en edited the *Hsin Ch'ing-nien* in which science and
democracy were promoted as the two pillars for New China.
In the same magazine, the Confucian tradition was relentlessly discredited. Ch'en was a forerunner of the literary
revolution and became, in 1917, professor and dean of the
School of Letters at Peking University. After his conversion to Marxism, Ch'en and Li Ta-chao were leaders of the
Communist Party. In 1925, Ch'en was elected a member of the
Central Executive Committee of the coalition government of
the Kuomintang and the Chinese Communist Party. Ch'en found
the personality of the historical Jesus admirable, but many
Christian doctrines were to him incredible on scientific
ground.

33
   Ch'en Tu-hsiu, "Ou-hsiang p'o-huai lun" (On the destruction of idols), *HCN* 5.2 (1918):89; translated by Kwok,
Scientism in Chinese Thought, p. 71. Also "K'e-hsüeh yü
shen-sheng" (Science and deity) in *Tu-hsiu wen-ts'un*
(Collected Essays of Tu-hsiu) 4 vols. (Shanghai, 1922;
reprint ed., Shanghai, 1933), 2:5.

34
   PFCTC, p. 11.

35
   Ibid., p. 28.

36
   Ibid., p. 30

37
   Ibid., p. 29.

38
   Liu Po-ming, "Fei tsung-chiao yün-tung p'ing-i" (A
critical study of the anti-religious movement), *Hsüeh Heng*
(The Critical Review) 6 (June 1922).

39
   Wang Chih-hsin, *Chung-kuo tsung-chiao ssu-hsiang shih
ta-kang* (Outline of Chinese religious thought) (Shanghai:
Chung-hua shu-chu, 1933), p. 224.

40
   Liang Ch'i-ch'ao, "Ou-yu hsin-ying lu, chieh-lu" (A condensed record of impressions of travels in Europe), in *Yin-ping
shih ho-chi, chüan-chi,* (Shanghai: Chung-hua Shu-chü, 1936),
5.23:38.

41
   For a good summary of the Debate, see Kwok, *Scientism in
Chinese Thought*, pp. 135-60. Also see a contemporary treat-
ment of the issue by Lo Chih-hsi, *K'e-hsüeh yü hsüan-hsüeh*
(Science and metaphysics) (Shanghai: Commercial Press,
1927).

42
   The Debate began with a lecture on "Philosophy of Life",
delivered by Chang Chün-mai at Tsing Hua College at Peking
on February 14, 1923. Chang argued that science cannot
solve the problem of philosophy of life which is more
governed by the internal world than by the external.

Spiritual values, rather than scientific values, must be
consulted. Chang was supported by Chang Tung-sun and, to
some extent, by Liang Ch'i-ch'ao and Lin Tsai-p'ing.

On the other side, Ting Wen-chiang insisted on the suffi-
ciency of science. He held that sensory perception is the
sole basis of knowledge and that the ultimate reality is
unknowable apart from it. Ting's company included Ch'en Tu-
hsiu, Hu Shih, Wang Hsing-kung, T'ang Yüeh and Jen Shu-yung.

43
    Hu Shih, "K'e-hsüeh yü jen-sheng kuan hsü", pp. 12-13.

44
    Hsin Ch'ao (New Tide) (January 1919), pp. 1-3; trans-
lated by Chow Tse-tsung, *The May Fourth Movement*, p. 60.

45
    "Christian Renaissance: The Aims of the Peking Apolo-
getic Group", *The Chinese Recorder* 51 (August 1920):636;
hereinafter cited as *CR*.

46
    See the discussion regarding the position of the Chinese
individual in society in Y. P. Mei, "The Status of the
Individual in Chinese Thought and Practice", in *The Chinese
Mind*, ed. Charles A. Moore (Honolulu: University of Hawaii
Press, 1967), pp. 323-39.

47
    Hu Shih, "I-pu-sheng chu-i" (Ibsenism), *HCN* 4.6 (June
1918).

48
    The May Fourth Incident took place on May 4, 1919, when
Chinese students at Peking, prompted by the patriotic anti-
foreign sentiment, demonstrated in protest against the
nation's humiliating policy toward Japan. The immediate
cause of the Incident was the Shantung question at the
Versailles Peace Conference when Japan sought to take over
the German privilege in China. See Chow Tse-tsung, *The May
Fourth Movement*, pp. 84-116.

49
    Lo Yün-yen (R. Y. Lo) was born in 1890 in Kiangsi. He
received his early education at the William Nast College at
Kiukiang. Lo entered Baldwin-Wallace College at Berea, Ohio
and got his B.A. degree in 1911. Then he studied economics

and political science at Syracuse University from 1911-14.
From the University of Michigan, Lo got his M.A. in 1912 and
PH.D. in 1914, writing his thesis on "The Social Teachings
of Confucius". After returning to China, Lo served as
editor of the Chinese *Christian Advocate* and the *Young
People's Friend*. He was also appointed as a member of the
Legislative Yüan of the National Government. His writings
included *The Social Teachings of Confucius* (1914), *Chris-
tianity and New China* (1922), *What is Democracy?* (1924), and
China's Revolution From the Inside (1930).

50
    R. Y. Lo (Lo Yün-yen), *China's Revolution From the
Inside* (New York: The Abingdon Press, 1930), p. 62

51
    Liu T'ing-fang (Timothy T. Lew) was born in 1891 at
Wenchow, Chekiang. He got his preliminary education at
Wenchow College and St. John's University. He won the
Horace Russell Prize in psychology at the University of
Georgia, and then entered Columbia University where he
received his A.B., M.A. and PH.D. degrees. Liu also studied
theology at Union Theological Seminary and got his B.D.
(magna cum laude). He served as dean of the graduate school
of education at Peking Government Teacher's College, professor of psychology at National Peking University and
member of the theological faculty of Yenching University.
He was elected dean of the school of theology in Yenching
University from 1921-26. He was editor of *Sheng-ming* (1920-
24), editor of *Chen-li chou-k'an* (1924-26), associate editor
of the *Journal of New Education* (1922-25), and editor of
Chen-li yü Sheng-ming for several years.

52
    Timothy T. Lew (Liu T'ing-fang), "China's Renaissance
--the Christian Opportunity", *CR* 52 (May 1921):303.

53
    Lo Yün-yen, "Hsin ssu-ch'ao ho chi-tu-chiao" (New
Thought Movement and Christianity), *SM* 2.1 (June 1921):2-5.

54
    Hsü Pao-ch'ien (1892-1944) was born in Shang-yü, Chekiang,
and was brought up in a traditional Chinese family. Visits
to China of Sherwood Eddy and John R. Mott had contributed
to his Christian conversion. Hsü went to the United States
in 1921 and studied at the Union Theological Seminary in
New York and Columbia University.

Returning to China in 1924, Hsü taught in Yenching University in religion and philosophy. In 1930, he served as travelling secretary of the World's Student Christian Federation. He received the PH.D. degree in 1933 from Columbia University with a dissertation, published that year, entitled *Ethical Realism in Neo-Confucian Thought*. Hsü was an influential leader in Christian circles, and his writings appeared in *Sheng-ming* and *Chen-li yü sheng-ming*.

55
    P. C. Hsü (Hsü Pao-ch'ien), "The Christian Renaissance", *CR* 51 (June 1920):459.

56
    Liu T'ing-fang, "China's Renaissance--Christian Opportunity", p. 314.

57
    For example, see Frank W. Price, "Chung-kuo hsin ssu-ch'ao ho chi-tu-chiao ti kuan-hsi" (The relationship between the New Thought Movement and Christianity in China), translated by Liu T'ing-fang and Hu Hsüeh-ch'eng, in *SM* 2.1 (June 1921); 1-11. Cf. the discussion of John Childs, "Chi-tu-chiao yü Chung-kuo ti hsin ssu-ch'ao" (Christianity and the New Thought Movement in China), translated in *SM* 2.1 (June 1921):1-6.

58
    "A Liberal Religion for New China", *Christian China* 7.7 (May 1921).

59
    Chien Yu-wen (Timothy Jen) was born in 1896 in Canton. He went to the United States for education and received his B.A. from Oberlin College in 1917. In 1920, Chien received his M.A. from the University of Chicago and attended Union Theological Seminary in New York in 1920-21. Upon his return to China, he served as editorial secretary of the National Committee of the YMCA. From 1924-27, he became an associate professor of philosophy and religion at Yenching University. During the regime of the National Government, Chien held different official posts and was a member of the Legislative Yüan from 1933-46. Chien is best known for his historical scholarship in the study of Taiping Rebellion. See Chien's autobiography, "Ch'ung-sheng liu-shih-nien" (Sixty Years After Rebirth), *Ching Feng* 28 (Spring 1971):49-60 and 29 (Summer 1971):51-78.

60

Chien Yu-wen, "She-mo shih chi-tu-chiao"? (What is Christianity?), *SM* 2.1 (June 1921):1. See also Chien's "The Meaning of Christianity", *Christian China* 7.2-3 (December 1920 to January 1921):90-96.

61

Chien Yu-wen, "She-mo shih chi-tu-chiao"?, *SM* 2.2 (September 1921):6.

62

Wei Ch'üeh (Sidney K. Wei) was a Christian educator in our period. He received higher education in the United States and graduated from Oberlin College and the University of Chicago. Many of his views on religion were expressed in the *Christian China*, a representative organ of Chinese Christians in the United States. Back in China, Wei filled several important positions, for example, Commissioner of Education in Kwang-tung, Secretary in the Ministry of Foreign Affairs, Professor of Canton Christian College, and Dean of the College of Education, National Central University, Nanking. Wei was also a member of the Educational Commission of the Nationalist government, which prepared the regulations for the registration of schools.

63

Sidney K. Wei, "Some Characteristics of Religious Experience", *The Chinese Students' Christian Journal* 6.3 (January 1920):134-37.

64

Ibid., p. 137.

65

Mei Yi-pao (1900-) received secondary education at Nankai Middle School. Mei studied at Tsing Hua University and, after graduation in 1922, served as travelling secretary for the National YMCA. He went to the United States and got his B.A. degree from Oberlin College in 1924 and his PH.D. from the University of Chicago in 1927. Upon his return to China, Mei taught philosophy at Yenching University for a number of years. Later, he became Dean of the College of Arts and Letters, and Acting President of Yenching University, 1928-49. His major publications include *The Ethical and Political Philosophy of Motse* (1929) and *Motse, The Neglected Rival of Confucius* (1934).

66
    Mei Yi-pao, "Tsung-chiao ti shih-chi" (The substance of
religion) *Chen-li yü sheng-meng* 6.7 (May 1932):1-9. Hereinafter referred to as *CLYSM*.

67
    Ibid., pp. 6-9.

68
    Chao Tzu-ch'en was born on February 14, 1888 in Chekiang.
(There has been some discussion about the exact date of
Chao's birth. See Philip West, *Yenching University and
Sino-Western Relations, 1916-1952* (Cambridge: Harvard
University Press, 1976), p. 265, footnote 51. The majority
of scholars put it in 1888. The date given above is taken
from L. D. Cio (Chu Li-teh), ed., "Who's Who Among Chinese
Christian Leaders", in *China Christian Year Book* 1936-1937
(Shanghai: Christian Literature Society, 1937), p. 430).
He got his B.A. from Soochow University in 1910. Chao went
to study in the United States and received from Vanderbilt
University his M.A. in 1916 and B.D. in 1917. He returned
to teach Sociology and Religion at Soochow University, and,
in 1922, he joined the faculty of Yenching University. In
1928, Chao became Dean of the School of Religion. He authored
a number of books, including *Chi-tu-chiao che-hsüeh* (1925),
Yeh-su-ch'uan (1935), *Chi-tu-chiao chin-chieh* (1947), *Sheng
pao-luo ch'uan* and *Shen-hsüeh ssu-chiang* (both 1948). Chao
was elected one of the six vice-presidents of the World
Council of Churches in 1948. The major thrust of Chao's
thought in the twenties were in social reconstruction and
indigenous church movement.

69
    Chao Tzu-ch'en, "Tsung-chiao yü lun-li" (Religion and
ethics) *CLYSM* 4.7 (November 1929):1-2. Also see Chao "The
Appeal of Christianity to the Chinese Mind", *CR* 49 (1918):
287-96.

70
    Chao's comment in the Preface to Chien Yu-wen, ed.,
Tsung-chiao yü jen-sheng (Religion and life) (Shanghai: The
Association Press, 1923).

71
    Chao Tzu-ch'en, "Tsung-chiao yü ching-pien" (Religion
and circumstantial changes), *Ch'ing-nien chin-pu* 30 (February 1920):30f; hereinafter cited as *CNPC*.

72

Wang Ming-tao, *Yeh-su shih-shei* (Who is Jesus?) (1927; reprint ed., Hong Kong: Hung Tao Press, 1962), pp. 3-4.

73

Wang Ming-tao, *Jen-neng chien-she t'ien-kuo ma?* (Can the kingdom of heaven be established by man?) (1933; reprint ed., Hong Kong: The Alliance Press, 1962), pp. 9-12.

74

Sidney K. Wei, "How the Religious Needs of China May Be Met", *Christian China* 7.5 (March 1921): 211.

75

See statement in *CR* 51 (September 1920): 636.

76

Liu T'ing-fang, "Chinese Renaissance--Christian Opportunity", pp. 319-20.

77

Lo Yün-yen, *Chi-tu-chiao yü hsin Chung-kuo* (Christianity and New China) (Shanghai: Methodist Press, 1923), p. 3

78

Chao Tzu-ch'en, *Chi-tu-chiao che-hsüeh* (Christian Philosophy) (Shanghai: Chung-hua chi-tu-chiao wen-she, 1926), p. 65.

79

Hsieh Hung-lai, *Chi-tu-chiao yü k'e-hsüeh* (Christianity and science) (Shanghai: Ch'ing-nien hsieh-hui shu-chü, 1921), pp. 9-12. Chu Ching-nung, "K'e-hsüeh yü tsung-chiao" (Science and religion), *Wen-she yüeh-k'an* 1.11-12 (October 1926):16-17; hereinafter cited as *WS*.

80

Wang Li-chung, "Chi-tu-chiao yü ssu-hsiang chieh" (Christianity and the intellectual) *CLYSM* 2.1 (January 1927): 14-16.

81

Liu Chung-fu, "Wo ti erh-shih shih-chi tsung-chiao kuan" (My religious view in the twentieth century), *SM* 3.10 (June 1923): 12-13.

82
   Liu T'ing-fang, "Shih-chiu shih-chi ko-chung ssu-ch'ao
ti yün-tung tui-yü chi-tu-chiao hsin-yang shang so fa-sheng
ti yin-hsiang" (The influences on Christianity due to the
various intellectual movements in the nineteenth century),
CLYSM 3.17 (January 1929). Liu analytically traced how ideologies of the previous century affected the development of
Christian thought even before the New Culture Movement in
China.

CHAPTER 2

1
   See the discussion in Mary C. Wright, *The Last Stand of
Chinese Conservatism: The T'ung-Chih Restoration, 1862-1874*
(Stanford: Stanford University Press, 1957).

2
   From *Records of the General Conference of the Protestant
Missionaries of China Held at Shanghai, May 10-24, 1877*
(Shanghai: American Presbyterian Mission Press, 1878),
pp. 32-33.

3
   Evangelization was regarded as conquest. See Rufus
Anderson, *Chinese Repository* 15 (1846):489-90; D. Z.
Sheffield, "Christianity is a religion of conquest", *CR* 14
(1883): 93-94.

4
   Marshall Broomhall, *The Jubilee Story of the China
Inland Mission* (Shanghai, 1915), p. 193.

5
   Kenneth Scott Latourette, *A History of Christian Missions
in China* (London: Society for Promoting Christian Knowledge, 1929), p. 386.

6
   Lewis S. C. Smythe, "Changes in the Christian Message
for China by Protestant Missionaries" (PH.D. dissertation,
University of Chicago, 1928), p. 31. Also C. William
Mesendick, "The Protestant Missionary Understanding of the
Chinese Situation and the Chinese Task from 1890 to 1911",
(PH.D. dissertation, Columbia University, 1958).

7
James Legge, *The Religions of China* (London: Hodder and Stoughton, 1880), p. 284.

8
See the discussion of F. S. Turner in *CR* 1 (1869):31.

9
Peter Duus, "Science and Salvation in China: The Life and Work of W. A. P. Martin (1827-1916)" in *American Missionaries in China*, ed. Kwang-ching Liu (Cambridge: Harvard University Press, 1966), p. 35.

10
A. R. Kepler, "The Need for a Changed Approach to the People in Our Missionary Enterprise", *CR* 51 (January 1920): 21-31.

11
The remark of Ch'en Tu-hsiu in "Chi-tu-chiao yü Chung-kuo jen", in *KNCS*, pp. 37-38.

12
Hsü Pao-ch'ien, "The Prospects for Christianity in China", p. 320.

13
Liu T'ing-fang, "Chinese Renaissance--The Christian Opportunity", p. 19.

14
Hsü Pao-ch'ien, ed., "The Future of Christianity in China", *CLYSM* (Special English Number) 2.3 (February 1927): 3.

15
Chao Tzu-ch'en, "The Appeal of Christianity to the Chinese Mind", p. 287.

16
Ibid., p. 288.

17
Wu was born in 1870 in Kiangsu and was educated in strict Confucian tradition. He got his *chin-shih* in 1898. Wu served as headmaster in the Chekiang Provincial College from 1905-1909 and then in *Chin-shih kuan* for a year. Wu was appointed civil magistrate of Hangchow for sometime after

Hangchow declared independence from the imperial government
in 1911. From 1912-25, he served in the board of education
at Peking as senior assistant. He was converted to Christianity in 1914, and was actively involved in church ministry. Wu edited the *Chen-li chou-k'an* from 1923-26. In
1926, the magazine was joint with the *Sheng-ming* of the Life
Fellowship. Wu began teaching in Yenching in 1922, and was
appointed the first Chinese vice-president in 1926 and chancellor in 1929. See West, *Yenching University*, pp. 62-66.

18
    Wu Lei-ch'uan, *Chi-tu-chiao yü Chung-kuo wen-hua* (Chris-
tianity and Chinese Culture) (Shanghai: Ch'ing-nien hsieh-
hui shu-chü, 1936), p. 10; also "Lun chi-tu-t'u tang ju-ho
hsiao-f a shang-ti" (How can a Christian imitate God) *CLYSM*
4.9 (January 1930): 8-11.

19
    Hsü Pao-ch'ien, ed., "The Future of Christianity", pp.
3-4.

20
    Wu Lei-ch'uan, "Tso chi-tu-t'u ti liang-ko wen-t'i"
(The Why and How of Being a Christian) *CLYSM* 8.4 (June
1934).

21
    Hsü Pao-ch'ien, "Uniqueness of Jesus from a Chinese
Standpoint", *CLYSM* (Special English Number) 2.3 (February
1927): 30.

22
    Hsü adopted William Hocking's terms 'effortless' and
'effortful' to describe the dual experience. See "She-mo
shih tsung-chiao"? (What is Religion?) *CLYSM* 4.6 (June 1929):
9-11.

23
    Hsü Pao-ch'ien, ed., "The Future of Christianity in
China", p. 4.

24
    Hsü Pao-ch'ien, "The Prospects for Christianity in
China", p. 20.

25

Chien Yu-wen, "She-mo shih-chi-tu-chiao", *SM* 2.1 (June 1921):1-3. We see in this article how Chien's view was influenced by Western scholars in the same generation.

26

Ibid., p. 6.

27

Pao Kuang-lin, *Yeh-su ti yen-chiu* (Studies on Jesus) (Shanghai: Chung-hua chi-tu-chiao wen-she, 1928); and Wu Yao-tsung, *Wo so jen-shih ti Yeh-su* (The Jesus that I know) (Shanghai: Ch'ing-nien hsieh-hui shu-chü, 1929).

28

Chu's essay first appeared in the "Jesus Issue" in *Ch'ien-she* (December 1919). Copies of the essay were distributed in an evangelistic meeting during the Christmas time of the next year. During the anti-Christian movement in 1922, this essay was again used by the anti-Christians as an effective tool of attack. Later the same writing was printed by the Propaganda Board of the Kuomintang Party Committee in Kiangsu, with a preface of 2000 words which added fuel to the fire of antagonism. The influence of Chu could be thus estimated. See Chang I-ching, "Lun Kuangchou ta pu-tao ti ch'eng-chi ho fan-hsiang" (Comment on the Result of Mass Evangelism and Reaction in Canton) and "Tu-liao Kiangsu sheng tang-wu cheng-wei-hui hsüan-ch'uan-pu yin Chu Chih-hsin 'Yeh-su shih she-mo tung-hsi' ti chuan t'ou yü i-hou" (After Reading the Preface to Chu Chih-hsin's 'What a Thing is Jesus' printed by the Propaganda Board of the Kuo-mintang Party Committee at Kiangsu) in Chang I-ching, ed., *Kuan-yü Chu chih-hsin "Yeh-su shih she-mo tung-hsi" ti tsa-p'ing* (Collection of Criticism of Chu Chih-hsin's 'What a Thing is Jesus') (Shanghai: Mei Hua Chin-hsin-hui shu-chü, 1930).

29

Chu Chih-hsin, "Yeh-su shih-she-mo tung-hsi" (What a Thing is Jesus), in *KNCS*, p. 37.

30

Ch'en Tu-hsiu, "Chi-tu-chiao yü Chung-kuo jen" (Christianity and the Chinese People) *HCN* 7.3 (February 1920); reproduced in *KNCS*, pp. 37-50. Before Ch'en became a Marxist, it seemed that he was quite open to ideological alternatives that might help solve the national crisis. This article was

written before his conversion in September 1920. See
Benjamin I. Schwartz, *Chinese Communism and the Rise of Mao*
(Cambridge: Harvard University Press, 1966), pp. 18-24.

31
    KNCS, p. 41.

32
    Liang Chün-mo (1899-1975) was born in Kwangtung and
accepted Christianity in 1918. He graduated from the Kwangtung Higher Teacher College in 1923 and taught at P'ei-
ching chung hsüeh at Canton. Liang became editor of the
Chin-yen chou-k'an, a magazine devoted to the study of
Christianity in relation to social problems. Liang planned
to study theology in the United States but was sent back to
China upon arrival at San Francisco by the immigration
officers. As an active member in the Central Committee of
the Kuomintang, Liang did secretarial work for Wang Ching-
wei, Sun Fo and others. When Sun Fo became president of the
Legislative Yüan in 1932, Liang was appointed Secretary of
the Yüan. During the anti-Christian movement in the 1920s,
he wrote extensively to defend the Christian faith.

33
    This magazine was a Baptist journal in the South, repre-
sentative of conservative theological viewpoints. During
the anti-Christian movement, many apologetic writings
appeared in this magazine. Even T. C. Chao commended their
intellectual effort as rare among conservative denominations.
See T. C. Chao, "Christian and Non-Christian Reply to the
Anti-Christian Movement", *CR* 53 (December 1922):743-48.

34
    Liang Chün-mo, "P'i-p'ing Chu Chih-hsin chu Yeh-su shih
she-mo tung-hsi chih miou-wang" (Critique of the error of
Chu Chih-hsin's "What a Thing is Jesus"), in *PFCTC*, pp. 163-
67.

35
    Chien Yu-wen, "Yeh-su shih szu-sheng tzu ma"? (Is Jesus
an illegitimate child?), *Chen-li chou-k'an* 2.40 (December
28, 1924); also Chao Tzu-ch'en, *Chi-tu-chiao che-hsüeh
(Christian Philosophy)* (Shanghai: Chung-hua chi-tu-chiao
wen-she, 1926), pp. 223-24.

36
    Liang Chün-mo, "P'i-p'ing Chu Chih-hsin", p. 167.

37

In the meeting sponsored by the Christian Association at Canton, the speakers included Chou Ch'uan-hsin, Ou Ch'ih-tang, Yü Jih-chang, and Chang Li-ts'ai. Over 3,000 conversions were recorded, the best result in the recent history of evangelism of the Chinese Church. See Chang I-ching, "Lun Kuang-chou ta pu-tao".

38

Chang I-ching was born in 1871 and was educated in the traditional Chinese way. A most articulate Christian voice in South China, Chang was one of the leading apologists in the 1910s and 1920s. He served as editor of the *Chung-kuo shen-pao*, *Chen-kuang yüeh-k'an* in Canton, *Chen-kuang tsa-chih*, and *Ta-kung jih-pao* in Hong Kong. After that, he became the head of the *Chen-kuang tsa-chih* in Shanghai.

39

Chang I-ching, "Lun Kuangchou ta pu-tao".

40

Ch'en Tu-hsiu, "Chi-tu-chiao yü chi-tu-chiao-hui" (Christianity and the Christian Church), in *KNCS*, pp. 190-92.

41

Chang I-ching, "Yü Ch'en Tu-hsiu hsien-sheng shuo 'Chi-tu-chiao yü chi-tu-chiao-hui'" (Discussion with Mr. Ch'en Tu-hsiu regarding his "Christianity and the Christian Church"), in *PFCTC*, pp. 191-213.

42

Ibid., p. 196.

43

Ibid., pp. 195-96. Chang quoted and translated fairly correctly from Flavius Josephus, *Jewish Antiquities*, 18. 3. 3.

44

Ibid., p. 197.

45

Hu I-ku (Y. K. Woo) was an outstanding Christian writer and editor of *Ch'ing-nien pao*, a magazine that promoted moral, physical, and intellectual development of the young people. He was the executive secretary of the publication department of the National Y.M.C.A. Many of his writings in the twenties advocated patriotism and social reform and appeared in *Ch'ing-nien chin-pu*, the representative organ of Y.M.C.A. Hu was best known for his work, *Jen-ko yü shiu-yang* (Character and cultivation) and for his translation of H. E. Fosdick's *The Meaning of Faith*.

46
   Hu I-ku, "Chi-tu-chiao yü Yeh-su chi-tu" (Christianity and Jesus Christ), in *Hsien-tai ssu-hsiang chung ti chi-tu-chiao* (Christianity in the Light of Today) ed. Hu I-ku (Shanghai: Association Press of China, 1926).

47
   Chao Tzu-ch'en, "Jesus and the Reality of God", *CLYSM* 7.5 (March 1933):1. For further discussion, see Chao Tzu-ch'en, *Chi-tu-chiao-che-hsüeh*, pp. 225-28, 232-39.

48
   Chao Tzu-ch'en, "Jesus and the Reality of God", p. 9.

49
   Chao Tzu-ch'en, "Yeh-su ti shang-ti kuan" (Jesus' conception of God), *SM* 2.2 (September 1921):1-15.

50
   Ibid., p. 3.

51
   Hsü Pao-ch'ien, "Uniqueness of Jesus from a Chinese Standpoint", p. 30.

52
   Hsü Pao-ch'ien, ed., "The Future of Christianity in China", p. 4.

53
   Wu Lei-ch'uan, "Ts'ung Ju-chia ssu-hsiang lun chi-tu-chiao" (Discussion of Christianity from the Standpoint of Confucian Thought), *CLYSM* 4.13 (1930):3-6; and Wu Lei-ch'uan, "Chi-nien Yeh-su tan-sheng ti wo-chien" (My view of commemoration of Jesus birth), *CLYSM* 7.3 (December 1932):1-6.

54
   A full treatment is given in Wu Lei-ch'uan, *Chi-tu-chiao yü Chung-kuo wen-hua* (Christianity and Chinese Culture) (Shanghai: Chin-nien hsieh-hui, 1936), pp. 82-98.

55
Wang Ching-wei (1883-1944) was a revolutionary leader of Kuomintang and close political associate of Dr. Sun Yat-sen. During early twenties, Wang occupied an important political position at Canton. He was elected a member of the Central Executive Committee of the Kuomintang in the First National Congress in 1924 and served as Chief Secretary to Dr. Sun. After Sun's death, he was elected Chairman of the National Government in July, 1925. While Chiang Kai-shek ruled the right wing, the left wing of the Party was under Wang's leadership. In religious matters, Wang was antagonistic toward Christianity, as revealed in some of his writings. His position in the South had lent weight to the anti-Christian movement. For a biographical sketch, see Boorman, *Biographical Dictionary* 3:369-73.

56
Chang I-ching, "P'i-p'ing Wang Ching-wei ti li-ch'ih Yeh-chiao san ta miou" (A critique of Wang Ching-wei's 'Rebutting the three big errors of Christianity'), in *PFCTC*, p. 87.

57
The third error, in Wang's view, was the teaching of Creation, which was against the theory of evolution and of all sciences.

58
Ling Ken's essay was translated by Chao Tzu-ch'en in *CR* 52 (March 1921):177-86.

59
Chang I-ching, "P'i-p'ing Wang Ching-wei", p. 88.

60
Chang I-ching, "Po Wang Ching-wei ti tsung-chiao tu-min lun" (Rebutting Wang Ching-wei's 'Religion as poison to the people'), in *PFCTC*, p. 122.

61
Hsü Pao-ch'ien, ed., "The Future of Christianity in China", p. 6.

62
Chang Ch'in-shih, "Wo ko-jen ti tsung-chiao ching-yen" (My Personal Religious Experience), *SM* 3.7-8 (April 1923).

63
Wu Yao-tsung, "How One Christian Looks at the Five Year Movement", *CR* 61 (1930):147-48. The Five Year Movement was a movement of the Christian churches in China inaugurated on January 1, 1930. Its goals consisted in achieving deeper spiritual life in its various dimensions and in evangelizing the society.

64
Wu Lei-ch'uan, "Tsung Ju-chia ssu-hsiang lun chi-tu-chiao", pp. 6-8.

65
Ibid., p. 5.

66
Wu quoted from the Gospel of John 14:6. The translation is taken from the Revised Standard Version.

67
During the twenties, Chou Tso-jen was a well-known writer and translator of Western works into vernacular Chinese. Chou was professor in the College of Arts of Peking University. An advocate of language reform, he and his brother Lu Hsün brought new shape to Chinese literature. His writings were filled with the sense of social realism and humanitarianism. During the anti-Christian movement, Chou and others issued an important statement to defend the freedom of religious belief in China. See *KNCS*, p. 199.

68
See "Hsin wen-hua chung chi-wei hsüeh-che tui-yü chi-tu-chiao ti t'ai-t'u" (Attitudes toward Christianity among scholars of the New Culture Movement), *SM* 2.7-8 (March 1922): 1-10, for the views of Chou Tso-jen, Kao I-han, Hu Shih, Ch'en Tu-hsiu and Ch'ien Hsuan-t'ung.

69
Ch'ien Hsüan-t'ung (1887-1939) was professor of Peking University for a number of years where his scholarly contribution was in the field of classical studies and philology. With Ch'en Tu-hsiu and Hu Shih, Ch'ien advocated the use of *pai-hua* (the vernacular) to replace the classical Chinese language. He served in the six-man editorial committee of the magazine *Hsin Ch'ing-nien*. In cooperation with Li Chin-hsi, Y. R. Chao and Lin Yü-tang, he compiled a dictionary of the Chinese language on phonetic principles.

70
  During the initial outbreak of the anti-Christian movement in 1922, a special issue, entitled, "Fei chi-tu-chiao
hsüeh-sheng t'ung-meng hao", was published by the Anti-
Christian Student Federation. See *Hsien-ch'ü* (The Vanguard)
(March 15, 1922). This issue contained several provocative
articles that opposed Christianity. In Chang I-ching's
edited volume, *PFCTC*, each of them was criticized from a
Christian standpoint. In it was Ch'ih Kuang's essay, "Chi-
tu-chiao yü shih-chieh kai-tsao".

71
  Chang I-ching, "P'i-p'ing Ch'ih Kuang ti chi-tu-chiao yü
shih-chieh kai-tsao" (A critique of Ch'ih Kuang's "Christianity and World Reform"), in *PFCTC*, pp. 53-61.

72
  Liang Chün-mo, "P'i-p'ing Ch'i Yüan ti chi-tu-chiao yü
kung-ch'an chu-i" (A critique of Ch'i Yüan's "Christianity
and Communism"), in *PFCTC* pp. 74-76. Ch'i Yüan was another
anti-Christian critic whose writing appeared in the special
issue of the Anti-Christian Student Federation.

73
  Ch'ang Nai-te was a non-Christian observer of the anti-
Christian movement who was provoked by the excess of the
anti-Christian propaganda. He did not believe in the necessity of religion in the modern scientific age. In his defense of democracy and liberty of thought, Ch'ang felt that
much anti-Christian antagonism was groundless. His essay in
Chang I-ching's collection was a blow to the position of
anti-Christian movement.

74
  Ch'ang Nai-te, "Tui-yü fei tsung-chiao ta t'ung-meng chih
cheng-yen" (A word of remonstration to the Anti-Religion
Federation), in *PFCTC*, pp. 263-66.

75
  Liang Chün-mo, "P'i-p'ing Ch'i Yüan", p. 79.

76
  Ch'ang Nai-te, "Tui yü fei tsung-chiao", pp. 265-66.

77
  Their understanding of the Medieval society in its cultural and intellectual activity was very inadequate. Historical research in our time has already shown that the "Dark
Ages" were not dark at all.

78
    See T'u's lecture in *KNCS*, pp. 87-106.

79
    See Ch'ien's view in "Hsin wen-hua chung chi-wei hsüeh-che", pp. 9-10.

80
    Ch'en Tu-hsiu, "Chi-tu-chiao yü Chung-kuo jen", in *KNCS*, pp. 46-48.

81
    See Chou's view in "Hsin wen-hua chung chi-wei hsüeh-che", pp. 1-3.

82
    Chien Yu-wen, "She-mo shih chi-tu-chiao", *SM* 2.2 (September 1921):6.

83
    T. C. Chao, "Can Christianity be the Basis of Social Reconstruction in China"? *CR* 53 (May 1922):316.

84
    Chang Ch'in-shih, "Ching-shen fu-hsin" (Revival of the spirit), *SM* 2.4 (November 1921). Also see Chang Ch'in-shih, "Wo ko-jen ti tsung-chiao ching-yen" (My personal religious experience) *SM* 3:7-8 (April 1923).

85
    Cf. Hu I-ku, "Yeh-su chi-tu neng kai-tsao shih-chieh ma"? (Can Jesus Christ reform the world?), in *Hsien tai ssu-hsiang chung ti chi-tu-chiao* (Christianity in the light of today) (Shanghai: Association Press of China, 1926), pp. 21-35.

86
    For a detailed discussion of the movement of the Church of Christ in China, see Wallace C. Mervin, *Adventure in Unity: The Church of Christ in China* (Grand Rapids: Wm. B. Eerdmans Publishing Co., 1974).

87
    Bulletin of the Bible Union of China 1.2 (April 1921):4; also the "Tentative Statement", in 1.1 (January 1921):3.

88
    Hsü Pao-ch'ien, "The Prospects for Christianity in
China", p. 23. For a good discussion of the controversy
see Paul Hutchinson, "Conservative Reaction in China",
Journal of Religion 2 (July 1922):337-61; Griffith W. H.
Thomas, "Modernism in China", *Princeton Theological Review*
(October 1921):630-71. Also M. Searle Bates, "The Theology
of American Missionaries", in *The Missionary Enterprise in
China and America*, ed. John K. Fairbank (Cambridge: Harvard
University Press, 1974), pp. 150-57.

89
    Hsü Pao-ch'ien, ed., "The Future of Christianity in
China", p. 6.

90
    Andrew C. Y. Ch'eng, "Interpreting Christianity to
China", *Christian China* 8.1 (October 1921):38-39.

91
    Ch'eng Ching-yi (C. Y. Ch'eng) received his early edu-
cation in mission schools and graduated from the theological
school of the London Missionary Society at Tientsin in 1900.
He went to London to help the revision of the Chinese New
Testament from 1903-1908. Ch'eng represented the Chinese
churches of the London Missionary Society in the World
Missionary Conference at Edinburgh in 1910 and was appointed
in 1913 secretary to the China Continuation Committee until
1922. He campaigned against the attempt made by Ch'en Huan-
chang to establish Confucianism as the state religion of
China in 1915. Ch'eng started the "China for Christ Movement" in 1919 and was chairman of the National Christian
Conference in 1922. Later he studied in the United States,
and upon his return, he became the General Secretary of the
National Christian Council of China until the end of 1933.
In 1927, Ch'eng was elected moderator of the Church of Christ
in China.

92
    C. Y. Ch'eng, "Problems of the Chinese Church", in *China
Her Own Interpreter*, ed. M. Stauffer (New York: Missionary
Education Movement of the United States and Canada, 1927),
p. 97.

CHAPTER 3

1
   In current missiological studies, the term 'contextualization' has replaced 'indigenization'. Indigenization
is a missiological necessity in cross-cultural evangelism,
taking into consideration a particular cultural setting. It
is pointed out that 'contextualization' includes all that is
implied in 'indigenization' and carries a forward-looking
significance. For example, see the essays on Asian theology
in Douglas J. Elwood, ed., *What Asian Christians Are Thinking: A Theological Source Book* (Quezon City, Philippines:
New Day Publishers, 1976). In the 1920s, the Chinese term
used was 'pen-se' (indigeneity). Chinese Christians did not
entertain the distinction that we now make. For them, indigenization was the theological effort to deal with the cultural tradition and the contemporary problems.

2
   See the discussion of the Jesuit missions in K. S.
Latourette, *A History of Christian Missions in China*, pp.
78-101.

3
   Ibid., pp. 133-35.

4
   C. Y. Ch'eng, "Problems of the Chinese Church", pp. 99-
100.

5
   Latourette, *History of Christian Missions*, pp. 567-616.

6
   For a good analysis of the Chinese thinking by a contemporary scholar, see T. C. Chao (Chao Tzu-ch'en), "The Appeal
of Christianity to the Chinese Mind", *CR* 49 (1918): 287-96,
371-80

7
   Liang Chün-mo, "Wo-men tui tzu-tzu fei chi-tu-chiao hsüeh-
sheng t'ung-meng ti kan-hsiang ho t'ai-tu" (Our feeling and
attitude toward the Anti-Christian Student Federation), in
PFCTC, pp. 1-5; and Liu T'ing-fang, "Chi-tu-chiao tsai Chung-
kuo chin-jih tang ju-ho tzu-hsiu i chih-pang" (How should
Christianity cultivate itself to stop people's scandal in
China today), *SM* 6.2 (November 1925).

8

For the documents of the Conference, see F. Rawlinson,
Helen Thoburn, and D. MacGillivray, ed., *The Chinese Church
as Revealed in the National Christian Conference held in
Shanghai, May 2 to 11, 1922* (Shanghai: The Oriental Press,
1922).

9

Before this year, four national missionary conferences
were held in 1877, 1890, 1907, and 1913 respectively. In
the 1913 conference, only one-third of those in attendance
were Chinese. See "Findings of the Continuation Committee
Conferences Held in Asia, 1912-1913", (New York, 1913).

10

Conference Document, *The Chinese Church*, p. viii.

11

Timothy T. Lew (Liu T'ing-fang) "The Message of the
Church", in *The Chinese Church*, p. 502.

12

See "Interpretive Introduction", in *The Chinese Church*,
p. xi. F. Rawlinson was a representative missionary statesman in China and editor of *The Chinese Recorder* of the
Presbyterian Mission Press. He seemed to have done more
work than other missionaries in the creation of an indigenous
theology. His *Naturalization of Christianity in China*
(Shanghai: Presbyterian Mission Press, 1927) was a leading
statement among missionaries in the decade.

13

See the analysis in Chow Tse-tsung, *The May Fourth Movement*, pp. 218-28.

14

Ying Yüan-tao, "Chin wu-nien lai Chung-kuo chi-tu-chiao
ssu-hsiang chih shih-tai pei-ching ho ch'i nei-jung chih ta-
kai" (A general survey of the background and content of
Christian thought in China during the past five years), *Wen-
she yüeh-k'an* 1.9-10 (September 1926):4-6; hereinafter cited
as *WS*. Also refer to *The National Christian Council: A
Five Years' Review, 1922-1927* (Shanghai, n.d.), p. 20.

15

A detailed discussion of the May Thirtieth Incident is
given on pp. 96-98 infra.

16
   C. Y. Ch'eng, "Chairman's Opening Address", in *The Chinese Church*, p. 32.

17
   Latourette, "Christian Missions as Mediators of Western Civilization", in *Christian Missions in China: Evangelists of What?* ed. J. G. Lutz (Boston: D. C. Heath and Co., 1965), pp. 83-93.

18
   See statement in "Christian Renaissance in China", *CR* 51 (September 1920):637.

19
   Ying Yüan-tao, "Chin wu-nien lai Chung-kuo", p. 8

20
   "Tung Hsi min-chu ken-pen ssu-hsiang chih ch'a-i" (The basic difference in the way of thinking between the Oriental and the Western people), *HCN* 1.4 (December 15, 1915):1-4.

21
   Chow Tse-tsung, *The May Fourth Movement*, p. 59.

22
   "Wo-men tui-yü Hsi-yang chin-tai wen-ming ti t'ai-tu" (Our attitude toward the recent Western civilization), *Hu Shih wen-ts'un, san chi* (Collected essays of Hu Shih, third collection) 4 vols., 9 chüan (Shanghai: Ya-tung t'u-shu-kuan, 1930), 3.1:8. (Hereinafter referred to as *HSWT*).

23
   "Tung Hsi wen-hua ti chien-hsien" (The line of demarcation between the cultures of East and West), *HSWT* 3.1:51-52. Cf. Kuo Chan-po, *Chin wu-shih nien Chung-kuo ssu-hsiang shih, pu-pien* (A history of Chinese thought during the last fifty years; a supplement) (Hong Kong: Lung-meng shu-tien, 1966), pp. 27-31.

24
   See "Wo-men tui-yü Hsi-yang chin-tai wen-ming ti t'ai-t'u", pp. 20-21.

25
   "Tu Liang Sou-ming hsien-sheng ti Tung Hsi wen-hua chi ch'i che-hsüeh", *HSWT* 2.2:83. In Hu Shih's criticism of Chinese culture, his attitude was not contemptuous. He also spoke of choosing the best elements from the cultures of East and West, but his Western emphasis was unmistakable. See Grieder, *Hu Shih and the Chinese Renaissance*, pp. 151-169.

26

Liang Sou-ming, *Tung Hsi wen-hua chi ch'i che-hsueh* (The cultures of East and West and their philosophies) (Shanhai, 1922), p. 199.

27

Ibid., pp. 54-56.

28

Ibid., p. 203. Cf. the discussion in Grieder, *Hu Shih and the Chinese Renaissance*, pp. 135-48.

29

Liang's three major works in the last decade of his life included *History of Chinese Political Thought in the Pre-Ch'in Period, Intellectual Trends in the Ch'ing Period,* and *History of Chinese Thought in the Last Three Hundred Years.*

30

Liang Ch'i-ch'ao, "Ou-yu hsin-ying lu, chieh-lu" (A condensed record of impressions of the European journey), *Yin-ping-shih ho-chi, chüan-chi,* 5.23:1-162.

31

Ibid., pp. 10-11.

32

Ibid., pp. 37-38. In Philip Huang's view, Liang took a middle way between the radical iconoclasts and the conservative traditionalists. Cf. *Liang Ch'i-ch'ao and modern Chinese Liberalism* (Seattle: University of Washington, 1972), pp. 141-45. Huang's work, in general, improves on Joseph R. Levenson's interpretation of Liang in his *Liang Ch'i-ch'ao and the Mind of Modern China* (Cambridge: Harvard University Press, 1953).

33

Cf. Kuo Chan-po, *Chin wu-shih nien Chung-kuo ssu-hsiang shih, pu-pien,* pp. 61, 75-77.

34

In Joseph R. Levenson's view, Ts'ai's appeal to cultural harmony was "a balm for cultural defeatism". See J. R. Levenson, *Confucian China and Its Modern Fate: A Trilogy* (Berkeley and Los Angeles: University of California Press, 1968), p. 111. Levenson may have read too much into Ts'ai's psychology, but that Ts'ai was thoroughly a Confucianist is quite clear. See Tai Chin-hsiao, "The Life and Work of Ts'ai Yüan-p'ei" (Ph.D. dissertation, Harvard University, 1952) pp. 41-42.

35
   T. C. Chao, "Our Cultural Heritage", p. 1.

36
   Chao Tzu-ch'en, "Chi-tu-chiao yü Chung-kuo wen-hua"
(Christianity and Chinese Culture), *CLYSM* 2.9-10 (1927):247-
60; and his later and more comprehensive work, *Chi-tu-chiao
chin-chieh* (An interpretation of Christianity) (Shanghai:
Association Press of China, 1947), pp. 36-40.

37
   Wei Cho-min (Francis Wei) was born in 1888 and was
brought up in a traditional Chinese family. He graduated
with honor in 1911 from Boone University, Wuchang, and
received his M.A. in 1915 with a thesis on the political
principles of Mencius. Wei studied at Harvard University in
1918 and got his M.A. in philosophy in 1919. Without com-
pleting the doctorate program, Wei returned to China, teaching in Boone University. After the establishment of Huachung
University at Wuchang in 1924, Wei became dean of the faculty
of sciences and arts and administrative vice-president. He
left for England briefly where he received a D. Phil. degree
from London University in 1929. Upon return, he served as
president in the newly reopened Huachung University, a school
devoted to educate Christian leaders in China. Among his
writings, he is best known for *The Spirit of Chinese Culture*,
a series of Hewett lectures published in 1947. See Boorman,
Biographical Dictionary, 3:403-5.

38
   Francis C. M. Wei, *The Spirit of Chinese Culture* (New
York: Charles Scribner's Sons, 1947), p. 3.

39
   For example, see T. M. Van (Fan Tzu-mei), "Chung-kuo lun-
li wen-hua yü Chi-tu-chiao" (Chinese ethical culture and
Christianity), in *Tung Hsi wen-hua chih i-kuan* (Civilization:
East and West) (Shanghai: Association Press of China, 1925),
p. 5. Chao Tzu-ch'en commented that the Chinese philosophy
of life is mainly Confucian, stemming from the doctrine of
Confucius and Mencius and embracing, later on, elements of
other philosophical schools, like Taoism and Buddhism. See
Chao Tzu-ch'en, *Chi-tu-chiao chin-chieh*, p. 41. Wei Cho-min
also said, "China is thoroughly Confucian because Confucianism is so typically Chinese. . . . It is the culture of the
Chinese People". Wei, *The Spirit of Chinese Culture*, p. 94.

40
   Levenson, *Confucian China*, p. 105.

41

Ch'eng Ching-yi, "Pen-se chiao-hui chih shang-ch'üeh" (Discussion of indigenous church), *WS* 1.6 (May 1926):1-17.

42

Liu T'ing-fang, "Wei pen-se chiao-hui yen-chiu Chung-hua min-tsu tsung-chiao ching-yen ti yi-ko tsao-an" (A draft of the study of the religious experience of the Chinese people on behalf of the indigenous church), *CLYSM* 1.7 (August 1926): 187.

43

Ch'eng Ching-yi, "Pen-se chiao-hui chih shang-ch'üeh", pp. 9-10.

44

T. C. Chao, "Indigenous Church", *CR* 56 (August 1925):497.

45

Liu T'ing-fang, "Wei pen-se chiao-hui", p. 186.

46

Cf. Wang Chih-hsin, "Pen-se chiao-hui yü pen-se chu-tso" (Indigenous church and indigenous writings), *WS* 1.6 (May 1926):1-17.

47

It has to be pointed out that, in the analysis of the following patterns, not every one is by itself unique and distinct. This analysis is based on the different emphases by contemporary Chinese Christians in tackling the indigenous problem. Some overlap is recognizable, especially the same Scriptural texts are quoted and similar Confucian doctrines are discussed. But their theological presuppositions and approaches in relating Christianity to Chinese culture are closely reflected in the different emphases.

48

Chao Tzu-ch'en, "Wu Lei-ch'uan hsien-sheng hsiao-chüan" (A biographical sketch of Mr. Wu Lei-ch'uan), *CLYSM* 10.8 (January 1937):418.

49

Wu Lei-ch'uan, "Chi-tu-chiao yü Ju-chiao" (Christianity and Confucianism), *Chen-li chou-k'an* 1.43 (January 12, 1923). Hereinafter cited as *CL*.

50
    Wu Lei-ch'uan, "Pen-chou-k'an chou-nien chi-nien ching-kao tu-che chu-chün" (Exhortation to our weekly's readers in the celebration of the anniversary), *CL* 2.1 (March 30, 1924).

51
    Wu Lei-ch'uan, "Wo tui-yü chi-tu-chiao-hui ti kan-hsiang", *SM* 1.4 (November 1920):3-4; translated by T. C. Chao as "Problems of the Christian Church in China: A Statement of Religious Experience", *CR* 52 (February 1921):101-102.

52
    Wu Lei-ch'uan, "Ts'ung Ju-chia ssu-hsiang lun chi-tu-chiao", pp. 3-6.

53
    Ibid., pp. 5-6.

54
    Wu Lei ch'uan, "Chi-tu-chiao ching yü Ju-chiao ching" (The Christian scripture and the Confucian documents), *SM* 3.6 (March 1923):1-6.

55
    Wu has quoted here from "Kung-sun Ch'ou p'ien 22", in *Meng Tzu* (The Book of Mencius). See Shen Chih-fang, ed., *Ssu Shu tu-pen* (The Four Classics: A Reader) (Taiwan: Ch'i-ming shu-chü, 1952).

56
    Wu Lei-ch'uan, *Chi-tu-chiao yü Chung-kuo wen-hua*, pp. 57-58.

57
    Wu has quoted here from "Yen Yüan p'ien", in *Lun Yü (The Analects)* 12. See Wu Lei-ch'uan, "Chi-tu-chiao ching", pp. 3-5.

58
    Wu Lei-ch'uan, *Chi-tu-chiao yü Chung-kuo wen-hua*, p. 57.

59
    Wu Lei-ch'uan, "Ts'ung Ju-chia ssu-hsiang lun chi-tu-chiao", p. 8.

60

Wang Chih-hsin, "Chung-kuo wen-hua yü Chi-tu-chiao jung-hua k'o-neng chung chih i-tien" (A point of possible harmonization between Chinese culture and Christianity), in *Chung-kuo wen-hua yü chi-tu-chiao* (Chinese Culture and Christianity) Shanghai: Association Press of China, 1927), pp. 1-9.

61

Wang Chih-hsin was born in 1881 in Chekiang. After getting the second degree of *chü jen*, he taught Chinese for more than ten years. He edited the Chinese *Christian Advocate* from 1913-18, and joined the faculty of Nanking Theological Seminary as professor of Chinese Philosophy in 1921. From 1926-28, Wang was editor-in-chief of the Christian Literature Association. He was dean of the Arts College in Fukien Christian University from 1928-34. After that he served as head of the Department of Chinese in the University of Shanghai. He authored several books of importance, including *The Idea of God in Chinese History, The Place of San Min Chu I in Chinese Culture, A History of Chinese Religions,* and *The Philosophy of Confucius.*

62

Wang Chih-hsin, "Pen-se chiao-hui", pp. 1-5.

63

Wang has quoted from "Wei Cheng p'ien", in *Lun Yü* 2 that "learning without thinking is illusive; thinking without learning is futile". See his "Chung-kuo wen-hua yü chi-tu-chiao", p. 4.

64

Ibid., p. 9.

65

Wang Chih-hsin, "Chi-tu-chiao yü Chung-kuo wen-hua" (Christianity and Chinese Culture), in *Chen-kuang tsa-chih* 26.6 (1927).

66

Wang has quoted from "Tseng Tzu ta-hsiao", in *Ta Tai Li Chi* 4.10.

67

Wang Chih-hsin, "Chi-tu-chiao yü Chung-kuo wen-hua", p. 3.

68

According to Wang, 'love-for-others' is described in I Cor. 13:1-3 and 'love-for-self' in I Cor. 13:4-7.

69
Wang Chih-hsin, "Chung-kuo wen-hua", p. 6.

70
Ibid., p. 7.

71
Fan Tzu-mei (T. M. Van) was brought up in traditional
Confucian background, which had left a mark in many of his
writings. In the 1920s, Fan had already established himself
as a well-known figure in the world of Christian literature.
He was co-editor of the *Wan-kuo kung-pao* and also editor of
the *Chin-pu tsa-chih*, later *Ch'ing-nien chin-pu*. His works
included *Tao chih fu* (The basis of truth), *Shih tao p'ien*
(A chapter on the relevance of truth), *Tung Hsi wen-hua chih
i-kuan* (Civilization: East and West).

72
Fan Tzu-mei, "Chung-kuo ku-tai Shang-ti kuan" (The God-
idea in ancient China), in *Tung Hsi wen-hua chih i-kuan*,
p. 56.

73
Fan Tzu-mei, "Chung-kuo lun-li ti wen-hua yü chi-tu-
chiao" (The Chinese Ethical culture and Christianity), in
Tung Hsi wen-hua chih i-kuan, pp. 1-2.

74
In Nietzsche's ethical view, the weak is inferior to the
strong, and Christianity belongs to the former. Fan used
'weak' and 'strong' in Nietzschean sense, but he rejected
such ethics by comparing contemporary Germany and historical
China. It was the 'weak' which was in the long run superior.
See Fan Tzu-mei, "Ho-p'ing hsing-chih ti Chung-kuo wen-hua
yü chi-tu-chiao tsai hsien shih-chieh chih ho-tso" (The
cooperation in the present world between the peace-natured
Chinese culture and Christianity), in *Tung Hsi wen-hua chih
i-kuan*, pp. 20-38.

75
Ibid., p. 38.

76
Fan Tzu-mei, "Chung-kuo lun-li", p. 13.

77
Ibid.

78
  Ying Yüan-tao, "Erh-shih-nien lai chih Chung-kuo chi-tu-chiao chu-tso-chieh chi ch'i tai-piao jen-wu" (The literary world and its representatives of the Chinese Church during the last twenty years), *WS* 1.5 (April 1926):13-14.

79
  Fan Tzu-mei, "Chung-kuo lun-li", p. 16.

80
  Chao Tzu-ch'en, for example, criticized the proponents of total westernization as ignoring the difference between culture *(wen-hua)* and civilization *(wen-ming)*, and the inevitability of cultural exchanges. See his *Chi-tu-chiao chin-chieh*, p. 38.

81
  Francis C. M. Wei, *The Spirit of Chinese Culture*, pp. 28-29.

82
  Ch'eng Ching-yi, "Problems of the Chinese Church", p. 104. Also T. C. Chao, "The Indigenous Church", p. 497.

83
  Ch'eng Ching-yi, "Problems of the Chinese Church", p. 104.

84
  Wei Cho-min disagreed with William Hocking in his program of cultural eclecticism. See William Hocking, *Living Religion and a World Faith* (New York, 1940), pp. 190, 198; and Francis C. M. Wei, *The Spirit of Chinese Culture*, pp. 24-27.

85
  This group includes Chao Tzu-ch'en, Liu T'ing-fang, Wei Cho-min, Hsieh Sung-kao, and Ch'eng Ching-yi. This section will mainly deal with them.

86
  Francis C. M. Wei, "Synthesis of Cultures East and West", in *China Today Through Chinese Eyes* ed. Chao Tzu-ch'en et al. (2nd Series: New York, 1927), pp. 74-85.

87

Cf. Liang Ch'i-ch'ao and Ts'ai Yüan-p'ei in their cultural views. In Levenson's description of Ts'ai, Ts'ai was trying to save the face of Chinese cultural defeatism. But this motive, if Levenson is correct, was not detected among these Christian leaders.

88

T. C. Chao, "Our Cultural Heritage", p. 17.

89

T. C. Chao, "Christianity and Confucianism", *International Review of Missions* 17 (1928):595.

90

Hsieh Sung-kao (Zia Zong-kao) was born in 1895 in Hangchow. He got his B.A. from Soochow University and M.A. from Boston University. Hsieh did his graduate studies in Auburn Theological Seminary in 1921. Upon his return to China, Hsieh taught in Nanking Theological Seminary and also in the Comparative Law School in China. Later on, he was involved in Mass education and joined the staff of the Christian Literature Society. He also pastored the Fitch Memorial Church. Among his writings, Hsieh translated over thirty books, including *The Christ at the Round Table* by E. Stanley Jones. He edited the *Shining Light* and *People's Magazine*.

91

Z. K. Zia (Hsieh Sung-kao), "The Confucian Theory of Moral and Religious Education and its Bearing on the Future Civilization of China", *CR* 55 (April 1924):231.

92

Francis C. M. Wei, "Making Christianity live in China", *CR* (February 1926):118. Wei presents the same view with fuller explanation in *The Spirit of Chinese Culture*, p. 23. The idea of Divine Life comes from Ernst Troeltsch; see Wei's book, p. 6.

93

Francis C. M. Wei, *The Spirit of Chinese Culture*, p. 24.

94

Ch'eng Ching-yi, "Problems of the Chinese Church", p. 97.

95

Chao Tzu-ch'en, "Chi-tu-chiao yü Chung-kuo wen-hua", p. 248.

96
    T. C. Chao, "Our Cultural Heritage", p. 15.

97
    Francis C. M. Wei, *The Spirit of Chinese Culture*, p. 180.

98
    T. C. Chao, "Our Cultural Heritage", p. 5.

99
    T. C. Chao, "Christianity and Confucianism", pp. 589-90.

100
    In Chao's view, this is the dominant school of Chinese thought. He is aware that, among important Confucianists, Hsün Tzu taught the need of subduing nature for human and social purposes. See T. C. Chao, "Our Cultural Heritage", pp. 3-4.

101
    Francis C. M. Wei, *The Spirit of Chinese Culture*, pp. 176-77.

102
    See the discussion in Tsu Yu-yue (Chu Yu-yü), "The Confucian God-Idea", in *Christian China* 7.4 (February 1921): 138-48.

103
    Z. K. Zia, "The Confucian Theory", p. 653.

104
    Ibid., p. 654.

105
    Tsu Yu-yue (Chu Yu-yü) was born in 1887. He got his A.B. from St. John's University and Ph.D. from Columbia University. He received theological training in General Theological Seminary, New York. Tsu served as secretary to the religious and social work department of the Peiping Union Medical College from 1924-32. He was visiting lecturer in Pacific School of Religion at Berkeley, California, from 1922-34. He then worked as secretary of the National Christian Council. He wrote *The Spirit of Chinese Philanthrophy*.

106
    Tsu Yu-yue, "The Confucian God-Idea", p. 143. Both Tsu
and Zia adopted Soothill's argument in the *Three Religions
of China* (1913) that the personal qualities are attributed
to both *Shang-ti* and *T'ien*.

107
    Chao Tzu-ch'en, *Chi-tu-chiao chin-chieh*, p. 43.

108
    Chao Tzu-ch'en, "Chi-tu-chiao yü Chung-kuo wen-hua",
p. 254. Chao points out that from Mo Tzu to Tung Chung-shu
(in his *Ch'un-ch'iu fan-lu*) of the Former Han era, (ca.
first century B.C.), the same position was held. Even in
Neo-Confucianism, scholars like Chang Tsai (in *Hsi-ming*,
i.e., his famous "Western Inscription", translated in Wing-
tsit Chan, *A Source Book in Chinese Philosophy* (Princeton:
Princeton University Press, 1963),) could not get away from
this naturalistic expression of the ultimate reality.

109
    T. C. Chao, "Our Cultural Heritage", p. 9.

110
    Z. K. Zia, "The Confucian Theory", *CR* 54 (1923):726.

111
    T. C. Chao, "Our Cultural Heritage", p. 13 and his
Chi-tu-chiao chin-chieh, p. 56. In Wei's view, the structure
of Confucian ethics is based on the cosmic principle, *ch'eng*,
the harmony with the universe. As this principle is appro-
priated by men, it is *jen*. As *jen* manifests in life situation, it is *yi*. The highest virtue of man is to be in conformity with nature. See Wei, "Making Christianity Live in
China". Hsieh is careful to point out in this connection
that ancestral worship was not originated by Confucius.
Confucius was interested in the making of a Man rather than
in the making of a Son. Hsieh agreed with Hu Shih that the
emphasis of filial piety should be ascribed to Neo-Confucian-
ists, not to Confucius. See Z. K. Zia, "The Confucian Theory",
p. 722.

112
    Z. K. Zia, "The Confucian Theory", p. 726.

113
    Francis C. M. Wei, *The Spirit of Chinese Culture*, p. 172.

114
   T. C. Chao, "Christianity and Confucianism", p. 598.

115
   Cf. Chao Tzu-ch'en, *Chi-tu-chiao chin-chieh*, pp. 62-66.

116
   T. C. Chao, "Christianity and Confucianism", p. 595.

117
   Wang Ming-tao was born in 1900 in a traditional Chinese
family. He received education in mission schools and became
a Christian convert in 1914. In 1927, Wang established the
Spiritual Food, a magazine published quarterly; and in 1937,
the Christian Tabernacle was founded. Wang represented the
mainstream of conservative Chinese Christianity, and from
his magazine flowed a lot of writings on practical Christian
living. His works included *Wu-shih-nien lai*, *Ch'ung-sheng
chen-i*, and *Yeh-su shih-shei*. Wang was well-known for his
martyrdom in Communist China during the 1950s.

118
   Wang Ming-tao, *Ch'ung-sheng chen-i* (The true meaning of
rebirth) (1933; reprint ed., Hong Kong: Alliance Press,
1967), pp. 64-65.

119
   Wang Ming-tao, *Yeh-su shih-shei*, p. 3.

120
   Wang Ming-tao, *Chi-tu ti hsin-fu* (The Bride of Christ)
(1926; reprint ed., Hong Kong: Bellman House, 1970), pp.
1-6.

121
   Wang-Ming-tao, *P'u-shih jen-lei tu-shih Shen ti erh-tzu
ma?* (Are all men Sons of God?) (1934; reprint ed., Hong Kong:
Alliance Press, 1962), p. 12.

122
   Wang Ming-tao, *Wu-shih nien lai* (These Fifty Years)
(1950; reprint ed., Hong Kong: Bellman House, 1967), pp. 71-
73.

123
   Wang Ming-tao, *Chen-yi fu-yin pien* (Debate between true
and false Gospel) (1936; reprint ed., Hong Kong: Sung-en
Press, 1963), p. 5.

124
   It does not mean that Wang did not face social problems.
He wrote a lot about Christian living with his own theologi-
cal approach. See his *Chi-tu-t'u yü hun-yin* (Christian and
Marriage), *Hsin-t'u ch'u-shih ch'ang-shih* (General knowledge
on Christian living), and *Hsieh-ke ch'ing-nien ti chi-tu-t'u*
(Written for young Christians).

125
   Cf. Ng Lee Ming's comment in "Christianity and Social
Change: The Case In China: 1920-1950", (Th.D. dissertation,
Princeton Theological Seminary, 1971), p. 80.

126
   See, for example, Ng's dissertation, pp. 70-75.

127
   Wang Ming-tao, *Ch'ung-sheng chen-i*, pp. 7-10; and his
Wu-shih nien-lai, pp. 15, 20.

128
   Wang Ming-tao, *Jen neng chien-she t'ien-kuo ma?* (Can
the Kingdom of Heaven be established by man?) (1933; reprint
ed., Hong Kong: Alliance Press, 1962).

129
   Hendrik Kraemer, *The Christian Message in a Non-Christian
World* (3rd ed., Grand Rapids: Kregel Publications, 1956),
p. 316.

130
   In the numerous writings of Chang, there are three lines
of apologetic literature. First, as seen in chapter one, he
dealt with the young intellectuals in the New Thought Movement, which opposed Christianity from the standpoint of
science and democracy. Secondly, Chang also addressed himself to the advocates of Buddhism and Taoism in order to show
their inadequate views. Thirdly, he debated with Confucian
scholars from the principles of Christianity. Ying Yüan-tao,
"Chung-kuo chi-tu-chiao ch'u-tso chieh", pp. 19-20, lists all
the writings of Chang in these three areas.

131
   Chang took issue with Chinese traditional customs and
practices. For example, Chang made a thorough study of the
origin and development of ancestral worship and declared its
futility in modern Chinese society. See Chang I-ching, "Chi-
hsien yüan-liu k'ao" (Investigation of the origin of ances-

tral worship), in *Chen-kuang ts-ung k'an* (Shanghai: China
Baptist Publication Society, 1928) 4:9-29. Similarly, he did
an extensive analysis of the Ch'ing Ming Festival and recommended a Christian memorial service in place of the traditional
tomb-sweeping sacrifice. See Chang's "Ch'ing Ming sao-mu
k'ao", in *Chen-kuang ts'ung-k'an* 4:1-9.

132
    Chang I-ching, "Tai yu-jen ta-fu i lao-hsüeh-chiu"
(Answer to an old scholar on behalf of a friend), *Chen-kuang
ts'ung-k'an* 2:192.

133
    Chang I-ching, "Yeh Ju pien" (Debate between Chris-
tianity and Confucianism), *Chen-kuang ts'ung-k'an* 2:32-33.
In another essay, Chang used 'sun-lamp' analogy; see "Tai yu-
jen ta-fu", p. 180. In the same essay, he also used the
'sun-famous hill' metaphor, p. 218.

134
    Chang I-ching, "Yeh Ju pien", p. 32-33.

135
    Chang I-ching, "P'i-p'ing Miou Feng-lin chih fei Yeh-
chiao" (A critique of the anti-Christian view of Miou Feng-
lin), in *PFCTC*, p. 221.

136
    Ibid.

137
    Chang I-ching, "Yeh Mo pien" (Debate between Chris-
tianity and Mohism), *Chen-kuang ts'ung-k'an* 2:37.

138
    Chang I-ching, "Tu Ch'en Huan-chang po-shih K'ung-chiao
chiang-i pien-miou" (A critique of Dr. Ch'en Huan-chang's
lecture on Confucian religion), in *Chen-kuang ts'ung-k'an*
2:118.

139
    Ibid., pp. 128-29.

140
    Ibid., pp. 113-14.

141
    Ibid., p. 149.

142
    Chang I-ching, "Tai yu-jen ta-fu", pp. 198-99.

143
    Ibid., pp. 218-19.

144
    H. Richard Niebuhr, *Christ and Culture* (New York:
Harper and Row, Publishers, 1951), pp. 1-3.

145
    The terms 'Christ against culture' and 'Christ of cul-
ture' are used in Niebuhr's book.

146
    For example, in the recent debate over the theological
interpretation of Communist China, we see these patterns at
work. In relating Christianity to the Chinese Communist
culture, some sinologists regard the communist reconstruction
in China as the work of the Christian God. Others take the
opposite view that Chinese Communism is the foe of Christianity. Apart from these two positions, we have scholars
who consider the achievements in New China as a combination
of divine grace and judgment. See the symposium, *Christianity and New China*, (South Pasadena: Ecclesia Publication, 1976) and Charles C. West, "Some Theological Reflections on China--I" and "Responses" in *China Notes* 14.4 (Fall,
1976); West, "Some Theological Reflections in China--II",
and R. M. Brown, "A Response to Charles West's 'Theological
Reflection on China--II'", in *China Notes* 15.2 (Spring, 1977).
Furthermore, see the papers from the Conference on "China:
The Religious Dimension", held at the University of Notre
Dame, June 29-July 2, 1977.

CHAPTER 4

1
    Levenson, *Confucian China*, pp. 98-100.

2
    Benjamin I. Schwartz, *In Search of Wealth and Power:
Yen Fu and the West* (Cambridge: Harvard University Press,
1964).

3
    CNCP 50 (February 1922) and *SM* 2.7 (March 1922), the
special number of the *WSCF* Conference.

4
KNCS, pp. 187–88.

5
For the telegram, see *PFCTC*, p. 22.

6
It has been difficult to gather biographical information about these students in the Anti-Christian Student Federation. Chang Ch'in-chih made reference to the identity of this group of students in his essay "The Anti-Religion Movement" in *CR* 54 (August 1923). Chang said, "A tiny group of Bolshevik students in Shanghai read this special number, dismissed the only Christian member of their group, and wrote the proclamation of the Non-Christian Student Federation". This special number was the edition of *Ch'ing-nien chin-pu* in February, 1922. In Chang I-ching's exhaustive critique of the manifesto and telegram, he took this group as members of the Chinese Communist organization. Five days after the telegram, *Hsien-chü*, a fortnightly magazine published by the Socialist Youth Corps in Shanghai, had a special issue of the Anti-Christian Student Federation, containing the manifesto and the constitution of the Federation. See also the discussion in Yip Ka-che, "The Anti-Christian Movement in China, 1922-1927, with special reference to the experience of the Protestant missions" (Ph.D. dissertation, Columbia University, 1971), pp. 98-102.

7
KNCS, p. 193.

8
"Welding the Christian World Spirit", *CR* 53 (May 1922): 319.

9
Ibid.

10
From "Reports and Findings of Open Forum Discussions of the Eleventh Conference of *WSCF*", pp. 26-27 as cited by Kiang Wen-han, *The Chinese Student Movement*, p. 64.

11
"Welding the Christian World Spirit", p. 324.

12
PFCTC, pp. 143-45; *KNCS*, pp. 201-206.

13
  For Wang's telegram, see *Chen-kuang tsa-chih* 21.10-11
(June 1922):42.

14
  Wang Ching-wei, "Li-ch'ih Yeh-chiao san ta-miou" (Rebutting the three big errors of Christianity), in *PFCTC*, pp.
87-88; and "Tsung-chiao tu-min lun" (Discussion of religion
as a poison to the people), in *PFCTC*, pp. 118-20.

15
  Quoted in Yip Ka-che, "Anti-Christian Movement", p. 123.

16
  The Washington Conference was held from November 12,
1921 to February 6, 1922, attended by nine Powers which had
diplomatic relation with the Far East. It was intended and
sponsored by the United States to take up the unfinished
business of the Paris Peace Conference.

17
  Cf. Immanuel C. Y. Hsü, *The Rise of Modern China*, 2nd
ed. (New York: Oxford University Press, 1975), pp. 623-29.

18
  See the declaration of Kuomintang Congress in Tsou Lu,
Chung-kuo Kuomintang shih-kao (A draft of history of
Kuomintang) (Taipei, 1965), pp. 377-88.

19
  Maurice Meisner, *Li Ta-chao and the Origins of Chinese
Marxism* (Cambridge: Harvard University Press, 1967), pp.
239-42.

20
  C. Martin Wilbur and Julie Lien-ying How, eds., *Docu-
ments on Communism, Nationalism, and Soviet Advisers in
China, 1918-1927* (New York, 1956), pp. 146-49.

21
  N. Z. Zia (Hsieh Fu-ya), "Chin-nien fei tsung-chiao ho
fei chi-tu-chiao yün-tung kai-shu" (A survey of the anti-
religion and anti-Christian movement in recent years), *Chung-
hua Chi-tu-chiao-hui nien-chien* (1925), pp. 17-24.

22
  Tsou Lu, *Chung-kuo Kuo-min-tang Shih-kao*, pp. 130-32.

23
   Wu Chih-hui, "Ch'iang-nu chih-mo ti chi-tu-chiao"
(Christianity on the verge of collapse) *Chüeh-wu* (August 19,
1924):2-4.

24
   Li Jung-fang, "Fei chi-tu-chiao yün-tung" (Anti-Christian Movement), *CL* 2.45 (February 2, 1925).

25
   "The Anti-Christian Movement" (editorial), *CR* 56 (February 1925):71.

26
   Hsien-ch'ü 4 (March 15, 1922). Some essays are repro-
duced in *PFCTC*. The names of the authors, such as Ch'ih
Kuang, Ch'i Yüan, and Lu Shu are hard to identify.

27
   "Fei chi-tu-chiao hsüeh-sheng t'ung-meng hsüan-yen"
(The manifesto of the Anti-Christian Student Federation), in
KNCS pp. 187-88.

28
   See discussion in Liang Chün-mo, "P'i-p'ing Lu Shu ti
chi-tu-chiao yü tzu-pen chu-i" (A critique of Lu Shu's
"Christianity and Capitalism"), in *PFCTC*, p. 67.

29
   Chang I-ching, "P'i-p'ing Ch'ih Kuang ti chi-tu-chiao
yü shih-chien kai-tsao", pp. 54-55.

30
   See Ch'ih Kuang's view, ibid., p. 54.

31
   See discussion in Liang Chün-mo, "P'i-p'ing Ch'i Yüan",
p. 76

32
   Quoted in Chang I-ching, "Yü Ch'en Tu-hsiu hsien-sheng",
p. 208.

33
   Chang I-ching, "P'i-p'ing Ch'ih-kuang", p. 55.

34
   PFCTC, p. 22.

35
  Ibid., p. 67.

36
  Ibid., p. 66. See also Chang I-ching, "Yü Ch'en Tu-hsiu hsien-sheng", p. 202.

37
  PFCTC, p. 75.

38
  Ibid., p. 74.

39
  Ibid., p. 139.

40
  It appeared in early December, 1924. The four articles were: Li Ch'un-fan, "Evangelism and Imperialism", Mei Tien-lung, "Christianity and China"; Ts'ai Ho-shen, "Modern Christianity"; and Chu Chih-hsin, "What a thing is Jesus"?

41
  Ying Yüan-tao, "Chin wu-nien lai Chung-kuo", p. 4.

42
  "Fei chi-tu-chiao ta t'ung-meng hsuan-yen" (Manifesto of the Great Anti-Christian Federation),*Chüeh-wu* (August 19, 1924).

43
  Ibid.

44
  Ibid.

45
  Wu Chih-hui, "Ch'iang-nu chih-mo", p. 3.

46
  Ibid.

47
  Li Ch'un-fan, "Ch'uan chiao yü ti-kuo chu-i" (Evangelism and Imperialism), *Chüeh-wu* (August 19, 1924).

48
 Mei Tien-lung, "Chi-tu-chiao yü Chung-kuo" (Christianity and China), *KNCS*, pp. 388-90.

49
 Ibid., p. 393.

50
 Ibid., p. 392.

51
 Schwartz, *Communism and the Rise of Mao*, p. 52.

52
 Tung-fang tsa-chih has a special issue on the May 30th Incident, published in July 1925. Also Dorothy Borg, *American Policy and the Chinese Revolution* (New York: American Institute of Pacific Relations and the Macmillan Co., 1947), pp. 20-30.

53
 The Kuomintang benefited much from the Shaki Incident. See David T. Griggs, "The Anti-Imperialist Theme in Chinese Nationalism, 1919-1926" (PH.D. dissertation, Harvard University, 1952), p. 417.

54
 Hung Yeh (William Hung), "A Meditation", *SM* 5.9 (June 1925):1.

55
 Hu Shih, "Tso-chan ti pu-tsou" (The Steps to Battle), *SM* 5.9 (June 1925):61.

56
 Chiao-yü pan-yüeh k'an (June 15, 1925) has a special issue entitled "Abrogation of Unequal Treaties Number".

57
 Wang Chih-hsin, "Wu-san Shih-pien yü chiao-hui chih ying-hsiang" (The Influence of the May Thirtieth Incident to the Church), *Chung-hua chi-tu-chiao-hui nien-chien* (1925), p. 26.

58
    Translated by D. Willard Lyon in "What are Chinese
Christians saying to one another at this time"? *CR* 56 (July
1925): 478-79.

59
    "An Appeal to the Christian People of the World from
Chinese Christians of Peking", *CR* 56 (July 1925):476. This
appeal was issued by the Union of Chinese Christian Churches
of Peking on June 7, 1925.

60
    Wu Lei-ch'uan, "Hu-an yü Chung-kuo chi-tu-chiao ti ch'ien-
tu" (The Shanghai Case and the Future of Christianity in
China), *SM* 5.9 (June 1925).

61
    Yü Jih-chang (David Z. T. Yui), "Letter by the N. C. C.
to the Chairman of the Municipal Council, Shanghai", *CR* 56
(July 1925): 469.

62
    Yü Jih-chang was the General Secretary of the national
YMCA. He was a graduate from St. John University in 1902.
He got his M.A. degree with honors from Harvard University
in 1910. After returning to China, Yü was the dean of Boone
University at Wuchang. Since the revolution in 1911, he
served as private secretary to Vice-President Li Yüan-hung.
Yu was once editor of the Peking Daily News, and later became
the Executive Secretary of the Lecture Department of the
National YMCA. Since 1916, Yü was the General Secretary of
the National Committee of the YMCA. In 1921, Yü was a dele-
gate to the Washington Conference on the reduction of arma-
ments. During the National Christian Conference in 1922, he
was elected Chairman.

63
    See the Statement in *CR* 56 (July 1925):474. It was in
1926 that the resolution was passed to elect three Chinese
to the Municipal Council, which had been controlled by nine
foreigners. But this offer of membership was not accepted
by the Chinese until it was changed to five in 1930.

64
    See Manifesto of the Yenching University Faculty in *SM*
5.9 (June 1925).

65

Hu Shih, "Tso-chan ti pu-tsou", p. 61.

66

See the Peking Manifesto in *SM* 5.9 (June 1925).

67

Chang I-ching, "Chin-jih chiao-hui ssu-ch'ao chih ch'ü-shih" (Trends of Thought in the Church Today), *Chung-hua chi-tu-chiao-hui nien-chien* (1927), p. 22.

68

Quoted in D. Willard Lyon, "What are Chinese Christians saying to one another at this time"? *CR* 56 (July 1925):480.

69

Chang I-ching, "Chin-jih chiao-hui", pp. 31-32.

70

Lo Yün-yen, "Ch'uan-chiao t'iao-yüeh yü chiao-hui chih kuan-hsi" (Relation between missionary treaties and the Church), *Chung-hua chi-tu-chiao-hui nien-chien* (1927), p. 29.

71

Chang I-ching, "Chin-jih chiao-hui", pp. 30-31.

72

Chien Yu-wen, "Wo-meng ti yao-ch'iu" (Our Request), *Kuang-chou ch'ing-nien* (June 29, 1925); reproduced in *SM* 5.9 (June 1925). Also Chu Yen-sheng, "Hsi hsüan-chiao-shih ti shih-chin-shih--Hu-an" (The Shanghai Case: A Testing Stone for Western Missionaries), *CL* 3.11 (June 14, 1925).

73

Wu Lei-ch'uan, "Hu-an yü chi-tu-chiao". Also his "Fan chi-tu-chiao yün-tung yü kuo-chia chu-i" (Anti-Christian movement and nationalism), *CL* 3.39 (December 27, 1925).

74

Statement by a group of British missionaries in Peking on June 6, 1925; see *SM* 5.9 (June 1925).

75

Liu T'ing-fang, "Chi-tu-chiao yü Chung-kuo kuo-min hsing" (Christianity and the characteristics of the Chinese people), *SM* 5.9 (June 1925):12.

76

For the letter of the Shanghai Missionary Association, see *CR* 56 (July 1925):470.

77

Ibid., pp. 470-71.

78

It must also be noted that many missionaries were not bothered by the question, thinking that God had opened the Gospel door for them in China through the unequal treaties. Others were not aware of the issue. Cf. Harold Balme, "Missionaries and Special Privilege", *China Christian Year Book, 1926* (Shanghai: Christian Literature Society, 1926), p. 25. Hereinafter cited as *CCYB*.

79

Wang Chih-hsin, "Wu-san shih-pien", p. 27.

80

See the Resolution in *CCYB*(1926), pp. 480-82.

81

H. F. MacNair, "The Protestant Christian Movement and Political Events", *CCYB* (1926), pp. 5-6.

82

Shu Hsin-ch'eng, *Shou-hui chiao-yü-ch'üan yün-tung* (The movement for restoring educational rights) (Shanghai: Chunghua shu-chü, 1927), p. 15. Also "Educational Department", *CR* 38 (1907):104. The Commissioner of Education in Kwangtung, for example, gave recognition to mission schools. See Latourette, *History of Christian Missions*, pp. 644-45.

83

Latourette, *History of Christian Missions*, pp. 644-45.

84

M. T. Stauffer, ed., *The Christian Occupation of China: General Survey of the Numerical Strength and Geographical Distribution of the Christian Forces in China, 1918-1921* (Shanghai: China Continuation Committee, 1922), pp. 33-34, 38-39, 407,419.

85

Kiang Wen-han, *The Chinese Student Movement*, p. 66.

86

"Review of *The Christian Occupation in China*", in *CR* 53 (May 1922):330.

87

Quoted also in E. W. Wallace, "The Educational Commission--and After", *China Mission Year Book, 1923* (Shanghai: Christian Literature Society, 1923), p. 157.

88

Christian Education in China: A Study Made by an Educational Commission Representing the Mission Boards and Societies Conducting Work in China (New York 1922), p. 15.

89

For a more detailed discussion, see Jessie G. Lutz, *China and the Christian Colleges, 1850-1950* (Ithaca and London: Cornell University Press, 1971), pp. 174-89.

90

The First effort to restrict educational activities in the 1920s was taken against Japanese schools in South Manchuria. See Shu Hsin-ch'eng, *Shou-hui chiao-yü ch'üan*, p. 47; H. C. Tsao, "The Nationalist Movement and Christian Education", *CCYB* (1928), p. 173; and Yip Ka-che, "The Anti-Christian Movement", pp. 148-49.

91

Ts'ai Yüan-p'ei, Chiao-yü tu-li i" (Independence of Education), *Hsin Chiao-yü* 4 (1922):317-19. Ts'ai's speech was reiterated in the meeting of the Great Anti-Religion Federation in April 1922.

92

"Resolution regarding Religious Education in Primary Schools", *KNCS*, pp. 271-72.

93

Yü Chia-chü, "Chiao-hui chiao-yü wen-t'i" (The problem of Christian Education), *Shao-nien Chung-kuo* 4.7 (February 1923); reproduced in *KNCS*, pp. 305-37.

94

KNCS, pp. 335-57.

95
    Chang Shih-chang, "Shou-hui chiao-yü-ch'üan yün-tung ti
yen-chiu" (A study of the Movement for Restoring Educational
Rights), *CNCP* 92 (April 1926):3.

96
    Yang Hsiao-ch'un, "Chi-tu-chiao chih hsüan-ch'uan yü
shou-hui chiao-yü ch'üan yün-tung" (Christian propaganda and
the Movement for the Restoration of Educational Rights),
Chung-hua chiao-yü chieh 14.8 (February 1925). Hereinafter
cited as *CHCYC*. Also Jessie G. Lutz, *China and the Christian Colleges*, pp. 239-46.

97
    N. Z. Zia (Hsieh Fu-ya), "The Anti-Christian Movement
in China: A Bird's-eye View", *China Mission Year Book, 1925*
(Shanghai: Christian Literature Society, 1925), pp. 54-55.

98
    Chang Shih-chang, "Shou-hui chiao-yü ch'üan yün-tung ti
yen-chiu", p. 3.

99
    Ch'en Ch'i-t'ien, "Hsin kuo-chia-chu-i yü kuo-min chiao-
yü ti kai-tsao" (New nationalism and the reconstruction of
national education), *CHCYC* 14.3 (September 1924).

100
    Ch'en Ch'i-tien, "Wo-meng chu-chang shou-hui chiao-yü
ch'üan ti li-yu yü pan-fa" (Our reasons and methods in promoting the restoration of educational rights), *CHCYC* 14.8
(February 1925); also in *KNCS* pp. 342-65.

101
    Christian Education in China, pp. 9, 29, 39, and 315.

102
    KNCS, p. 348. Cf. Ch'en Ch'i-t'ien, "Kuo-chia-chu-i
chiao-yu ti yao-i" (The essence of national education),
CHCYC 15.1 (July 1925).

103
    KNCS, p. 354.

104
    Chang Shih-chang, "Shou-hui chiao-yü-ch'üan yün-tung ti
yen-chiu", p. 4.

105
    For the resolution, see *Chung-hua chi-tu-chiao chiao-yü chi-k'an* 1.3 (September 1925).

106
    See Statement in Appendix I.

107
    Fan Yüan-lien, "Hu-an yü chiao-yü" (The Shanghai Case and education), *CHCYC* 15.2 (August 1925).

108
    For the resolution, see *KNCS*, pp. 395-400. It was translated in *CCYB* (1926), pp. 480-83.

109
    See the Resolution of the Students' Union in *CCYB* (1926), p. 483.

110
    Leon Weiger, ed. and trans., *Chine Moderne*, 10 vols. (Hsien-hsien, China, 1920-1932), vol. 5: *Nationalisme, Xenophobie, Anti-Christianisme*, p. 65.

111
    See Appendix II for the New Education Regulation.

112
    E. W. Wallace, "Christian Education in 1925", *CCYB* (1926), pp. 225.

113
    Fong F. Sec, "Recent Development in China Government Education", *CCYB* (1926), pp. 236-49.

114
    E. W. Wallace, "Christian Education in 1925", p. 226.

115
    Frank W. Lee, "Registration of Christian Schools: A Chinese Christian Statement", *CR* 57 (May 1926):341.

116
    Ch'en Ch'i-t'ien, "P'ing chiao-hui hsüeh-chiao li-an pan-fa" (Comment on the policy of registration of Christian schools), *CHCYC* 15.7 (January 1926). The two major demands were: 1. transfer of Christian education from foreign hands to Chinese hands; 2. separation of religion from education. The New Regulation was too moderate for them.

117
    Wu Lei-ch'uan, "Chi-tu-chiao chiao-yü", p. 62.

118
    For a good summary account of the Northern Expedition,
see I. C. Y. Hsü, *The Rise of Modern China*, pp. 629-39.

119
    Wang Chih-hsin, "Ch'ing-t'ien pai-jih ch'i-hsia ti chi-
tu-chiao" (Christianity under the Flag of the Chinese Republic), *WS* 2.6 (April 1927):1. Also see Chao Kuan-hai, "Kuo-
min cheng-fu hsia chih chi-tu-chiao" (Christianity under
the Kuomintang Government), *WS* 2.7 (May 1927): 13-27.

120
    H. T. Hodgkin, "Political Events of 1927 and their
Effects on the Christian Church", *CCYB* (1928), p. 6.

121
    In July, Kuo T'ai-ch'i, Commissioner for Foreign Affairs
at Shanghai intimated to John K. Davis, American Consul at
Nanking that many soldiers simply ignored the orders of
General Chiang. Yip Ka-che, "The Anti-Christian Movement",
p. 237.

122
    Cf. Pearl Buck, *My Several Worlds* (New York, 1954),
p. 206; and M. Searle Bates, "The Ordeal of Nanking", *World
Call* (May 1927), pp. 2-4.

123
    Latourette, *History of Christian Missions*, p. 820.

124
    Hodgkin, "Political Events of 1927", p. 10.

125
    Lutz, *China and the Christian Colleges*, p. 255.

126
    F. P. Lockhart to the Secretary of State, December 5,
1925; Department of State Archives. Quoted in Paul A. Varg,
Missionaries, Chinese, and Diplomats (Princeton: Princeton
University Press, 1958), pp. 191-92.

127
    C. L. Boynton, "The Evacuation and Return of Mission-
aries", *CCYB* (1928), p. 158.

128
F. Rawlinson, "Introduction: Reconstruction Crises", *CCYB* (1928), p. 2.

129
For missionary views of the Communists and the Kuomintang, see Paul A. Varg, "Response to the Nationalist Revolution", in *The Missionary Enterprise in China and America*, ed. John K. Fairbank (Cambridge: Harvard University Press, 1975), pp. 317-26.

130
"Government Proclamations Affecting Christian Institutions", *CR* 58 (July 1927):465.

131
Shirley Stone Garrett, "Why They Stayed: American Church Politics and Chinese Nationalism in the Twenties", in *The Missionary Enterprise in China and America*, p. 292.

132
Francis C. M. Wei, "Viewpoints on the Present Situation: Some Aspects of the Relation of the 'People Revolution' to the Christian Movement", *CR* 58 (March 1927): 219-20.

133
Hodgkin, "Political Events of 1927", p. 13.

134
See the proclamation of the Fourth Plenary Meeting of the Kuomintang in February 1928. H. C. Tsao, "Nationalist Movement and Christian Education", p. 184. Also see "Order of the Nationalist Government Regarding Discipline of Student", *Educational Review* (hereafter *ER*) 21 (1929): 197-98; and "To Provincial and Municipal Educational Presidents of Government Universities", *ER* 20 (1928): 394-95.

135
Quoted in H. C. Tsao, "Nationalist Movement and Christian Education", pp. 183-84.

136
Ibid.

137
"Niu-Chang t'i-i shih-hsing hsin-chiao tzu-yu" (The proposal of Niu and Chang to implement freedom of religious belief), *Shen Pao* (February 18, 1928).

138
   See the text of the reply of the Central Executive
Committee in *ER* 20 (1928): 196.

139
   Yeh Sheng, "Tsung-chiao wen-t'i: ho Chang-Niu liang
hsien-sheng tso i-ko shang-ch'üeh, (religious Problem: Discussion with Mr. Chang and Mr. Niu) *WS* 3.5 (March 1928): 49-52.

140
   Yüan Yeh-yü, "Lun ch'u-hsiao ta-tao tsung-chiao k'ou-
hao", (Discussing the abrogation of the slogan "Down with
Religion") *WS* 3.5 (March 1928).

141
   Yüan Yeh-yü, "Tui-yü Chang-Niu ti-an chih shang-ch'üeh"
(Discussion of the Chang-Niu Proposal), *WS* 3.5 (March 1928).

142
   Chang Chen-chen, "Wo ti tsung-chiao kuan" (My Concept
of Religion), *WS* 3.5 (March 1928): 56-60.

143
   Sun Yat-sen, *San Min Chu I*, trans. Frank W. Price
(Shanghai: Commercial Press, 1928), p. xii.

144
   H. C. Tsao, "The Nationalist Movement and Christian
Education", p. 188.

145
   For a detailed book list approved by the University
Council, see Cyrus H. Peake, *Nationalism and Education in
Modern China* (New York: Columbia University Press, 1932),
pp. 176-80.

CHAPTER 5

1
   A fairly acceptable definition of nationalism among
scholars of political science is given by Carlton J. H. Hayes
in *Essays on Nationalism* (New York: Macmillan Co., 1926),
p. 6. Also his *Nationalism: A Religion* (New York: Macmillan Co., 1960), pp. 1-5.

2
The Book of Filial Piety VII; translation by Hsieh Yu-wei, "Filial Piety and Chinese Society", in *The Chinese Mind*, ed. Charles A. Moore (Honolulu: University of Hawaii Press, 1967), p. 176.

3
Wu Lei-ch'uan, "Lun Chung-kuo chi-tu-t'u tui-yü kuo-chia ying-fu ti tse-jen" (Discussion of the responsibility of Chinese Christians toward the country), *SM* 5.5 (February 1925): 5-7.

4
The Book of Mencius, IV A. 19; translation by Hsieh Yu-wei, "Filial Piety", p. 176.

5
C. H. Peake, *Nationalism and Education in Modern China*, pp. 120-23.

6
Levenson, *Confucian China and its Modern Fate*, p. 104.

7
Stephen Neill, *Colonialism and Christian Missions* (New York: McGraw-Hill Book Co., 1966), pp. 117-18.

8
Yü Jih-chang (David Z. T. Yui), "Chin-jih Chung-kuo cheng-chih hsien-hsiang ti kuan-ch'a" (Observations on the present political situation in China), *CNCP* 91 (March 1926): 4-5.

9
Hu I-ku (Y. K. Woo), "Chung-kuo kuo-chia chu-i" (Chinese Nationalism), *CNCP* 93 (May 1926): 4, 8.

10
Sun Yat-sen, *Tsung-li ch'üan-shu* (Complete Works of the President), 12 vols. (Taipei: The Central Committee of the Kuomintang, 1956), 5: 175; 7-A: 141-42.

11
Chinese communism as formulated by Li Ta-chao and Mao Tse-tung was strongly nationalistic in outlook. In a good treatment of Chinese communism during the twenties Maurice Meisner says:

For Mao, as well as for Li, the salvation and rebirth
of the Chinese nation was the major concern, but it
was to be a socialist rebirth, China's precapitalist
social and economic structure notwithstanding, for
China was not to be allowed to fall behind in the
progressive march of history. It was to achieve this
rebirth that both undertook to transform Marxist
doctrine. . . .

Although their confidence in this rebirth was based
upon their faith in the energies of the people,
particularly the youth, who were to write a new
Chinese history in accordance with the new Marxist
ideals and values which had come from the West, this
very real rejection of the values of old China was
accompanied by a nationalistic attachment to Chinese
traditions and a feeling of pride in the glories of
the Chinese past.

From Maurice Meisner, *Li Ta-chao and the Origins of Chinese
Marxism* (Cambridge: Harvard University Press, 1967), p. 263.

12
    The complexity of socialism in the 1920s renders an exact
definition difficult. Simply put, socialism can be regarded
as a movement of the people with the intention of reconstructing the existing society by opposing private ownership of
property.

13
    Liang Ch'i-ch'ao, "She-hui chu-i yen-chiu" (A Study of
Socialism), *Kai-tsao* 3.6, noted in Chang Shih-chang, "Chung-
kuo chi-tu-chiao yü she-hui chu-i" (Chinese Christianity and
Socialism), *CNCP* 56 (October 1922): 17.

14
    Chang Shih-chang, "Chung-kuo chi-tu-chiao yü she-hui
chu-i", p. 17.

15
    Cf. Chow Tse-tsung, *The May Fourth Movement*, p. 247.

16
    Chang I-ching, "P'i-p'ing fei chi-tu-chiao-hsüeh-sheng
t'ung-meng hsüan-yen" (A Critique of the Manifesto of the
Anti-Christian Student Federation), *PFCTC*, p. 18.

17

    Liang Chün-mo, "P'i-p'ing Lu Shu", p. 65.

18

    Chang Shih-chang, "Chung-kuo chi-tu-chiao yü she-hui chi-i", p. 6.

19

    Liang Chün-mo, "P'i-p'ing Lu Shu", pp. 63-65.

20

    Chang I-ching, "P'i-p'ing fei chi-tu-chiao", p. 18.

21

    Liang Chün-mo, "P'i-p'ing Lu Shu", p. 63; translation taken from the Revised Standard Version (*RSV*).

22

    Cf. Chang I-ching's comment in *PFCTC*, p. 2.

23

    Mi Hsing-ju, "Chi-tu-chiao tui-yü tzu-pen-chi hsia san ta wen-t'i ying-yu ti t'ai-tu" (What should be the Christian attitude toward the three big questions in Capitalism?) *CNCP* 66 (October 1923): 50.

24

    Ibid., p. 49.

25

    Quoted in Wang Chao-hsiang, "Chi-tu-chiao tui-yü tsui-chin shih-chü tang-yu ti t'ai-t'u ho ts'o-shih" (Christian attitude and policy regarding the recent situation), *WS* 2.8 (June 1927): 8.

26

    Ch'en Li-t'ing was born in 1894, and in 1914 he went to the United States to study at Yale University. After graduation in 1917, Ch'en continued his further study at Harvard University. Upon his return to China, Ch'en served in the National Committee of YMCA to take charge of the repatriation work of Chinese laborers in Shantung. In 1928, he became General Secretary of YMCA in Peiping and lecturer on contemporary history at the National University. In 1929, he served as executive secretary in the China Council, Institute of Pacific Relations.

27
    Ch'en Li-t'ing, "Chi-tu-chiao yü ti-kuo chu-i" (Christian-
ity and Imperialism), *CNCP 99* (January 1927): 8.

28
    Ch'en Yün, "Chi-tu-chiao tui-yü tsui-chin shih-chü tang-
yu ti t'ai-t'u ho ts'o-shih" (Christian attitude and policy
regarding the recent situation), *WS* 3.3 (January 1928): 6.

29
    Ch'en Li-t'ing, "Chi-tu-chiao yü ti-kuo chu-i", p. 9.

30
    Cf. Wei Cho-min, "Synthesis of Cultures East and West",
pp. 74-80.

31
    Ch'en Li-t'ing, "Chi-tu-chiao yü ti-kuo chu-i". p. 11.

32
    Hsü Pao-ch'ien, "Fan chi-tu-chiao yün-tung yü wu-jen
chin-hou ying-ts'ai chih fang-chen" (The anti-Christian
movement and our policy from now on), *SM* 6.3 (March 1926): 1.

33
    Chang Shih-chang, "Chung-kuo ti chi-tu-chiao yü she-hui
chu-i" (Christianity and Socialism in China), *CNCP* 56
(October 1922): 4-6.

34
    Ibid., pp. 6-7.

35
    This passage was quoted by many contemporary writers, for
example, in Liang Chun-mo's "P'i-p'ing Ch'i Yüan", p. 82 and
Chan Wei, "Chi-tu-chiao yü kung-ch'an chu-i ti Chung-kuo she-
hui kai-tsao-kuan" (The view of reform of Chinese society in
Christianity and Communism), *CNCP* 94 (June 1926): 2.

36
    Liang Chün-mo, "P'i-p'ing Ch'i Yüan", pp. 82-83. Also
Hsü Shih-kuei, "Yeh-su chi-tu ho she-hui chu-i ti wo-chien"
(My view of Jesus Christ and Socialism), *CNCP* 66 (October
1923): 44-47.

37
    Chan Wei, "Chi-tu-chiao yü kung-ch'an", p. 94.

38
Li Huang, "She-hui chu-i yü tsung-chiao" (Socialism and Religion), *Fei tsung-chiao-lun*, pp. 1-6.

39
Ibid., p. 6.

40
Ibid.

41
Chan Wei, "Chi-tu-chiao yü kung-ch'an", pp. 1-13.

42
Ibid., p. 11.

43
Chang Shih-chang, "Chung-kuo ti chi-tu-chiao yü she-hui chu-i", pp. 4-6.

44
Hsü Pao-ch'ien, "Fan chi-tu-chiao yün-tung", p. 5.

45
Liang Chün-mo, "P'i-p'ing Ch'i Yüan", p. 80.

46
Ibid., p. 78.

47
Yü Mu-jen, "Chi-tu-chiao kai-tsao she-hui ti fang-fa" (The Christian method of social reform), *CNCP* 66 (October 1923): 32.

48
Wang Chao-hsian, "Chi-tu-chiao tui-yü shih-chü," p. 17.

49
Ibid., pp. 17-18. Also cf. Wang Chien-yu, "Chi-tu-chiao yü she-hui chu-i" (Christianity and Socialism), *SM* 6.5 (February 1926): 1-6.

50
Yü Jih-chang (David Z. T. Yui), "Chi-tu-chiao yü cheng-chih" (Christianity and Politics), *CNCP* 98 (December 1926): 9-13.

51
William Hung (Hung Wei-lien), "Christianity and Politics", *Christian China* 7.9 (July 1921): 418.

52
Hsü Ch'ien (1871-1940) was a *chin-shih* and became head
of the Law Codification Bureau of the Ministry of Justice in
1907. In March 1912, he accepted the position of vice-
Minister of Justice in the first Republican cabinet. When
the Chinese protestants and Catholics at Peking founded the
General Association for Religious Freedom, Hsü was elected
President. In 1918, Hsü led the formation of the Christian
National Salvation Association. At the Paris Peace Conference in 1919, Hsü opposed the signing of the Treaty regarding
the Shantung question. He supported Dr. Sun's alliance with
the communists and became a notable leader in the Wuhan
regime in 1926-27.

53
Hsü Ch'ien, *Chi-tu-chiao chiu-kuo chu-i k'an-hsing chih-
san* (The theory of national salvation through Christianity,
III) (Shanghai: Chi-tu-chiao chiu-kuo-hui, 1920), pp. 1-3;
and his "Kung-ho chen-li" (Christianity the basis for a
republic), *SM* 1.1 (November 1919).

54
See the resolutions and address of the Anti-Christian
Mass meeting in Wuchang in *KNCS*, pp. 401-405.

55
Hsü Ch'ien, *Chi-tu-chiao chiu-kuo-hui ch'eng-li chih li-
yu* (Reasons for the establishment of the Christian National
Salvation Association) (Shanghai: Chi-tu-chiao chiu-kuo-hui,
1920), pp. 8-10.

56
Wu Lei-ch'uan, "Hu-an yü chi-tu-chiao ti lien-hsiang"
(Thought on the Shanghai Affair and Christianity), *CL* 3.13
(June 28, 1925). In another article, "Chi-tu-t'u chiu-kuo"
(National Salvation by Christians), *CL* 1.4 (April 22, 1923),
Wu was critical of the Christian terminology in relation to
national salvation. Non-Christians would dislike 'Chi-tu-
chiao chiu-kuo', as if the task was only confined to Chris-
tianity. 'Chi-tu chiu-kuo' also had difficulty for those
who insisted on the separation between Church and State.
Thus, Wu suggested 'Chi-tu-t'u chiu-kuo' to combine the significance of both.

57
Wu Lei-ch'uan, "Kuo-chia-chu-i yu chi-tu-chiao shih-fou
ch'ung-t'u" (Do Nationalism and Christianity Conflict?) *SM*
5.4 (January 1925): 4-5.

58

Cf. Wu Lei-ch'uan, "Chi-tu-chiao yü ke-ming" (Christianity and revolution), *CLYSM* 5.4 (February 1931): 4-5. Even in the 1930s, Wu entertained the same political conviction regarding the relationship of revolution and the Christian faith, as seen in his work, *Chi-tu-chiao yü Chung-kuo wen-hua*.

59

Sun Fo, "Kuomintang yü chi-tu-chiao" (Kuomintang and Christianity), *SM* 6.3 (February 1926).

60

Chang Chih-chiang, "Chi-tu-chiao yü kuo-min ke-ming" (Christianity and the people's revolution), *WS* 3.3 (January 1928).

61

William Hung, "Christianity and Politics", pp. 420-21.

62

Yü Jih-chang, "Chi-tu-chiao yü cheng-chih", pp. 9-10.

63

Chao Tzu-ch'en, "Chi-tu-chiao yü cheng-chih" (Christianity and Politics), *WS* 3.2 (December 1927): 13-15.

64

Ibid., p. 14.

65

Chao Tzu-ch'en, "Fu-yin ti hsiao chu-chieh" (A brief explanation of the Gospel), *CLYSM* 8.8 (January 1935). Even in the thirties, Chao's conflict remained despite the change of the political situation.

66

Hu I-ku (Y. K. Woo), "Chung-kuo ti kuo-chia chu-i" (China's Nationalism), *CNCP* 93 (July 1926): 3-5.

67

Yü Jih-chang, "Kuo-chia chu-i yü kuo-chi chu-i" (Nationalism and Internationalism), *CNCP* 99 (January 1927): 4-5; also Lucius Porter, "Nationalism", *CLYSM* 7.1 (October 1932).

68

Hsü Pao-ch'ien, "Christianity and Nationalism--a plea for the objective attitude", *SM* 5.10 (January 1925): 3.

69
  Lucius Porter, "Nationalism", p. 7.

70
  Hsü Pao-ch'ien, "Christianity and Nationalism", p. 2.

71
  William Hung, "Christianity and Politics", p. 421.

72
  Yü Jih-chang, "Chi-tu-chiao yü cheng-chih", p. 13.

73
  Lo Yün-yen, "Ch'uan-chiao t'iao-yüeh", pp. 29-30.

74
  Chao Kuan-hai, "Chi-tu ti kuo-chia kuan-nien" (Christ's
View of Nationalism), *CNCP* 87 (November 1925): 31-34; also
Hsü Pao-ch'ien, "Tsai chih kuo-chia chu-i che" (Again to
the Nationalists), *CL* 3.24 (September 13, 1925).

75
  See the discussion in Chao Kuan-hai, "Chi-tu ti kuo-chia
chu-i", pp. 31-33; Yü Jih-chang, "Chi-tu-chiao yü cheng-chih",
p. 12; and Frank Lee, "Christianity and Internationalism",
CR 56 (June 1925): 362.

76
  Hsü Pao-ch'ien, "Christianity and Nationalism," p. 3.

77
  Fan Tzu-mei, "K'ung Tzu ti cheng-chih-kuan" (The political view of Confucius), *CNCP* 96 (October 1926): 31-36.

78
  Hu I-ku, "Chung-kuo ti kuo-chia chu-i", pp. 4-6.

79
  Yü Jih-chang, "Kuo-chia chu-i yü Kuo-chi chu-i", pp. 4-5.

80
  Frank Lee, "Christianity and Internationalism", p. 361.

81
  Ch'ao K'un-lin, "Ai-kuo chu-i kuo-chi chu-i ho chi-tu-
chiao-hui" (Patriotism, Internationalism, and the Christian
Church), *SM* 3.1 (September 1922).

82
Yü Jih-chang, "Kuo-chia chu-i yü kuo-chi chu-i", p. 5.
Cf. the view of Chao Kuan-hai, "Chi-tu ti kuo-chia kuan-
nien", pp. 33-34. Some Christian apologists pointed out that
the Confucian political doctrine was most congenial to the
promotion of internationalism in China, cf. Fan Tzu-mei,
"K'ung Tzu cheng-chih-kuan", and Hu I-ku, "Chung-kuo ti kuo-
chia chu-i".

83
Sun Yat-sen, *San Min Chu I*, trans. by F. W. Price and
ed. by L. T. Ch'en (Shanghai: China Committee, Institute
of Pacific Relations, 1927), p. 75.

84
Ibid., p. 76.

85
Cf. the discussion in Chao Kuan-hai, "Chi-tu ti kuo-
chia kuan-nien", pp. 35-36.

86
Wu Lei-ch'uan, "Fan Chi-tu-chiao yün-tung yü kuo-chia
chu-i" (Anti-Christian Movement and Nationalism), *CL* 3.39
(December 17, 1925).

87
Wu Lei-ch'uan, "Tsai-lun chi-tu-chiao tsai chung-kuo ti
ch'ien-t'u"(Further discussion of the future of Christianity
in China), *SM* 5.10 (July 1925): 2.

88
E. W. Wallace, "The Educational Commission--and After",
China Mission Year Book (1923), p. 159. The point of the
question was: how is this religious force employed? This
led missionaries of both conservative and liberal background
into a hot debate, actively participated in by their Chinese
colleagues. On the one side, Christian educators insisted
on obligatory religious courses and chapel service as part
of the school curriculum. On the other side, the principle
of voluntarism was espoused as the proper way to achieve the
objective of Christian education. See the discussion in G.
Poteats, "Shall We Surrender the Christian Character of our
School"? *CR* 56 (May 1925): 333-34; E. D. Burton, "The Purpose of Christian Education in China", *CR* 56 (July 1925):
457-58; Chester S. Miao and Frank W. Price, *Religion and
Character in Christian Middle Schools* (Shanghai: China
Christian Educational Association, 1929), pp. 37-43.

89
Ch'eng Hsiang-fan, "Shih-nien lai chih chi-tu-chiao chiao-yü" (Christian education in the past decade), *CNCP* 100 (February 1927): 152-53.

90
See Statement in Appendix I.

91
Ibid.

92
Ibid.

93
This was also the decision of the First Meeting of the Council of Primary and Secondary Education held in Shanghai, in March 1925. It was recommended by the Council that "no action should be taken which would involve the surrender of the rights of the Christian community with reference to religious education of their children". See discussion in *CR* 56 (May 1925): 340.

94
Cf. *Chiao-yu chi-k'an* 1.1 (March 1925).

95
Hsieh Fu-ya (N. Z. Zia) was born in 1892 in Chekiang. He received education from Tungwen College, Tokyo, and later went to the United States to study in the University of Chicago and Harvard University. Returning to China, Hsieh served as Secretary of the National Committee of YMCA. He also taught philosophy at Lingnan University. Hsieh's writings during the 1920s and 1930s included *Philosophy of Religion, Outline of Christianity* and *Cultivation for Personality*.

96
N. Z. Zia (Hsieh Fu-ya), "Are Party Education and Christian Education Conflicting"? *ER* 20 (1928): 185-86.

97
Cf. Chao Tzu-ch'en, "The Future of Religious Education", *ER* 20 (1928): 162-71.

98
Quoted in Miao and Price, *Religion and Character*, p. 58.

99
    Chang Shih-chang, "Kuomintang ti tsung-chiao hua" (The Religious Dimension of the Kuomintang), *WS* 3.4 (February 1928): 2-4.

100
    E. R. Hughes, "Will Sanminism Survive"? *CR* 59 (October 1928): 631. Cf. Lyon Sharman, *Sun Yat-sen: His Life and Its Meaning* (New York, 1934), p. 292, for the discussion of the so-called 'cult of Sun Yat-sen'.

101
    Sun Yat-sen, *Fundamentals of National Reconstruction* (Taipei: China Cultural Service, 1953), pp. 160-61.

102
    Chang Shih-chang, "Tang chiao ho-tso lun ti ken-chü" (The basis of cooperation between the Party and religion), *WS* 3.5 (1928); cf. Yüan Yeh-yü, "Tui-yü Chang-Niu ti-an chih shang-ch'üeh".

103
    N. Z. Zia, "Are Christian Education and Party Education Conflicting"?, p. 186.

104
    Ibid.

105
    F. W. Price, "The Teaching of *San Min Chu I* in Christian Schools", *ER* 20 (1928): 23.

106
    Chu Ching-nung was born in 1886 at Pukiang, Chekiang. He studied in Japan and joined the revolutionary organization under the leadership of Dr. Sun. After the establishment of the Republic, he served as editor of the *National Herald* in Peking. Chu went to America in 1916 and received his B. A. and M. A. degrees from George Washington University. He did graduate studies at Columbia University. After returning to China in 1920, Chu filled several important posts, including professor at Peking University, 1922; editor of the Commercial Press, 1923; dean of Kwanghua University, Shanghai, 1925-26; director of elementary and secondary education of the Ministry of Education, 1928-30; and president of Cheeloo University, 1931-32.

107
    Chu Ching-nung, "Sun Chung-shan hsien-sheng hsüeh-shuo
ti yen-chiu" (A study of the teachings of Sun Yat-sen), *Tung-
fang tsa-chih* (April 1925); trans. by F. R. Millican in *CR*
57 (November 1926): 774-84.

108
    Wang Chih-hsin, "Sun Wen chu-i yü Yeh-su chu-i"
(Sanminism and Jesusism), *WS* 2.3 (January 1927): 1-25.

109
    Ibid., pp. 24-25.

110
    Ibid., p. 22.

111
    Sun Yat-sen, *Tsung-li ch'üan-shu* (Complete Works of the
President), 12 vols. (Taipei: The Central Committee of the
Kuomintang, 1956), 7A:144; trans. Chester C. Tan in his
Chinese Political Thought in the Twentieth Century (Newton
Abbot: David & Charles, 1971), p. 150.

112
    Sun Yat-sen, *San Min Chu I*, trans. Frank W. Price
(Shanghai: Commercial Press, 1928), p. 65.

113
    Wang Chih-hsin, "Tui-yü ch'u-hsiao ta-tao tsung-chiao
k'ou-hao ti i-tien i-chien" (Some opinion about the abolition
of the slogan 'Down with Religion'), *WS* 3.5 (March 1928).
Cf. also Chang Shih-chang, "Wo yeh lai t'an-t'an 'Ch'u-hsiao
ta-tao tsung-chiao k'ou-hao' wen-t'i" (I also come to discuss
the problem regarding the abolition of the slogan 'Down with
Religion'), *WS* 3.4 (February 1928).

114
    Timothy Tingfang Lew, "Some of the Factors, Dangers and
Problems in the Christian Missionary Enterprise in China
Today through Chinese Eyes", *Addresses on China at the Thirty-
fourth Annual Session, Foreign Missions Conference of North
America, Atlantic City, N.J., January 11-14, 1927* (New York:
Foreign Missions Conference, 1927), p. 13.

115
    See the various interpretations of religion in Chapter
One.

116
   Carlton J. H. Hayes, *Nationalism: A Religion*, p. 15.

117
   Ibid., p. 176.

CONCLUSION

1
   See the discussion in Chapter Three, pp. 57–81.

Glossary

Chan Wei 詹渭

Chang Chen-chen 張振振

Chang Chih-chiang 張之江

Chang Ch'in-shih 張欽士

Chang Chün-mai 張君勱

Chang I-ching 張亦鏡

Chang Shih-chang 張仕章

Chang Tso-lin 張作霖

Ch'ang Nai-te 常乃德

Chao Kuan-hai 招觀海

Chao Tzu-ch'en 趙紫宸

Che-hsüeh 哲學

Chen-kuang tsa-chih 真光雜誌

Chen-kuang ts'ung-k'an 真光叢刊

Chen-li chou-k'an 真理週刊

Chen-li yü sheng-ming 真理与生命

Chen-tao 真道

Ch'en Ch'i-t'ien 陳啟天

Ch'en Huan-chang 陳煥章

Ch'en Li-t'ing 陳立廷

Ch'en Tu-hsiu 陳獨秀

Ch'en Yün 陳筠

Ch'eng Chih-yi (Andrew) 誠貿怡

Ch'eng Ching-yi 誠靜怡

Ch'eng Hsiang-fan 程湘帆

Chi-tu-chiao 基督教

Chi-tu-chiao-hui nien-chien 基督教會年鑑

Ch'i Yüan 綺園

Chiang Kai-shek 蔣介石

Chiao-an 教案

Chiao-yü chi-k'an 教育季刊

Chiao-yu pan-yüeh k'an 教友半月刊

Chien-kuo fang-lüeh 建國方略

Chien-kuo ta-kang 建國大綱

Chien-she 建設

Chien Yu-wen (Timothy Jen) 簡又文

Ch'ien Hsüan-t'ung 錢玄同

Ch'ih Kuang 赤光

Ch'ing-nien chin-pu 青年進步

Chiu-kuo 救國

Chou En-lai 周恩來

Chou Tso-jen 周作人

Chu Chih-hsin 朱執信

Chu Ching-nung 朱經農

Chu Tzu 朱子

chü-jen 舉人

Chüeh-wu 覺悟

Ch'un-ch'iu 春秋

Chün-tzu 君子

chung 忠

Chung-hua kuei-chu 中華歸主

Chung-kuo 中國

chung yung 中庸

fan-tui 反對

Fan Tzu-mei 范子美

fei chi-tu-chiao 非基督教

Feng Shen ch'uan 封神傳

Feng Yü-hsiang 馮玉祥

fu-ku 復古

han-lin 翰林

Hsiang-tao 嚮導

hsiao 孝

Hsiao Ching 孝經

Hsieh Fu-ya (N. Z. Zia) 謝扶雅

Hsieh Hung-lai 謝洪賚

Hsieh Sung-kao 謝頌羔

Hsien-ch'ü 先驅

Hsien-tai p'ing-lun 現代評論

Hsin-ch'ao 新潮

Hsin Chiao-yü 新教育

Hsin Ch'ing-nien 新青年

Hsin wen-hua 新文化

Hsin-yüeh 新月

hsiu-ts'ai 秀才

Hsü Ch'ien 徐謙

Hsü Pao-ch'ien 徐寶謙

hsüeh-ch'ao 學潮

Hu-an 滬案

Hu Han-min 胡漢民

Hu Hsüeh-ch'eng 胡學誠

Hu I-ku 胡貽穀

Hu Shih 胡適

Hung Yeh (Hung Wei-lien, William Hung) 洪業

jen 仁

jen-ko chiu-kuo 人格救國

Ju-chia 儒家

K'ang Yu-wei 康有為

K'e-hsüeh chiu-kuo 科學救國

K'e-hsüeh wan-neng 科學萬能

kuo-chia chu-i 國家主義

Kuomintang 國民黨

kung-ch'an 共產

K'ung Tzu 孔子

Li Chi 禮記

Li Ch'un-fan 李春蕃

Li Huang 李璜

Li Shih-tseng 李石曾

Li Ta-chao 李大釗

Li Yüan-hung 黎元洪

Liang Ch'i-ch'ao 梁啟超

Liang Chün-mo 梁均默

Liang Sou-ming 梁漱溟

Lien-O jung-kung 聯俄容共

Ling Ken 靈根

Liu Po-ming 劉伯明

Liu T'ing-fang (Timothy T. Lew) 劉廷芳

Lo Yün-yen (R. Y. Lo) 羅運炎

Lu Chih-wei 陸志韋

Lu Hsün 魯迅

Lu Shu 盧澍

Mei Tien-lung 梅電龍

Mei Yi-pao 梅貽寶

Mencius (Meng Tzu) 孟子

Mi Hsing-ju 米星如

Min-kuo jih-pao 民國日報

nan-Ch'en pei-Li 南陳北李

New Culture Movement 新文化運動

Niu Yung-chien 鈕永健

Ou-yu hsin-ying lu 歐遊心影錄

pa-tao 霸道

pai-hua 白話

pen-se 本色

p'i-p'ing 批評

San Min Chu I 三民主義

shang-ch'üeh 商榷

Shang-ti 上帝

Shao-nien Chung-kuo 少年中國

Shen Szu-chuang 沈嗣莊

Sheng-ming she 生命社

Sheng-ming yüeh-k'an 生命月刊

Shih Ching 詩經

Shou-hui chiao-yü ch'üan 收回教育權

shu 恕

Shu Ching 書經

ssu-hsiang 思想

Sun Fo (K'e) 孫科

Sun Yat-sen 孫逸仙

Sung Dynasty 宋朝

Ta Tai Li Chi 大戴禮記

ta-t'ung 大同

Tai Chi-t'ao 戴季陶

T'ao Chi 太極

T'ai-p'ing 太平

tang-hua 黨化

tao 道

t'i-yung 體用

t'iao-ho 調和

t'iao-yüeh 條約

T'ien Han 田漢

t'ien-hsia 天下

Ting Wen-chiang (V. K. Ting) 丁文江

Ts'ai Yüan-p'ei 蔡元培

Tsu Yu-yue (Chu Yu-yü) 朱友漁

tsung-chiao 宗教

T'u Hsiao-shih 屠孝實

Tuan Ch'i-jui 段祺瑞

Tung-fang tsa-chih 東方雜誌

T'ung-meng 同盟

tzu-pen 資本

tz'u-shu 辭書

Wang Chao-hsiang 汪兆翔

Wang Chih-hsin 王治心

Wang Ching-wei 汪精衛

Wang Hsing-kung 王星拱

Wang Li-chung 王理中

Wang Ming-tao 王明道

wang-tao 王道

wen-hua 文化

wen-ming 文明

Wen-she yüeh-k'an 文社月刊

Wei Cho-min (Francis Wei) 韋卓民

Wei Ch'üeh(Sidney K. Wei) 韋愨

Wu Chih-hui 吳稚暉

Wu Lei-ch'uan 吳雷川

Wu-san ts'an-an 五三惨案

Wu Yao-tsung 吳耀宗

Yeh Sheng 葉聲

Yeh-su 耶穌

yi 義

Yin Yang Wu Hsing 陰陽五行

Ying Yüan-tao 應元道

Yü Chia-chü 余家菊

Yü Jih-chang (David Z. T. Yui) 余日章

Yüan Shih-k'ai 袁世凱

Yüan Yeh-yu 袁業裕

yün-tung 運動

Abbreviations

CC	Christian China
CCYB	China Christian Year Book
CHCYC	Chung-hua chiao-yü-chieh
CK	Chen-kuang tsa-chih
CKTK	Chen-kuang ts'ung-k'an
CL	Chen-li chou-k'an
CLYSM	Chen-li yü sheng-ming
CMYB	China Mission Year Book
CNCP	Ch'ing-nien chin-pu
CR	The Chinese Recorder
CTCNC	Chung-hua chi-tu-chiao nien-chien
ER	Educational Review
FTCL	Fei tsung-chiao lun
HCN	Hsin Ch'ing-nien
HSWT	Hu Shih wen-ts'un

IRM	International Review of Missions
KNCS	Kuo-nei chin shih-nien lai chih tsung-chiao ssu-ch'ao
PFCTC	P'i-p'ing fei chi-tu-chiao yen-lun hui-k'an ch'üan-pien
SM	Sheng-ming yüeh-k'an
WS	Wen-she yüeh-k'an

Selected Bibliography

SOURCES IN WESTERN LANGUAGE

ALLEN, Roland
1927 "The Use of the Term 'Indigenous'", *IRM* 16: 262-70.

BALME, Harold
1925 *What is Happening in China*. London: Church Missionary Society.

———
1926 "Missionaries and Special Privilege". *CCYB*, pp. 25-34.

———
1928 "The Events of 1927 and the British Churches". *CCYB*, pp. 105-10.

BATES, Searle M.
1974 "The Theology of American Missionaries". In *The Missionary Enterprise in China and America*, pp. 150-57. Edited by John K. Fairbank. Cambridge: Harvard University Press.

BOORMAN, Howard L.
1967 ed. *Biographical Dictionary of Republican China*. 4
to   vols. New York: Columbia University Press.
1971

BORG, Dorothy
1947 *America Policy and the Chinese Revolution, 1925-1928.*
New York: American Institute of Pacific Relations.

ROYNTON, C. L.
1928 "The Evacuation and Return of Missionaries". *CCYB,*
pp. 155-59.

BRIERE, O.
1956 *Fifty Years of Chinese Philosophy, 1898-1950.* Translated by L. G. Thompson. London: Allen & Unwin.

BROOMHALL, Marshall
1925 *Notes on Crisis in China.* London: China Inland
Mission.

_____ 1925 *Opposition and Persecution in China.* London: China
Inland Mission.

BURTON, E. D.
1922 "Christian Education in China". *IRM* 11: 377-89.

_____ 1926 "The Purpose of Christian Education in China". *ER*
18 (January): 9-13.

CARTER, Paul A.
1954 "The Decline and Revival of the Social Gospel: Social
and Political Liberalism in American Protestant
Churches". Ph.D. dissertation, Columbia University.

CARTER, T. F.
1924 "The Three Dimensions of a Christian Civilization in
China". *IRM* 13: 555-64.

CHAN, Wing-tsit
1953 *Religious Trends in Modern China.* New York: Columbia University Press.

CHANG, C. S. (Chang Ch'in-shih)
1923 "The Anti-Religion Movement". *CR* 54 (August): 459-
67.

CHAO, T. C. (Chao Tzu-ch'en)
1918 "The Appeal of Christianity to the Chinese Mind".
CR 49: 287-96, 371-80.

_____ 1922 "Can Christianity be the Basis of Social Reconstruction in China"? *CR* 53 (May): 312-18.

_____ 1922 "Christian and Non-Christian Reply to the Anti-Christian Movement". *CR* 53 (December): 743-48.

_____ 1925 "The Indigenous Church". *CR* 56 (August): 496-505.

_____ 1927 "The Chinese Church Realizes Herself". *CR* 58 (May): 299-309.

_____ 1927 "Our Cultural Heritage". In *China Her Own Interpreter*, pp. 1-19. Edited by M. T. Stauffer, New York: Missionary Education Movement of the United States and Canada.

_____ 1928 "The Future of Religious Education in Christian Schools". *ER* 20 (April): 162-71.

_____ 1933 "Jesus and the Reality of God". *CLYSM* 7.5 (March): 1-10.

CHEN, Kwan-tou
  1928 "Problems Confronting the Christian Schools of Today". *ER* 20 (January): 87-93.

CHEN, L. T. (Ch'en Li-t'ing)
  1931 "Evolution of China Revolution". *CCYB*, pp. 43-53.

CHEN, Sanford C. C.
  1925 "The Anti-Christian Education Movement". *ER* 17 (April): 141-49.

_____ 1925 "General Development of Education in China". *CMYB*, pp. 259-69.

_____ 1927 ed. "New Movements in Chinese Education". *ER* 19 (January): 72-79.

CHENG, Andrew C. Y.
  1921 "Interpreting Christianity to China". *CC* 8.1
        (October): 35-39.

  1928 "How Shall We Think of Jesus"? *CR* 59 (March): 146-52.

CHENG, C. Y. (Ch'eng Ching-yi)
  1923 "The Development of an Indigenous Church in China".
        IRM 12: 368-88.

  1927 "Problems of the Chinese Church". In *China Her Own
        Interpreter*, pp. 96-105. Edited by M. T. Stauffer.
        New York: Missionary Education Movement of the
        United States and Canada.

  1929 "State of the Church". *CCYB*, pp. 146-58.

  1931 "Problems and Needs of the Church". *CCYB*, pp. 92-102.

  1927 *China in Chaos*. Shanghai: North China Daily News
        and Herald.

  1922 *China Today Through Chinese Eyes*. New York: George
        H. Doran Co.

  1927 *China Today Through Chinese Eyes*. Second Series.
        London: SCM.

  1925 *Chinese Christian Education: A Report of a Confer-
        ence Held in New York City, April 6, 1925*. Foreign
        Mission Conference of North America.

CHOW, Tse-tsung
  1960 *The May Fourth Movement: Intellectual Revolution
        in Modern China*. Cambridge: Harvard University
        Press.

  1960 "The Anti-Confucian Movement in Early Republican
        China". In *The Confucian Persuasion*, pp. 288-312.
        Edited by A. F. Wright, Stanford.

  1922 *Christian Education in China: A Study Made by an
        Educational Commission Representing the Mission Boards
        and Societies Conducting Work in China*. New York.

CIO, L. D. (Chu Li-teh)
1936 "Who's Who Among Chinese Christian Leaders". *CCYB*,
to pp. 428-57.
1937

COHEN, Paul A.
1961 "The Anti-Christian Tradition in China". *Journal of
Asian Studies* 20.2 (February): 169-81.

1963 *China and Christianity: The Missionary Movement
and Growth of Chinese Antiforeignism, 1860-1870.*
Cambridge: Harvard University Press.

CRESSY, Earl Herbert
1928 "Christian Education in 1928". *CCYB*, pp. 268-78.

1928 *Christian Higher Education in China. A Study for
the Year 1925-1926.* Shanghai: China Christian
Educational Association.

FAIRBANK, John K. and LIU, Kwang-ching
1950 ed. *Modern China: A Bibliographical Guide to Chinese Works 1898-1939.* Cambridge: Harvard University Press.

FAIRBANK, John K.
1974 ed. *The Missionary Enterprise in China and America.*
Cambridge: Harvard University Press.

FOSTER, John
1933 *The Chinese Church in Action.* London: Edinburgh
House Press.

FUNG, Yu-lan
1952 *A History of Chinese Philosophy.* Translated by
to Derk Bodde. 2 vols. Princeton: Princeton Univer-
1953 sity Press.

GRIEDER, Jerome B.
1970 *Hu Shih and the Chinese Renaissance.* Cambridge:
Harvard University Press.

GRIGGS, David T.
1952 "The Anti-Imperialist Theme in Chinese Nationalism,
1919-1926". Ph.D. dissertation. Harvard University.

HAYES, Carlton J. H.
  1926 *Essays on Nationalism*. New York: Macmillan Co.

_____ 1960 *Nationalism: A Religion*. New York: Macmillan Co.

HODGKIN, Henry T.
  1923 *China in the Family of Nations*. New York: George
        H. Doran Co.

_____ 1925 *Recent Events in China*. London: Friends Book Shop.

_____ 1928 "Events in China During 1927 and Their Effect on the
        Christian Church". *CCYB*, pp. 6-12.

_____ 1928 *The Missionary Situation in China*. In Foreign Mis-
        sions Conference of North America at Atlantic City
        January 10-13, pp. 86-103.

_____ 1928 "My Hopes for the Chinese Church". *CR* 59 (December):
        745-53.

_____ 1932 *Living Issues in China*. New York: Friendship Press.

HSÜ, Immanuel C. Y.
  1975 *The Rise of Modern China*. 2nd edition. New York:
        Oxford University Press.

HSÜ, P. C. (Hsü Pao-ch'ien)
  1921 "The Prospects for Christianity in China". *CC* 8.1
        (October): 18-25.

_____ 1921 "Recent Religious Activities in Peking". *CC* 7.6
        (April): 262-67.

_____ 1927 ed. "The Future of Christianity in China". *CLYSM*
        Special English Number, 2.3 (February): 1-11.

_____ 1927 "Uniqueness of Jesus from a Chinese Standpoint".
        CLYSM Special English Number, 2.3 (February).

1929 "Nationalism and Religion". *CCYB*, pp. 142-45.

1933 *Ethical Realism in Neo-Confucian Thought*. Peiping: Yenching University.

HU, Shih
1925 "The Present Crisis in Christian Education". *ER* 17 (July): 209-15.

1927 "China And Christianity". *The Forum*. 78.1 (July): 1-2.

1934 *The Chinese Renaissance*. Chicago: University of Chicago Press.

1931 "Religion and Philosophy in Chinese History". In *Symposium on Chinese Culture*, pp. 31-58. Edited by Sophia H. Ch'en Zen. Shanghai: China Institute of Pacific Relations.

HUANG, Philip
1972 *Liang Ch'i-ch'ao and Modern Chinese Liberalism*. Seattle: University of Washington Press.

HUGHES, E. R.
1928 "Will Sanminism Survives"? *CR* 59 (October): 629-36.

1930 "The Religious Experiment of Hsiao. An Enquiry into its Earlier History and an Estimate of its Religious Significance". *CLYSM* 4.10 (February): 1-30.

HUMMEL, W. F.
1925 "The Results of Compulsory Religious Education in Mission Schools". *CR* 56 (September): 565-70.

HUNG, William (Hung Yeh)
1920 "Christianity and Politics". *CC* 6.7 (May-June): 418-22.

1925 "A Meditation". *CLYSM* 5.9 (June): 1-2.

1928   "Consecration and Politics". *CR* 59 (April): 210-15.

1932   ed. *As It Looks to Young China.* London: SCM Press.

HUTCHINSON, Paul
  1921   "The Future of Religion in China". *CC* 7.4 (February):
          156-59.

1922   "Conservative Reaction in China". *Journal of Religion* 2 (July): 337-61.

1924   *China's Real Revolution.* New York: Missionary Education Movement.

ISAACS, Harold R.
  1951   *The Tragedy of the Chinese Revolution.* Revised ed.,
          Stanford: Stanford University Press.

ISRAEL, John
  1966   *Student Nationalism in China, 1927-1937.* Stanford:
          Stanford University Press.

JEN, Timothy (Chien Yu-wen)
  1920   "The Meaning of Christianity". *CC* 7. 2-3 (December-
  to   January): 90-96.
  1921

KEPLER, A. R.
  1920   "The Need for a Changed Approach to the People in Our
          Missionary Enterprise". *CR* 51 (January): 21-31.

KIANG, Wen-han (Chiang Wen-han)
  1948   *The Chinese Student Movement.* New York: King's
          Crown Press.

KOO, Telly H.
  1921   "The Naturalization of Christianity in China". *CC*
          7.5 (March): 201-6.

KOO, T. Z. (Ku Tzu-jen)
  1927   "The Future of Christianity in China". In *China Her
          Own Interpreter*, pp. 143-56. Edited by M. T. Stauffer.
          New York: Missionary Education Movement of the
          United States and Canada.

1927 "The Nationalism of Jesus". *CR* 58 (March): 163-69.

1931 "Trends in National Thinking". *CCYB*, pp. 30-42.

KRAEMER, Hendrik
1956 *The Christian Message in a Non-Christian World.* 3rd
ed. Grand Rapids: Kregel Publications.

KWOK, D. W. Y.
1965 *Scientism in Chinese Thought, 1900-1950.* New Haven:
Yale University Press.

LATOURETTE, Kenneth Scott
1920 "Nationalism and Christianity". *CC* 6.6 (April): 319-
21.

1922 "Impressions of Some Present Tendencies in the Christian Movement in China". *CR* (November): 681-88.

1928 "Retaining the Christian Character of Educational
Foundations". *IRM* 17: 663-74.

1929 *A History of Christian Missions in China.* London:
Society for Promoting Christian Knowledge.

1965 "Christian Missions as Mediators of Western Civilization". In *Christian Missions in China: Evangelists
of What?* pp. 83-93. Edited by Jessie G. Lutz.
Boston: D. C. Heath and Co.

LEE, Frank
1925 "Communism and the Anti-Christian Movement". *CR* 56
(April): 233-35.

1925 "Christianity and Internationalism". *CR* 56 (June):
361-65.

LEE, Y. L. (Li Ying-lin)
1925 "The Anti-Christian Movement in Canton". *CR* 56
(April): 220-26.

LEGGE, James
   1880 *The Religions of China*. London: Hodder and
         Stoughton.

LEVENSON, Joseph R.
   1953 *Liang Ch'i-ch'ao and the Mind of Modern China*.
         Cambridge: Harvard University Press.

   1968 *Confucian China and Its Modern Fate: A Trilogy*.
         Berkeley & Los Angeles: University of California
         Press.

LEW, Timothy T. (Liu T'ing-fang)
   1922 "Making the Christian Church in China Indigenous".
         CR 53 (May): 297–312.

   1925 "Chinese Christian and Dr. Sun". *SM* 5.9 (June): 1–7.

   1926 "My Creed in Christian Education". *ER* 18 (October):
         475–78.

LI, Chien-nung
   1956 *The Political History of China, 1840-1928*. Trans-
         lated and edited by Ssu-yu Teng and Jeremy Ingalls.
         Princeton: D. Van Nostrand Co.

LI, Yung-fang
   1924 "The Function of the Educational Missionary in China
         During the Next Ten Years". *CR* 55 (January): 35–38.

LINEBARGER, Paul Myron Anthony
   1937 *The Political Doctrines of Sun Yat-sen*. Baltimore:
         John Hopkins Press.

LIU, Chün-jo
   1964 *Controversies in Modern Chinese Intellectual History:
         An Analytical Bibliography of Periodical Articles,
         Mainly of the May Fourth and Post-May Fourth Era*.
         Harvard East Asian Monograph, no. 15. Cambridge:
         Harvard University Press.

LIU, Herman C. E. (Liu Chan-en)
   1925 "Chinese Students and Religion Today". *CMYB*, pp.
         42–50.

LIU, Kwang-ching
  1966 ed. *American Missionaries in China.* Cambridge:
      Harvard University Press.

LIU, K. S.
  1922 "The Anti-Religion Movement, Christianity and Reli-
      gion". *CR* 53 (December): 748-54.

LO, R. Y. (Lo Yün-yen)
  1921 "Modern Thought Among Chinese Students". *CR* 52
      (April): 257-67.

  1930 *China's Revolution From the Inside.* New York:
      Abingdon Press.

LOBENSTINE, E. C.
  1926 "Christianity in the Treaties between China and Other
      Nations". *CCYB*, pp. 51-70.

LOH, Pichon P. Y.
  1955 "The Popular Upsurge in China: Nationalism and
      Westernization, 1919-1927". Ph.D. dissertation.
      University of Chicago.

LUTZ, Jessie G.
  1965 *Christian Missions in China: Evangelists of What?*
      Boston: D. C. Heath and Co.

  1971 *China and the Christian Colleges, 1850-1950.* Ithaca
      and London: Cornell University Press.

LYMAN, Eugene W.
  1922 "Influence of Modern Science and Philosophy Upon
      Religious Thinking". *CC* 8.3 (March): 185-90.

LYON, Willard D.
  1929 "Education and Religion". *CCYB*, pp. 279-88.

  1927 *Religious Values in Confucianism.* A Source of Facts
      and Opinions Prepared for Use in Connection with the
      Enlarged Meeting of the International Missionary
      Council to be held at Jerusalem 1928. New York:
      Committee of Reference and Counsel.

MAC GILLIVRAY, D.
  1929 "Effect of Chinese Environment on Imported Faiths".
        CR 60 (December): 755-66.

MEISNER, Maurice
  1967 *Li Ta-chao and the Origins of Chinese Marxism*.
        Cambridge: Harvard University Press.

MERVIN, Wallace C.
  1974 *Adventure in Unity: The Church of Christ in China*.
        Grand Rapids: Wm. B. Eerdmans Publishing Co.

MIAO, Chester S. (Miao Ch'iu-sheng)
  1931 "Status of Registration". *CCYB*, pp. 237-52.

MIAO, Chester S. and PRICE, Frank W.
  1929 *Religion and Character in Christian Middle Schools*.
        Shanghai: China Christian Educational Association.

MILLS, W.P.
  1931 "The Kuomintang and Religion". *CCYB*, pp. 77-91.

MONROE, Paul
  1922 "The Place of Mission Education in a National System".
        ER 14 (April): 134-51.

  1925 "Education and Nationalism". *ER* 17 (July): 355-57.

  1927 *China: A Nation in Evolution*. New York: Macmillan
        Co.

MOORE, Charles A.
  1967 ed. *The Chinese Mind*. Honolulu: University of
        Hawaii Press.

NATIONAL CHRISTIAN COUNCIL
  1925 *Annual and Biennial Reports, 1924 and 1925*. Shanghai.

NG, Lee Ming
  1971 "Christianity and Social Change: The Case in China,
        1920-1950". Th.D. dissertation. Princeton Theolog-
        ical Seminary.

NIEBUHR, Richard H.
  1951 *Christ and Culture*. New York: Harper and Row Pub-
        lishers.

PEAKE, Cyrus H.
  1932 *Nationalism and Education in Modern China*. New York:
        Macmillan Co.

POLLARD, Robert T.
  1933 *China's Foreign Relations, 1917-1931*. New York:
        Macmillan Co.

PORTER, Lucius C.
  1924 *China's Challenge to Christianity*. New York: Mis-
        sionary Education Movement of the United States and
        Canada.

_____
  1932 "Nationalism: Negative or Positive". *CLYSM* 7.1
        (October): 1-8.

POTT, Hawks F.L.
  1922 "The Intellectual and Social Crisis in China".
        Journal of Religion (May): 291-302.

_____
  1925 "Some Present Day Problems of Christian Education".
        ER 17 (July): 248-54.

PRICE, Frank W.
  1928 "The Teaching of *San Min Chu I* in Christian Schools".
        ER 20 (January): 9-24.

_____
  1928 "Present Outlook for Religious Education". *CCYB*,
        pp. 207-16.

_____
  1926 "The New Program of Religious Education in the
        Chinese Church". *CR* 57 (January): 21-29.

RABE, Valentin H.
  1964 "The American Protestant Foreign Mission Movement,
        1880-1920". Ph.D. dissertation. Harvard University.

RAWLINSON, F.
  1919 "Some Chinese Ideas of God". *CR* 50: 461-68, 545-52,
        613-21.

_____
  1921 "The Approach to the Christian Message to China".
        CR 52 (August): 521-35.

1925   "The Anti-Christian Movement". *CR* 56 (February):
       71-77.

1927   *Naturalization of Christianity in China.* Shanghai:
       Presbyterian Mission Press.

1928   "Introduction--Reconstruction Crises". *CCYB*, pp.
       1-5.

_____; Thouburn, Helen and MacGillivray, D.
1922   ed. *The Chinese Church as Revealed in the National
       Christian Conference held in Shanghai, May 2-11, 1922.*
       Shanghai: Oriental Press.

RUSSELL, Bertrand
1922   *The Problem of China.* New York: Century Co.

SCHWARTZ, Benjamin I.
1951   "Ch'en Tu-hsiu and the Acceptance of the Modern West".
       Journal of History of Ideas 12: 61-74.

1951   *Chinese Communism and the Rise of Mao.* Cambridge :
       Harvard University Press.

1964   *In Search of Wealth and Power: Yen Fu and the West.*
       Cambridge: Harvard University Press.

SHEN, T. L.
1925   "A Study of the Anti-Christian Movement". *CR* 56
       (April): 227-33.

1928   "Religious Liberty in China". *CCYB*, pp. 47-59.

1928   "Christian Movement in a Revolutionary China". *CR*
       59 (August): 475-82.

SHRYOCK, John K.
1925   "Non-Compulsory Religious Instruction and Worship in
       Mission Schools". *CR* 56 (December): 782-87.

SMYTHE, Lewis S. C.
  1928 "Changes in the Christian Message for China by Pro-
        testant Missionaries". Ph.D. dissertation. Univer-
        sity of Chicago.

SPEER, Robert E. and KERR, Hugh T.
  1927 *Report on Japan and China of the Deputation sent by
        the Board of Foreign Missions of the Presbyterian
        Church in the U. S. A. to visit these fields and to
        attend a series of Evaluation Conferences in China
        in 1926.* New York: The Board of Foreign Mission of
        the Presbyterian Church in the U. S. A.

STAUFFER, M. T.
  1922 ed. *The Christian Occupation of China: General
        Survey of the Numerical Strength and Geographical
        Distribution of the Christian Forces in China, 1918-
        1921.* Shanghai: China Continuation Committee.

  1924 *Looking Towards a Christian China: A Discussion
        Course.* New York: Missionary Education Movement
        of the United States and Canada.

  1927 ed. *China Her Own Interpreter.* New York: Missionary
        Education Movement for S. V. M.

STUART, Leighton J.
  1917 "The Chinese Mind and the Gospel". *IRM* 6: 548-57.

  1923 "The Christian Dynamism for China". *CR* 54 (February):
        71-77.

  1925 "The Religious Policy at Yenching University". *ER*
        17 (April): 159-62.

  1928 "Christianity and Confucianism". Paper presented at
        the Jerusalem meeting of the International Missionary
        Council, March 24 - April 8, 1928. New York: Inter-
        national Missionary Council.

  1929 "Conflicts of Cultures in China". *CR* 60 (August):
        481-87.

SUN, Yat-sen
     1928 *San Min Chu I.* Translated by Frank W. Price, Edited
           by L. T. Chen. Shanghai: Commercial Press.

T'ANG, Leang-li
     1927 *China in Revolt: How a Civilization Became a Nation.*
           London: N. Douglas.

     1924 *The Anti-Christian Movement: A Collection of Papers
           Originally Issued by the Anti-Christian Movement and
           Translated for the Student Y. M. and Y. W. C. A. of
           China.* Shanghai.

     1923 "The Anti-Christian Movement: Symposium". *Chinese
           Social and Political Science Review.* 7.2 : 103-13.

     1927 "The Future of Christianity in China". *IRM* 16:
           321-38.

     1925 *The Present Situation in China and its Significance
           for Christian Missions.* New York: Foreign Missions
           Conference.

THOMAS, Griffith W. H.
     1921 "Modern in China". *Princeton Theological Review.*
           (October): 630-71.

     1921 "The Uniqueness of Christianity". *CR* 52 (July):
           483-85.

TSAO, H. C.
     1928 "The Nationalist Movement and Christian Education".
           CCYB, pp. 172-94.

TSIANG, Tingfu F.
     1922 "Christianity and Imperialism". *CC* 8.4 (May): 224-28.

TSU, Y. Y. (Tsu Yu-yue)
     1921 "The Confucian God-Idea". *CC* 7.4 (February): 85-89.

     1927 "Chinese Church Organization of the Future". *CR* 58
           (February): 85-89.

VARG, Paul A.
     1958 *Missionaries, Chinese, and Diplomats: The American
           Protestant Missionary Movement in China, 1890-1952.*
           Princeton: Princeton University Press.

1974 "The Missionary Response to the Nationalist Revolu-
      tion". In *The Missionary Enterprise in China and
      America*, pp. 311-35. Edited by John K. Fairbank.
      Cambridge: Harvard University Press.

WALLACE, Edward Wilson
1926 "Christian Education in 1925". *CCYB*, pp. 224-35.

1928 "The Outlook of Christian Education in China". *IRM*
      17 : 205-17.

WANG, Chengting T. (Tsi C. Wang)
1921 "Making Christianity Indigenous in China". *CR* 52
      (May): 323-29.

1928 *The Youth Movement in China*. New York: New Repub-
      lic, Inc.

1929 "Political Progress in 1928". *CCYB*, pp. 14-33.

WARD, Harry F.
1926 "China's Anti-Christian Movement". *Christian Cen-
      tury*. 43 (April 15).

WEBSTER, James B.
1923 *Christian Education and the National Consciousness
      in China*. New York: E. P. Dutton & Co.

WEI, Francis C. M. (Wei Cho-min)
1926 "Making Christianity Live in China". *CR* 57 (March):
      118-21.

1927 "Synthesis of Cultures East and West". In *China
      Today Through Chinese Eyes*, pp. 74-85. Second
      Series. London: SCM.

1927 "Viewpoints on the Present Situation: Some Aspects
      of the Relation of the 'People Revolution' to the
      Christian Movement". *CR* 58 (March): 219-20.

1947 *The Spirit of Chinese Culture*. New York: Charles
      Scribner's Sons.

WEI, Sidney K. (Wei Ch'üeh)
    1920 "Some Problems of Reconstructing Christianity for
          the Needs of China". *CC* 6.5 (March): 244-47; 6.7
          (May-June): 378-82.

    1928 "Government Control of Education". *ER* 20 (October):
          323-27.

    1928 "Education Under the Nationalist Government". *CCYB*,
          pp. 195-206

    1929 "Government Education, 1928-1929" *CCYB*, pp. 458-90.

WEIGER, Leon
    1920 ed. and trans. *Chine Moderne*. 10 vols. Hsien-
    to   hsien, China.
    1932.

WEST, Philip
    1976 *Yenching University and Sino-Western Relations, 1916-
          1952*. Cambridge: Harvard University Press.

WILBUR, C. Martin and HOW, Julie Lien-ying
    1956 ed. *Documents on Communism, Nationalism and Soviet
          Advisers in China 1918-1927*. New York: Columbia
          University Press.

          Who's Who in China. Shanghai: China Weekly Review
          Press, 1925, 1931 and 1936.

WOO, Y. K. (Hu I-ku)
    1921 "Latest Development of the Intellectual Awakening in
          China". *CC* 8.1 (October): 31-34.

    1926 "The Present Chinese Attitude Towards Christianity".
          CCYB, pp. 80-85.

WRIGHT, Mary C.
    1957 *The Last Stand of Chinese Conservatism: The T'ung-
          chih Restoration, 1862-1874*. Stanford: Stanford
          University Press.

WU, Y. T. (Wu Yao-tsung)
    1923 "Our Message". *CR* 54 (August): 485-89.

1928   "The Revolution and Student Thought". *CCYB*, pp. 223-34.

1930   "How One Christian Looks at the Five Year Movement". *CR* 61 (March): 147-48.

YAMAMOTO, Tatsuro & Sumiko
1953   "The Anti-Christian Movement in China, 1922-1927". *Far Eastern Quarterly* 12.2 (February): 133-47.

YANG, C. K.
1961   *Religion in Chinese Society*. Berkeley & Los Angeles: University of California Press.

YANG, Y. C.
        China's Religious Heritage. New York: Abingdon-Cokesbury Press, no date.

YIP, Ka-che
1970   "The Anti-Christian Movement in China, 1922-1927, with Special Reference to the Experience of Protestant Missions". Ph.D. dissertation. Columbia University.

YUI, David Z. T. (Yü Jih-chang)
1927   "The Needs of the Christian Movement in China". In *China Today Through Chinese Eyes*, pp. 140-51. London: SCM.

1927   "The Present Political Outlook in China". In *China Today Through Chinese Eyes*, pp. 1-9. London: SCM.

ZIA, N. Z. (Hsieh Fu-ya)
1925   "The Anti-Christian Movement in China: A Bird's-Eye View". *CMYB* , pp. 51-60.

1928   "Are Christian Education and Party Education Conflicting"? *ER* 20 (April): 181-87.

SOURCES IN CHINESE LANGUAGE

CHAN, Wei 詹渭

1926 "Kuo-chia chu-i ti chiao-hui chiao-yü" 國家主義的教會教育 (Nationalization of Christian Education). *CNCP* 90 (February): 27-37.

1926 "Chi-tu-chiao yü kung-ch'an chu-i ti Chung-kuo she-hui kai-tsao-kuan" 基督教與共產主義的中國社會改造觀 (The view of reform of Chinese society in Christianity and Communism). *CNCP* 94 (June): 1-13.

CHANG, Chen-chen 張振振

1928 "Wo ti tsung-chiao Kuan" 我的宗教觀 (My concept of religion). *WS* 3.5 (March): 56-60.

CHANG, Chih-chiang 張之江

1928 "Chi-tu-chiao yü kuo-min ke-ming" 基督教與國民革命 (Christianity and nationalist revolution). *WS* 3.3 (January).

1930 "Ke-ming yü tao-te" 革命與道德 (Revolution and morality). *CK* 29.8 (August).

CHANG, Ch'in-shih 張欽士

1921 "Ching-shen fu-hsing" 精神復興 (Revival of the spirit). *SM* 2.4 (November).

1923 "Wo ko-jen ti tsung-chiao ching-yen" 我個人的宗教經驗 (My personal religious experience). *SM* 3.7-8 (April).

1923 "Mei-kuo chiao-yü hsin-chiu liang-p'ai ti chan-cheng" 美國教育新舊兩派的戰爭 (Conflict between the old and new party in American education). *CL*1.19 (Aug. 5).

1927 ed. *Kuo-nei chin shih-nien lai chih tsung-chiao ssu-ch'ao* 國內近十年來之宗教思潮 (Religious Thought Movements in China During the Last Decade). Peking: Yenching School of Chinese Studies.

CHANG, I-ching 張亦鏡
1927　ed. *P'i-p'ing fei chi-tu-chiao yen-lun hui-k'an ch'-üan-pien* 批判非基督教言論彙刊全編 (Answering Attacks Upon Christianity).　Shanghai: China Baptist Publication Society.

————　"P'i-p'ing Ch'ih Kuang ti chi-tu-chiao yü shih-chieh kai-tsao" 批評赤光的基督教與世界改造 (A critique of Ch'ih Kuang's "Christianity and World Reform").　In *PFCTC*, pp. 53-61.

————　"P'i-p'ing Miou Feng-lin chih fei Yeh-chiao" 批評謬鳳林之非耶教 (A critique of the anti-Christian view of Miou Feng-lin).　In *PFCTC*, pp. 214-51.

————　"P'i-p'ing Wang Ching-wei ti li-ch'ih Yeh-chiao san ta-miou" 批評汪精衛的力斥耶教三大謬 (A critique of Wang Ching-wei's "Rebutting the three big errors of Christianity").　In *PFCTC*, pp. 87-101.

————　"Po Wang Ching-wei ti tsung-chiao tu-min lun" 駁汪精衛的宗教毒民論 (Rebutting Wang Ching-wei's "Religion as poison to the people").　In *PFCTC*, pp. 118-38.

————　"Yü Ch'en Tu-hsiu hsien-sheng shuo 'Chi-tu-chiao yü Chi-tu-chiao-hui'" 與陳獨秀先生說「基督教與基督教會」 (Discussion with Mr. Ch'en Tu-hsiu regarding his "Christianity and the Christian Church").　In *PFCTC* pp. 191-213.

1923　*Yü Ch'en Tu-hsiu Shen Hsüan-lu pien-tao* 與陳獨秀沈玄盧辯道 (Discussing Christianity with Ch'en Tu-hsiu and Shen Hsüan-lu).　Kwangtung: Mei-hua chin-hui shu-chü.

1927　"Chin-jih chiao-hui ssu-ch'ao chih ch'ü-shih" 今日教會思潮之趨勢 (Trends of thought in the Church today).　*CTCNC*, pp. 19-25.

1927 "Chi-tu-chiao yü ti-kuo chu-i" 基督教與帝國主義 (Christianity and imperialism). *CK* 26.4.

1928 ed. *Chen-kuang ts'ung-k'an.* 眞光叢刊 Shanghai: China Baptist Publication Society.

"Chi-hsien yüan-liu k'ao" 祭先源流考 (Investigation of the origin of ancestral worship). *CKTK* 4:9-29.

"Yeh Ju pien" 耶儒辯 (Debate between Christianity and Confucianism). *CKTK*, 2:25-35.

"Yeh Mo pien" 耶墨辯 (Debate between Christianity and Mohism). *CKTK*, 2:35-42.

"Tai yu-jen ta-fa i lao-hsüeh-chiu" 代友人答覆一老學究 (Answer to an old scholar on behalf of a friend). *CKTK*, 2:175-223.

"Tu Ch'en Huan-chang po-shih K'ung-chiao chiang-i pien-miou" 讀陳煥章博士孔教講義辯謬 (A critique of Dr. Ch'en Huan-chang's lecture on Confucian religion). *CKTK*, 2:106-65.

1930 *Kuan yu Chu Chih-hsin "Yeh-su shih she-mo tung-hsi" ti tsa-p'ing* 關於朱執信「耶穌是什麼東西」的雜評 (A collection of criticism of Chu Chih-hsin's "What sort of a thing is Jesus"). Shanghai: Mei-hua chin-hsin-hui shu-chü.

CHANG, Shih-chang 張仕章 "Chung-kuo ti chi-tu-chiao yü she-
1922 hui chu-i" 中國的基督教與社會主義 (Christianity and socialism in (China). *CNCP* 56 (October): 1-23.

1926 "Shou-hui chiao-yü ch'uan yün-tung ti yen-chiu" 收回教育權運動的研究 (A Study of the Movement for Restoring Education Rights). *CNCP* 92 (April): 1-15.

1927   "She-hui chu-i chia yen-kuang chung ti Yeh-su" 社會主義家眼光中的耶穌   (Jesus in the eyes of the socialist). *WS* 2.10 (October): 1-11.

1928   "Wo yeh-lai t'an't'an 'ch'u-hsiao ta-tao tsung-chiao k'ou-hao' ti wen-t'i'" 我也來談談「取消打倒宗教口的問題」(I also come to discuss the problem regarding "The abrogation of the slogan 'Down with religion'"). *WS* 3.4 (February).

1928   "Kuo-min-tang ti tsung-chiao-hua" 國民黨的宗教化 (The religious dimension of the Kuomintang). *WS* 3.4 (February): 2-4

1928   "Chung-shan hsien-sheng ti tsung-chiao hsin-yang" 中山先生的宗教信仰(The religious belief of Mr. Sun Yat-sen). *WS* 3.5 (March): 86-94.

1928   "Tang-chiao ho-tso lun ti ken-chü" 黨教合作論的根據 (Reasons for the cooperation of the Party and religion). *WS* 3.5 (March): 83-85.

1928   "Kuan-yü 'ch'ü-hsiao ta-tao tsung-chiao k'ou-hao' ti hsiao-hsiao pi-chan" 關於「取消打倒宗教口號」的小小筆戰 (A small debate concerning "The abrogation of the slogan 'Down with religion'"). *WS* 3.5 (March): 47-48.

1928   "Tu liao 'Wo ti tsung-chiao-kuan' i-hou" 讀了「我的宗教觀」以後(After reading "My concept of religion"). *WS* 3.5 (March): 60-62.

CHANG, Nai-te 常乃德
    "Tui-yü fei tsung-chiao ta t'ung-meng chih cheng-yen" 對於非宗教大同盟之諍言(A word of remonstration to the Anti-Christian Federation). In *PFCTC*, pp. 263-66.

CHAO, Kuan-hai 招觀海
  1925   "Chi-tu ti kuo-chia kuan-nien" 基督的國家觀念 (Christ's view of the nation). *CNCP* 87 (November): 31-36.

1925   "Chung-kuo pen-se chi-tu-chiao-hui yü chiao-hui tzu-
        li"中國本色基督教會與教會自立(The indigenization
        and independence of the Christian Church in China).
        WS 1.1 (October): 29-34.

1926   "San-ko Chung-kuo hsüeh-che ti fan-chiao t'an" 三個中
        國學者的反教談(The anti-religious conversation of
        three Chinese scholars). *WS* 1.7 (June): 53-56.

1926   "Fan-chiao feng-ch'ao chung chiao-hui ying-yu ti
        tzu-hsing"反教風潮中教會應有的自省(The needed self-
        examination of the Church during the anti-religious
        movement). *WS* 1.9-10 (September): 33-44.

1927   "Sheng-tan ku-shih chung ti min-tsu chu-i" 聖誕故事
        中的民族主義(Nationalism in the story of Christmas).
        WS 2.3 (January): 25-33.

1927   "Kuo-min cheng-fu hsia chih chi-tu-chiao" 國民
        政府下之基督教(Christianity under the Nationalist
        government). *WS* 2.7 (May): 13-28.

CHAO, Tzu-ch'en 趙紫宸
   1920   "Tsung-chiao yü ching-pien" 宗教與境變 (Religion
           and circumstantial changes). *CNCP* 30 (February):
           30-43.

   1920   "Ts'u-chin tsung-chiao ke-hsin ti shih-li"促進宗
           教革新的勢力(Promoting forces of religious reform).
           CNCP 31 (March): 34-51.

   1920   "Hsin-ching tui-yü chi-tu-chiao ti ch'i-hsiang"
           新境對於基督教的祈響(The Christian Church and the
           present situation in China). *SM* 1.4 (November):
           1-16.

   1921   "Yeh-su ti shang-ti kuan" 耶穌的上帝觀 (Jesus'
           conception of God). *SM* 2.2 (September): 1-15.

1923 "Wo-ti tsung-chiao ching-yen" 我的宗教經驗 (My religious experience). *SM* 4.3 (November): 1-16.

1924 "Chung-hua chi-tu-chiao ti kuo-chi wen-t'i" 中華基督教的國際問題(The problem of internationalism in Chinese Christianity). *CNCP* 73 (May): 15-26.

1924 "Pen-se chiao-hui ti shang-ch'üeh" 本色教會的商榷 (Discussion on the indigenous church). *CNCP* 76 (October): 8-16.

1926 *Chi-tu-chiao che-hsüeh.* 基督教哲學 (Christian Philosophy). Shanghai: Chung-hua chi-tu-chiao wen-she.

1926 *Yeh-su ti jen-sheng che-hsüeh* 耶穌的人生哲學(Jesus' philosophy of life). Shanghai: Christian Literature Society.

1927 "Chi-tu-chiao yü Chung-kuo wen-hua" 基督教與中國文化 (Christianity and Chinese culture). *CLYSM* 2.9-10: 247-60.

1926 "Yen-chiu Ju-chia shu-yü tsung-chiao pu-fen ti ts'ai-liao" 研究儒家屬于宗教部份的材料(Study material regarding the religious aspect of Confucianism). *CLYSM* 1.7 (August): 194-208.

1927 "Feng ch'ao chung fen-ch'i ti Chung-kuo chiao-hui" 風潮中奮起的中國教會(The Chinese Church arising from the storm). *CLYSM* 2.2: 25-30.

1927 "Hsin chi-tu ti kuo-min" 信基督的國民 (People who believe in Christ). *CLYSM* 2.1 (January): 7-9.

1927 "Ching-chih ch'uan-kuo chi-tu-t'u shu" 敬致全國基督徒書(A letter respectfully submitted to all Chinese Christians). *CLYSM* 2.4: 81-93.

1927   "Hsüeh Yeh-su" 學耶穌   (Imitation of Jesus). *CLYSM* 2.14: 395-99.

1929   "Tsung-chiao yü lun-li" 宗教與理論 (Religion and ethics). *CLYSM* 4.7 (November): 1-2.

1932   "Chi-tu-chiao yü Chung-kuo ti hsin-li chien-she" 基督教與中國的心理建設 (Christianity and the psychological reconstruction in China.) *CLYSM* 4.8 (June): 7-16.

1935   *Yeh-su chuan* 耶穌傳   (The life of Jesus). Shanghai: Association Press of China.

1947   *Chi-tu-chiao chin-chieh* 基督教進解 (Interpretation of Christianity). Shanghai: Association Press of China.

1948   *Shen-hsüeh ssu-chiang* 神學四講   (Four Talks on Theology). Shanghai: Association Press of China.

CH'EN, Ch'i-t'ien 陳啟天
1924   "Hsin kuo-chia chu-i yü kuo-min chiao-yü ti kai-tsao"新國家主義與國民教育的改造(New nationalism and the reconstruction of national education). *CHCYC* 14.3 (September).

1925   "Wo-men chu-chang shou-hui chiao-yü-ch'üan ti li-yu yü pan-fa"我們主張收回教育權的理由與辦法 (Our reasons and methods in promoting the restoration of educational rights). *CHCYC* 14.8 (February).

1925   "Kuo-chia chu-i chiao-yü ti yao-i"國家主義教育的要義 (The essence of nationalistic education). *CHCYC* 15.1 (July).

1926   "P'ing chiao-hui hsueh-hsiao li-an pan-fa" 評教會學校立案辦法 (Comment on the policy of registration of Christian schools). *CHCYC* 15.7 (January).

CH'EN, Li-t'ing 陳立廷
1927 "Chi-tu-chiao yü ti-kuo chu-i" 基督教與帝國主義
(Christianity and imperialism). *CNCP* 99 (January):
7-12.

CH'EN, Tu-hsiu 陳獨秀
1915 "Tung-hsi min-tsu ken-pen ssu-hsiang chih ch'a-i"
東西民族根本思想之差異 (The basic difference in the
way of thinking between the Oriental and the Western people). *HCN* 1.4 (December 15): 1-4.

1917 "K'e-hsüeh yü chi-tu-chiao" 科學與基督教 (Science
and Christianity). *HCN* 3.6 (August 1): 1-5.

1918 "Ou-hsiang p'o-huai lun" 偶像破壞論 (On the destruction of idols). *HCN* 5.2 (August 15): 89-92.

1920 "Chi-tu-chiao yü Chung-kuo jen" 基督教與中國人
(Christianity and the Chinese people). *HCN* 7.3
(February 1): 15-23.

1920 "Hsin wen-hua yün-tung shih she-mo"? 新文化運動是什麼？
(What is the New Culture Movement?) *HCN* 7.5 (April
1): 1-6.

1920 "Kuan-yü she-hui chu-i ti t'ao-lun" 關於社會主義的討論
(Discussion on socialism). *HCN* 8.4 (December 1):
1-24.

1927 "Chi-tu-chiao yü chi-tu-chiao-hui" 基督教與基督教會
(Christianity and the Christian Church). In *KNCS*,
pp. 190-92.

1933 *Tu-hsiu wen-ts'un* 獨秀文存 (Collected essays of
Tu-hsiu). 4 vols. Shanghai, 1922; reprint ed. Shanghai.

CH'EN, Yün 陳筠
1928 "Chi-tu-chiao tui-yü tsui-chin shih-chü tang-yu ti
t'ai-tu ho ts'o-shih 基督教對於最近時局當
有的態度和措施 (Christian attitude and policy regarding the recent situation). *WS* 3.3 (January): 1-38.

CH'ENG, Chih-yi 誠質怡
   1927 "Yeh-su ti lun-li yüan-tse" 耶穌的倫理原則 (The
         ethical principle of Jesus). *CLYSM* 2.18: 503-5.

CH'ENG, Ching-yi 誠靜怡
   1922 "Chung-kuo ti chiao-hui" 中國的教會 (The Chinese
         Church). *CNCP* 52 (April): 16-26.

   1926 "Pen-se chiao-hui chih shang-ch'üeh" 本色教會的商榷
         (Discussion of the indigenous church). *WS* 1.6
         (May): 4-13.

   1927 "Chung-kuo chi-tu-chiao ti hsing-chih ho chuang-t'ai"
         中國基督教的性質和狀態(The nature and the situation
         of Christianity in China). *WS* 2.7 (May): 53-64.

   1928 "Ch'üan-kuo chiao-hui kai-kuan" 全國教會概觀 (A
         survey of the Church in the country). *CTCNC*, pp.
         1-8.

   1929 "Liang-nien lai chih ch'üan-kuo chi-tu-chiao yün-
    to   tung niao-k'an"兩年來之全國基督教運動鳥瞰 (A bird's-
   1930 eye view of the Christian movement in the country in
         the last two years). *CTCNC*, pp. 1-7.

CH'ENG, Hsiang-fan 程湘帆
   1927 "Shih-nien lai chih chi-tu-chiao chiao-yü" 十年來之
         基督教教育(Christian education in the last decade).
         CNCP 100 (February): 148-59.

   1927 "Chi-tu-chiao yü cheng-chih wen-t'i" 基督教與政治問題
         (The problem of Christianity and politics). *WS* 3.2
         (December): 1-4.

   1925 "Chi-tu-chiao ko t'uan-t'i tui-yü Hu-an ti hsüan-
         yen" 基督教各團體對於滬案的宣言 (Announcements of
         various Christian organizations regarding the Shang-
         hai Affair). *SM* 5.9 (June): 33-58.

CHIEN, Yu-wen (Timothy Jen)簡又文
   1921 "She-mo shih chi-tu-chiao?" 什麼是基督教？(What is
         Christianity?) *SM* 2.1 (June): 1-8.

1921 "She-mo shih chi-tu-chiao"? 什麼是基督教？ (What is Christianity?) *SM* 2.2 (September): 1-6.

1922 "Min-tsu ti chiao-hui" 民族的教會 (The people's church). *CNCP* 52 (June): 33-44.

1922 "Fei tsung-chiao yün-tung yü hsin chiao-yü" 非宗教運動與新教育 *CNCP* 54 (October): 1-12.

1922 ed. *Hsin Tsung-chiao kuan* 新宗教觀 (New concepts of religion). Shanghai: Association Press of China.

1923 ed. *Tsung-chiao yü jen-sheng* 宗教與人生 (Religion and life). Shanghai: Association Press of China.

1924 "Tsung-chiao chen-li" 宗教眞理 (Religious Truth). *CL* 2.1 (March 30).

1924 "Chi-tu-chiao ti t'e-yu tien" 基督教的特優點 (The unique point of Christianity). *CL* 2.10 (June 1).

1924 "Yeh-su ti fu-wu li-hsiang" 耶穌的服務理想 (The service ideal of Jesus). *CL* 2.12 (June 15).

1924 "Wo-men yao-tso tsen-yang ti chi-tu-t'u" 我們要作怎樣的基督徒(What kind of Christian we should be). *CL* 2.38 (December 14).

1924 "Yeh-su shih szu-sheng tzu ma"? 耶穌是私生子嗎？
1925 (Is Jesus an illegitimate child?) *CL* 2.40 (December 28); 2.41 (January 5).

1925 "Fei-chi-tu-chiao yün-tung yü chi-tu-chiao" 非基督教運動與基督教(The Anti-Christian Movement and Christianity). *CL* 2.48 (February 22).

1925   "Chiu-kuo ti chi-tu-chiao" 救國的基督教 (Christianity that saves the nation). *CK* 24.11-12.

1925   "Wo-men ti yao-ch'iu" 我們的要求 (Our demand). *SM* 5.9 (June).

1926   "Yeh-su lun" 耶穌論 (Discussion on Jesus). *CLYSM* 1.1 (April 15); 1.3 (May 15).

1927   "Yeh-su shih-pu-shih i-ko ke-ming chia"? 耶穌是不是一個革命家 (Is Jesus a revolutionist?) *CLYSM* 2.4: 109-12.

CHOU, T'ai-hsuan 周太玄
   1927   "Tsung-chiao yü Chung-kuo ti chiang-lai" 宗教與中國的將來 (Religion and the future of China). In *KNCS*, pp. 155-83.

1922   "Tsung-chiao yü jen-lai ti chiang-lai" 宗教與人類的將來 (Religion and the future of mankind). In *FTCL*, pp. 1-30.

1925   "Fei tsung-chiao chiao-yü yü chiao-hui chiao yü" 非宗教教育與教會教育 (Non-religious education and Christian education). *CHCYC* 14.8 (February).

CHU, Chih-hsin 朱執信
   1929   *Yeh-su shih she-mo tung-hsi?* 耶穌是什麼東西 (What sort of a thing is Jesus). Shanghai: Hua-tung shu-chü.

CHU, Ching-nung 朱經農
   1926   "K'e-hsüeh yü tsung-chiao" 科學與宗教 (Science and religion). *WS* 1.11-12 (October): 5-20.

1930   ed. *Chiao-yü ta tz'u-shu* 教育大辭書 (A dictionary of educational terms). 2 vols. Shanghai.

1925   *Fan chi-tu-chiao chou-k'an* 反基督教週刊 (Anti-Christian Weekly). Canton, February-May.

1924   *Fan-tui chi-tu-chiao yün-tung* 反對基督教運動 (The
       Anti-Christian Movement). n.p. December.

FAN, Tzu-mei (Van, T.M.) 范子美
   1919   "Wo-chih kuo-ts'ui pao-ts'un kuan" 我之國粹保存觀
          (My view of preserving the national essence). *CNCP*
          26 (October): 10-13.

   1922   "Chi-tu-hua yü Chung-kuo chiao-hui" 基督化與中國教會
          (Christianization and the Chinese Church). *CNCP*
          52 (June): 27-32.

   1923   "Ju-chia pu-hsing ti chia-t'ing-kuan" 儒家不幸的家庭觀
          (The unfortunate view of the family in Confucian-
          ism). *CNCP* 61 (March): 62-65.

   1925   "Tung-fang ti chi-tu-chiao" 東方的基督教 (Chris-
          tianity of the East). *CNCP* 79 (January): 7-10.

   1925   "Chung-kuo ku-tai sheng-hsien ti nei-hsiu kung-fu
          yu shang-ti ti kuan-hsi" 中國古代聖賢的內修工夫與上
          帝的關係 (The relation between the practice of self-
          cultivation among the ancient sages and God in
          China). *CNCP* 87 (November): 37-40.

   1925   *Tung Hsi wen-hua chih i-kuan* 東西文化之一貫
          (Civilization: East and West). Shanghai: Asso-
          ciation Press of China.

   1926   "K'ung Tzu ti chia-t'ing kuan yü she-hui kuan" 孔子
          的家庭觀與社會觀 (Confucius' view of the family
          and society). *CNCP* 97 (November): 29-34.

   1926   "K'ung Tzu ti cheng-chih kuan" 孔子的政治觀 (Con-
          fucius' view of politics). *CNCP* 96 (October): 31-36.

   1927   "K'ung Tzu ti ke-ming ssu-hsiang" 孔子的革命思想
          (Confucius' thought of revolution). *CNCP* 103
          (May): 11-17.

1927   "Ju chia ti jen-ke kuan" 儒家的人格觀 (The Confu-
        cian view of personality). *CNCP* 104 (June): 13-14.

1925   *Fei chi-tu-chiao* 非基督教 (Anti-Christianity).
        n.p. November-December.

1922   *Fei tsung-chiao lun* 非宗教論 (Discussion on anti-
        religion). Peking: Hsin-chih shu-she.

FU, T'ung 傅銅
1922   "K'e-hsüeh ti fei tsung-chiao yün-tung yü tsung-
        chiao ti fei tsung-chiao yün-tung"科學的非宗教
        運動與宗教的非宗教運動(The scientific anti-religion
        movement and the religious anti-religion movement).
        Che-hsueh 哲學6 (June).

HSIEH, Fu-ya (Zia, N.Z.)謝扶雅
1925   "Chi-tu-chiao hsin ssu-ch'ao yü Chung-kuo min-tsu
        ken-pen ssu-hsiang" 基督教新思潮與中國民族根本思想
        (Christianity, New Thought Tide, and the basic thought
        of the Chinese people). *CNCP* 82 (April): 1-15.

1925   "Chin-nien fei tsung-chiao ho fei chi-tu-chiao yün-
        tung kai-shu" 近年非宗教和非基督教運動概迹(A sur-
        vey of the anti-religion and anti-Christian movement
        in recent years). *CTCNC*, pp. 17-24.

1925   *Hsin shih-tai ti hsin-yang* 新時代的信仰 (Beliefs
        in the new era). Shanghai: Association Press of
        China.

1926   "Pen-se chiao-hui wen-t'i yü chi-tu-chiao tsai
        Chung-kuo chih ch'ien-t'u"本色教會問題與基督教在中
        國之前途(The problem of indigenous church and the
        future of Christianity in China). *WS* 1.4 (January):
        27-31.

1926   *Chu-chiao yen-chiu* 諸教研究 (A short study of compara-
        tive religions). Shanghai: Christian Literature
        Society.

1927   "Cheng-chih ke-ming she-hui ke-ming yü ching-shen
        ke-ming" 政治革命社會革命與精神革命 (Political
        revolution, social revolution and spiritual revolu-
        tion). *CNCP* 107 (November): 4-9.

1928   *Tsung-chiao che-hsüeh* 宗教哲學   (Religious phil-
        osophy). Shanghai: Association Press of China.

HSIEH, Hung-lai 謝洪賚
1918   ed. *Cheng tao chi* 証道集 (Reasons for Christian faith).
        Shanghai: Association Press of China.

1920   *Sheng-tao kuan-k'uei* 聖道管窺 (The character of Jesus).
        Shanghai: Association Press of China.

1921   *Chi-tu-chiao yü k'e-hsüeh* 基督教與科學 (Christian-
        ity and science). Shanghai: Association Press of
        China.

1922   "Hsin wen-hua chung chi-wei hsüeh-che tui-yü chi-tu-
        chiao ti t'ai-t'u" 新文化中幾位學者對於基督教的態度
        (Attitudes toward Christianity among scholars of the
        New Culture Movement). *SM* 2.7-8 (March): 1-10.

HSÜ, Ch'ien 徐謙
1919   "Kung-ho chen-li" 共和眞理 (Christianity the basis
        for a republic). *SM* 1.1 (November).

1920   *Chi-tu-chiao chiu-kuo chu-i k'an-hsing chih-san*
        基督教救國主義刊行之三 (The theory of national sal-
        vation through Christianity, III). Shanghai: Chi-
        tu-chiao chiu-kuo-hui.

1920   *Chi-tu-chiao chiu-kuo-hui ch'eng-li chih li-yu*
        基督教救國會成立之理由 (Reasons for establishing the
        Christian National Salvation Association). Shang-
        hai: Chi-tu-chiao chiu-kuo-hui.

1925   "Wo tui-yü Sun Chung-shan hsien-sheng ti hsin-yang
        wei Yeh-su so ch'uan chih chen-tao tso cheng" 我對於孫
        中山先生的信仰爲耶穌所傳之眞道作証 (My testimony
        for the belief of Mr. Sun Chung-shan in the truth
        that Jesus preached). *CL* 3.3 (April 19).

HSÜ, Ch'ing-yü 徐慶譽
   1927   "Fei tsung-chiao t'ung-meng yü chiao-hui ke-ming"
          非宗教同盟與教會革命(Anti-Religion Federation
          and Church Revolution). In *KNCS*, pp. 212-239.

HSÜ, Pao-ch'ien 徐寶謙
   1920   "Hsin ssu-ch'ao yü chi-tu-chiao" 新思潮與基督教
          (The New Thought Movement and Christianity). *SM*
          1.2 (September): 1-4.

   1925   "Ching-kao chin chih t'i-ch'ang kuo-chia chu-i che"
          敬告今之提倡國家主義者(An exhortation to the advo-
          cates of nationalism). *SM* 5.4 (January): 1-3.

   1925   "Tsai chih kuo-chia chu-i che" 再質國家主義者(An-
          other message to the nationalist). *CL* 3.24 (Sep-
          tember 13).

   1926   "Fan chi-tu-chiao yün-tung yü wu-jen chin-hou ying
          ts'ai chih fang-chen" 反基督教運動與吾人今後應採
          之方針 (The anti-Christian movement and our policy
          from now on). *SM* 6.5 (February): 1-6.

   1926   "Yeh-su chi-tu ti yu-yüeh tien" 耶穌基督的優越點
          (The point of excellence in Jesus Christ). *CLYSM*
          1.4 (May): 96-101.

   1927   "P'ing tang-hua chiao-yü" 評黨化教育 (Comment on Party
          education). *CLYSM* 2.1: (January).

   1927   "Chi-tu-chiao yü shih-chü" 基督教與時局   (Chris-
          tianity and the present circumstances). *CLYSM* 2.2:
          23-25.

   1927   "Tui-yü i-pan fan-tui chiao-hui chiao-yü che so
          ch'ih li-yu ti fen-hsi" 對於一般反對教會教育者所
          持理由的分析 (An analysis of the reasons of those
          who are against Christian education). *CLYSM* 2.2:
          63-65.

1927 "Wo chiang kuo-chi chu-i ti ching-kuo" 我講國際主義的 經過(The history of my thought on internationalism). *CLYSM* 2.16: 11-15.

1927 "Chi-tu-chiao yü cheng-chih" 基督教與政治(Christianity and politics). *WS* 3.2 (December): 4-7.

1929 "She-mo shih tsung-chiao" 什麼是宗教 (What is religion?) *CLYSM* 4.6 (June): 9-11.

1932 "Chi-tu-chiao tui-yü shih-chieh ch'ao-liu chih ying-fu" 基督教對於社會潮流之應付(Christian response to the world trends). *CLYSM* 7.3 (December): 6-12.

1932 "Chi-tu-chiao tui-yü Chung-kuo ying-yu ti shih-ming" 基督教對於中國應有的使命(The Christian responsibility in China). *CLYSM* 7.3 (December): 12-16.

1934 "Shih-tai ti jen-shih yü wo-men ti hsin-yang: ts'ung chi-tu-chiao li-ch'ang k'an kuo-chia chu-i chi chieh-chi tou-cheng" 時代的認識與我們的信仰：從基督 教立場看國家主義及階級鬥爭 (A Christian critique of nationalism and the class struggle theory). *CLYSM* 8.2 (April): 47-52.

HU, Hsüeh-ch'eng 胡學誠
1922 "Wei fei tsung-chiao ta t'ung-meng chu-chün chin i-chieh"爲非宗教大同盟諸君進一解(An explanation for those in the Great Anti-Religion Federation). *SM* 3.3 (November).

1924 "Wo-men chin-hou tui-yü kuo-shih ying yu ti chüeh-wu"我們今後對於國事應有的覺悟(Our needed awakening regarding national affairs).*CL* 1.46 (Feb. 10).

HU, I-ku (Woo, Y. K.)胡貽穀
1922 "Shih-chieh kai-tsao yü Yeh-su chi-tu ti tan-sheng" 世界改造與耶穌基督的誕生d (World reconstruction and the birth of Jesus Christ). *CNCP* 58 (December): 32-40.

1925   "Hsin shih-tai ti hsin hsin-yang" 新時代的新信仰
       (New belief in the new era). *CNCP* 84 (June): 11-14.

1926   ed. *Hsien-tai ssu-hsiang chung ti chi-tu-chiao.*
       現代思想中的基督教(Christianity in the light of
       today). Shanghai: Association Press of China.

1926   "Chung-kuo ti kuo-chia chu-i" 中國的國家主義 *CNCP*
       93 (May): 1-13.

1927   "Kuo-min ke-ming yü shih-chieh ta-t'ung"國民革命
       與世界大同 (The people's revolution and world
       harmony). *CNCP* 103 (May): 1-5.

HU, Shih 胡適
  1918   "I-pu-sheng chu-i" 易卜生主義   (Ibsenism). *HCN*
         4.6 (June).

1919   "Shih-yen chu-i" 實驗主義   (Experimentalism).
       HCN 6.4 (April).

1919   "To yen-chiu hsieh wen-t'i, shao t'an hsieh 'chu-
       i'"多研究些問題,少談些主義(Study more problems,
       talk less of 'isms'). *Mei-chou p'ing-lun*. no. 31
       (July 20).

1919   "Hsin ssu-ch'ao ti i-i" 新思潮的意義   (The mean-
       ing of the new thought). *HCN* 7.1 (December).

1921   *Hu Shih wen-ts'un* 胡適文存   (Collected essays of
       Hu Shih). 2 vols., 4 chuan. Shanghai: Ya-tung t'u
       shu-kuan.

1922   "Kuo-chi ti Chung-kuo" 國際的中國   (China among
       the nations). *Nu-li chou-pao* no. 22 (October 1).

1927   "Pu-hsiu wo ti tsung-chiao"不巧,我的宗教(Immor-
       tality, my religion). In *KNCS* pp. 9-22.

1973   "K'e-hsüeh yü jen-sheng-kuan hsü" 科學與人生觀序
        (Preface to science and philosophy of life). In
        K'e-hsüeh yü jen-sheng-kuan lun-chan 科學與人生
        觀論戰(Debate over science and philosophy of life),
        pp. 1-33. Edited by Wang Meng-tsou. Shanghai,
        1923; reprint edition, Hong Kong: Chinese Univer-
        sity of Hong Kong.

1925   "Ai-kuo yün-tung yü ch'iu-hsüeh" 愛國運動與求學
        (The patriotic movement and receiving an educa-
        tion). *Hsien-tai p'ing-lun* 2.39 (September 5):
        5-9.

1926   "Wo-men tui-yü Hsi-yang chin-tai wen-ming ti t'ai-
        t'u" 我們對於西洋近代文明的態度(Our attitude toward
        modern Western civilization). *Hsien-tai p'ing-lun*
        4.83 (July 10): 3-11.

1929   "Hsin wen-hua yün-tung yü Kuomintang" 新文化運動與
        國民黨   (The New Culture Movement and Kuomintang).
        Hsin-yüeh 2.6-7 (September).

1930   *Hu-Shih wen-ts'un, san chi*胡適文存‧三集(Collected
        essays of Hu Shih, third collection). 4 vols., 9
        chüan. Shanghai: Ya-tung t'u-shu-kuan.

1925   "Kuan yü kuo-chia-chu-i ti chi-p'ien wen-chang"
        關於國家主義的幾篇文章(Several essays concerning
        the issue of nationalism). *SM* 5.4 (January).

KUO, Chan-po 郭湛波
1965   *Chin wu-shih nien Chung-kuo ssu-hsiang shih.*近五十
        年中國思想史   (A history of Chinese thought dur-
        ing the last fifty years). Peking, 1935; reprint
        edition, Hong Kong: Lung-meng shu-tien.

1966   *Chin wu-shih nien Chung-kuo ssu-hsiang shih, pu-
        pien.*近五十年中國思想史補編(A history of Chinese
        thought during the last fifty years, a supplement).
        Hong Kong: Lung-meng shu-tien.

LI, Ch'un-fan 李春蕃
 1924   "Ch'uan chiao yü ti-kuo chu-i" 傳敎與帝國主義
        (Evangelism and Imperialism). *Chüeh-wu* (August 19).

LI, Jung-fang 李榮芳
 1922   "Tsung-chiao k'e-hsueh yu che-li ti ko tzu fan-wei"
        宗敎科學與哲理的各自範圍 (The different realms of
        religion, science and philosophy). *CNCP* 54 (Octo-
        ber): 24-29.

_____
 1925   "Fei chi-tu-chiao yün-tung" 非基督敎運動 (The
        anti-Christian movement). *CL* 2.45 (February 1).

_____
 1925   "Hsien-shih hsi chiao-shih tsai Chung-kuo ying-yu
        ti chüeh-wu" 現時西敎士在中國應有的覺悟 (The needed
        awakening for Western missionaries in China today).
        SM 5.9 (June): 21-23.

_____
 1925   "Yeh-su yü chi-tu" 耶穌與基督   (Jesus and the
        Christ). *SM* 6.3 (December): 1-12. Shanghai: Chung
        Hua shu-chü.

LIANG, Ch'i-ch'ao 梁啟超
 1936   "Ai-kuo lun" 愛國論   (On patriotism). *Yin-ping
        shih ho-chi, wen-chi.*   2.3: 65-77. Shanghai: Chung
        Hua Shu-chü.

_____
 1936   "Hsin min shuo" 新民說   (On the new people). *Yin-
        ping shih ho-chi, chuan-chi.* 3.4: 1-162. Shanghai:
        Chung Hua shu-chü.

_____
 1936   "Ou-yu hsin-ying lu, chieh-lu" 歐遊心影錄 · 節錄
        (A condensed record of impressions of travels in
        Europe). *Yin-ping shih ho chi, chuan-chi.* 5.23:
        1-162.

_____
 1973   "Jen-sheng-kuan yü k'e-hsüeh" 人生觀與科學   (The
        philosophy of life and science). In *K'e-hsüeh yü
        jen-sheng-kuan lun-chan* 科學與人生觀論戰 (Debate
        over science and philosophy of life), pp. 171-84.
        Edited by Wang Meng-tsou. Shanghai, 1923: reprint
        edition, Hong Kong: Chinese University of Hong Kong.

1936   *Yin-ping shih ho-chi* 飲冰室合集 Collected works
from the Ice-drinker's studio). 40 vols. Shanghai.

1927   "P'i-p'ing fei tsung-chiao t'ung-meng" 批評非宗敎
同盟(A critique of the Anti-Religion Federation).
In *PFCTC*, pp. 251-60.

LIANG, Chun-mo 梁均默
"P'i-p'ing Ch'i Yüan ti chi-tu-chiao yü kung-ch'an
chu-i" 批評綺園的基督敎與共產主義 (A critique of
Ch'i Yüan's "Christianity and Communism"). In
PFCTC, pp. 74-86.

1927   "P'i-p'ing Lu Shu ti chi-tu-chiao yü tzu-pen chu-i"
批評 評盧淑的基督敎與資本主義 (A critique of Lu Shu's
"Christianity and Capitalism"). In *PFCTC*, pp. 62-
73.

1927   "P'i-p'ing Chu Chih-hsin chu Yeh-su shih she-mo
tung-hsi chih miou-wang"批評朱執信著耶穌是什麼東西
之謬妄(A critique of the error of Chu Chih-hsin's
"What sort of a thing is Jesus). In *PFCTC*, pp. 162-68.

1927   "Wo-men tui tz'u-tz'u fei chi-tu-chiao hsüeh-sheng
t'ung-meng ti kan-hsiang ho t'ai-t'u" 我們對此次非基
督敎學生同盟的感想和態度(Our feeling and attitude
toward the Anti-Christian Student Federation). In
PFCTC, pp. 1-5.

LIANG, Sou-ming 梁漱溟
1927   "Tsung-chiao wen t'i chih ssu" 宗敎問題之四   (The
problem of religion, IV). In *KNCS*, pp. 107-35.

1922   *Tung Hsi wen-hua chi ch'i che-hsüeh* 東西文化及其哲學
(The cultures of East and West and their philosophies). Shanghai.

LIN, Han-ta 林漢達
1928   "Wu-ch'an chieh-chi ti Yeh-su" 無產階級的耶穌
(Jesus a proletarian). *WS* 3.6 (April).

LIU, Chan-en 劉湛思
  1925 "Fan-tui chi-tu-chiao chiao-yü chih i-pan p'ing-
lun"反對基督教教育之一般評論(General comment
against Christian education). *CTCNC*, pp. 122-25.

LIU, Chung-fu 劉鍾孚
  1923 "Wo ti erh-shih shih-chi tsung-chiao kuan"我的二十
世紀宗教觀 (My religious view in the twentieth
century). *SM* 3.10 (June): 1-14.

LIU, po-ming 劉伯明
       "Tsung-chiao wen-t'i chih-wu" 宗教問題之五   (The
problem of religion, V). In *KNCS*, pp. 136-46.

  1922 "Fei tsung-chiao yun-tung p'ing-i" 非宗教運動平議
(A critical study of the anti-Religion Movement).
Hsüeh-heng no. 6 (June).

LIU, T'ing-fang (Lew, Timothy T.)劉廷芳
  1924 "Chung-kuo chi-tu t'u ai-kuo wen-t'i ti p'ing-i"
中國基督徒愛國問題的平議(Comment on the problem
of patriotism among Chinese Christians). *SM* 4.8
(April): 1-5; 4.9-10 (June): 1-8.

  1925 "Sun Chung-shan ti kung-hsien"孫中山的貢獻
(The contributions of Sun Chung-shan). *SM* 5.6
(March): 85-90.

  1925 "Chung-hua chi-tu-t'u yü Sun Chung-shan" 中華基督
徒與孫中山*SM* 5.6 (March): 90-93.

  1925 "Chi-tu-chiao yü Chung-kuo kuo-min hsing"基督教與
中國國民性 (Christianity and the characteristics
of the Chinese people). *SM* 5.9 (June): 5-16.

  1925 "Chi-tu-chiao tsai Chung-kuo chin-jih tang ju-ho
tzu-hsiu i chih-pang"基督教在中國今日當如何目修
以止謗 (How should Christianity cultivate itself to
stop people's scandal in China today). *SM* 6.2
(November): 3-16.

1925   "Ni-men shuo wo shih shei" 你們說我是誰 (Who do you say I am). *SM* 6.3 (December): 1-14.

1926   "Wei pen-se chiao-hui yen-chiu Chung-hua min-tsu tsung-chiao ching-yen ti i-ko ts'ao-an" 爲本色教會研究中華民族宗教經驗的一個草案 (A draft of the study of the religious experience of the Chinese people on behalf of the indigenous church). *CLYSM* 1.7 (August): 185-92.

1927   "Chung-kuo ti chi-tu-chiao yü Chung-kuo ti kuo-chi wen-t'i" 中國的基督教與中國的國際問題 (Christianity in China and the international problem of China). *CLYSM* 2.11: 290-95.

1929   "Shih-chiu shih-chi ko-chung ssu-ch'ao ti yün-tung tui-yü chi-tu-chiao hsin-yang shang so fa-sheng ti ying-hsiang" 十九世紀各種思潮的運動對於基督教信仰上所發生的影響 (The influence on Christianity due to the various intellectual movements in the nineteenth century). *CLYSM* 3.17 (January).

1929   "Chi-tu-chiao chung hsüeh-hsiao tsung-chiao chiao-yü ti yen-chiu hsü" 基督教中學校宗教教育的研究序 (Preface to the study of religious education in Christian middle schools). *CLYSM* 4.9 (December): 11-16.

1931   "Chi-tu-chiao tsai Chung-kuo tao ti shih ch'uan she-mo" 基督教在中國到底是傳什麼 (What does Christianity really preach in China). *CLYSM* 6.1 (October): 11-15.

LO, Chih-hsi 羅志希
1927   *K'e-hsüeh yü hsüan-hsüeh* 科學與玄學 (Science and metaphysics). Shanghai: Commercial Press.

LO, Yün-yen (Lo, R. Y.) 羅運炎
1921   "Hsin ssu-ch'ao ho chi-tu-chiao" 新思潮和基督教 (New thought movement and Christianity). *SM* 2.1 (June): 2-5.

1922   "Chi-tu-chiao yü cheng-chih" 基督教與政治 (Chris-
       tianity and politics). *SM* 3.3 (November): 1-4.

1923   *Chi-tu-chiao yü hsin Chung-kuo* 基督教與新中國
       (Christianity and New China). Shanghai: Methodist
       Press.

1927   "Ch'uan chiao t'iao-yüeh yü chiao-hui chih kuan-
       hsi 傳教條約與教會之關係(Relation between missio-
       nary treaties and the church). *CTCNC*, pp. 28-33.

1931   *Lo Yün-yen lun-tao wen-hsüan* 羅運炎論道文選 (Se-
       lected doctrinal essays of Lo Yün-yen). Shanghai:
       Christian Literature Society.

MAO, Pa 毛拔
  1926   "Tu liao 'Chung-kuo ti chi-tu-chiao' hou" 讀了中國
       的基督教後 (After reading "Christianity in
       China"). *WS* 1.11-12 (October).

1928   "Chi-tu-chiao yü ke-ming" 基督教與革命 (Chris-
       tianity and revolution). *WS* 3.8 (June): 26-31.

1928   "Chi-tu-chiao yü ti-kuo chu-i" 基督教與帝國主義
       (Christianity and imperialism). *CK* 27.9: 11-16.

1928   "Chiao-hui hsüeh-hsiao yü tang-hua chiao-yü"教會
       學校與黨化教育(Christian schools and Party edu-
       cation). *CK* 27.8 (August): 13-19.

MEI, Tien-lung 梅電龍
  1927   "Chi-tu-chiao yü Chung-kuo" 基督教與中國 (Chris-
       tianity and China). In *KNCS*, pp. 387-94.

MEI, Yi-pao 梅貽寶
  1932   "Tsung-chiao ti shih-chih" 宗教的實質 (The sub-
       stance of religion). *CLYSM* 6.7 (May): 1-9.

MI, Hsing-ju 米星如
1923 "Chi-tu-chiao tui-yü tzu-pen-chih hsia san ta wen-t'i ying-yu ti t'ai-tu" 基督教對於資本治下三大問題應有的態度 (The Christian attitude toward the three big problems in the capitalist system). *CNCP* 66 (October): 48-52.

NIEH, Wen-hui 聶文滙
1925 "Fei chi-tu-chiao wen-tzu so-yin" 非基督教文字索引 (Index to anti-Christian literature). *CTCNC*, pp. 142-76.

NIEH, Ch'i-chieh 聶其杰
1927 *P'i-Yeh p'ien* 闢耶篇 (An essay on anti-Christianity). Shanghai: Nieh-shih chia-yen hsün-k'an she.

PAO, Kuang-lin 寶廣林
1924 "Chi-tu-t'u yü kuo-min" 基督徒與國民 (The Christian and citizen). *SM* 4.8 (April): 1-3.

1924 "Yeh-su ch'u-shih ai-jen ti yüan-tse" 耶穌處世愛人的原則 (Jesus' principle of love and dealing with the world). *CL* 2.14 (June 29); 2.16 (July 13).

1926 "Chi-tu-chiao pan-hsüeh-hsiao ying-yu ti mu-ti yü fang-fa" 基督教辦學校應有的目的與方法 (The Christian aim and method in running schools). *CLYSM* 1.10 (October): 283-85.

1928 *Yeh-su ti yen-chiu* 耶穌的研究 (Studies on Jesus). Shanghai: Chung-hua chi-tu-chiao wen-she.

1928 "Chi-tu-chiao yü ta t'ung chu-i" 基督教與大同主義 (Christianity and the view of Great Harmony). *WS* 3.8 (June): 16-18.

P'ENG, Chin-chang 彭錦章
1923 "Hsin-yang yü tsung-chiao" 信仰與宗教 (Belief and religion). *CL* 1.3 (April 15).

1925 "Chi-tu-chiao yü ti-kuo chu-i" 基督教與帝國主義 (Christianity and imperialism). *CL* 2.44 (January 25).

SHEN, Ch'ing-lai 沈青來
  1923   *Chi-tu-chiao shih she-mo* 基督教是什麼 (What is
          Christianity). Shanghai: Association Press of
          China.

SHEN, Szu-chuang 沈嗣莊
  1926   "Ke-ming ti yeh-su" 革命的耶穌 (Jesus the revolu-
          tionist). *WS* 1.8 (July): 1-12.

  1927   "Min-sheng yü kung-ch'an" 民生與共產 (People's
          livlihood and communism). *WS* 2.7 (May): 1-11.

  1927   "I-chiu erh-ch'i nien sheng-tan-jih Chung-kuo chi-
          tu-t'u tui-yü shih-chü ti hsüan-yen 一九二七年聖誕日中
          國基督徒對於時局的宣言(The announcement regard-
          ing the national situation by Chinese Christians on
          the Christmas Day in 1927). *WS* 3.1 (November):
          1-18.

  1928   "Wo se jen-shih ti Yeh-su" 我所認識的耶穌 (The
          Jesus that I know). *WS* 3.7 (May): 12-25.

SHU, Hsin-ch'eng 舒新城
  1927   *Shou-hui chiao-yü ch'üan yün-tung* 收回教育權運動
          (The Movement for Restoring Educational Rights).
          Shanghai: Chung-hua shu-chü.

  1928   *Chin-tai Chung-kuo chiao-yü ssu-hsiang shih* 近代中
          國教育思想史(A history of educational thought in
          modern China). Shanghai.

  1923   ed. *Chin-tai Chung-kuo chiao-yü shih-liao* 近代中國
          教育史科 (Historical materials of modern Chinese
          education). 4 vols. Shanghai.

T'IEN, Han 田漢
  1927   "Shao-nien Chung-kuo yü tsung-chiao wen-t'i" 少年中
          國與宗教問題 (Young China and the problem of
          religion). In *KNCS*, pp. 51-58.

TS'ai, Yüan-p'ei 蔡元培
  1917   "I mei-yü tai tsung-chiao" 以美育代宗教 (Substi-
          tuting religion with aesthetic education). *HCN*
          3.6 (August): 1-5.

1920   "She-hui chu-i shih hsü" 社會主義史序 (Preface to
        the history of socialism). *HCN* 8.1 (September 1):
        1-4.

1922   "Chiao-yü tu-li i" 教育獨立議 (Independence of
        education). *Hsin Chiao-yü* no. 4: 317-19.

T'U, Che-yin 屠哲隱
1922   "Chi-tu-chiao-hui yü she-hui kai-tsao" 基督教會與社
        會改造 (The Christian church and social reform).
        CNCP 54 (October): 51-60.

1925   "Chi-tu-chiao yu fei chi-tu-chiao p'ing-i" 基督教
        與非基督教平議(Comment on Christianity and anti-
        Christianity). *SM* 5.7 (April): 54-57.

T'U, Hsiao-shih 屠孝實
1927   "Tsung-chiao wen-t'i chih-san" 宗教問題之三 (The
        problem of religion, III). In *KNCS*, pp. 87-106.

1922   "K'e-hsüeh yü tsung-chiao huo-chen pu-neng liang-
        li mo?" 科學與宗教果眞不能兩立麼?(Are science and
        religion really not able to exist together?) *SM*
        3.1 (September): 1-11.

WANG, Chao-hsiang 汪兆翔
1927   "Chi-tu-chiao tui-yü tsui-chin shih-chü tang-yu ti
        t'ai-t'u ho ts'o-shih"基督教對於最近時局當有的態度
        和措施 (Christian attitude and policy regarding
        the recent situation). *WS* 2.8 (June): 1-34.

1928   "Chi-tu-chiao yü min-sheng wen-t'i" 基督教與民生問題
        (Christianity and the problem of livelihood). *WS*
        3.3 (January): 9-28.

WANG, Chih-hsin 王治心
1925   "Chung-kuo pen-se chiao-hui ti t'ao-lun"中國本色教
        會的討論 (Discussion on the indigenous church in
        China). *CNCP* 79 (January): 11-16.

1925   "Wu-san shih-pien yü chiao-hui chih ying-hsiang"
        五三事變與教會之影响(The influence of the May
        Thirtieth Incident to the church). *CTCNC*, pp.
        25-28.

1926   "Pen-se chiao-hui yü pen-se chu-tso"本色教會與
        本色著作 (Indigenous church and indigenous writ-
        ings). *WS* 1.6 (May): 1-17.

1926   "Chung-hua chi-tu-t'u chih pen-se chia-t'ing sheng-
        huo"中華基督徒之本色家庭生活(The indigenous family
        life of Chinese Christians). *WS* 1.7 (June):65-70.

1926   "Chung-kuo chi-tu-chiao wen-tzu shih-yeh chih kuo-
        ch'u hsien-tsai yü wei-lai"中國基督教文字事業之過
        去現在與未來(The past, the present, and the future
        of the Christian literature work in China). *WS*
        1.8 (July): 59-70.

1926   "Chung-hua min-tsu ti tsung-chiao ching-yen"中華
        民族的宗教經驗 (Religious experiences of the
        Chinese people). *WS* 1.8 (July): 13-30.

1927   "Chi-tu-chiao yü Chung-kuo wen-hua"基督教與中國文化
        (Christianity and Chinese culture). *CK* 26.6: 1-6.

1927   "Sun Wen chu-i yü Yeh-su chu-i" 孫文主義與耶穌主義
        (Sun Yat-senism and Jesusism). *WS* 2.3 (January):
        1-25.

1927   ed. *Chung-kuo wen-hua yü chi-tu-chiao* 中國文化與
        基督教 (Chinese culture and Christianity). Shang-
        hai: Association Press of China.

1927   "Ch'ing-t'ien pai-jih ch'i-hsia ti chi-tu-chiao"
        青天白日旗下的基督教(Christianity under the flag
        of the Chinese Republic). *WS* 2.7 (April): 1-14.

1927   "Wo-men ti ke-ming-kuan" 我們的革命觀   (Our view of revolution). *WS* 2.7 (May): 28-36.

1927   *San Min Chu I tsai Chung-kuo wen-hua shang chih ken-chü* 三民主義在中國文化上之根據 (The basis of *San Min Chu I* in Chinese Culture). Shanghai: Chung-hua chi-tu-chiao wen-she.

1927   "Chin-nien sheng-tan ti hsin shih-ming" 今年聖誕的新使命 (The new mission for Christmas this year). *WS* 3.1 (November): 19-23.

1928   "Yeh-su shih she-mo tung-hsi" 耶穌是什麼東西 (What sort of a thing is Jesus). *WS* 3.7 (May): 71-82.

1933   *Chung-kuo tsung-chiao ssu-hsiang shih ta-kang* 中國宗教思想史大綱 (Outline of Chinese religious thought). Shanghai: Chung-hua shu-chü.

WANG, Chien-yu 王建猶
   1926   "Chi-tu-chiao yü she-hui chu-i" 基督教與社會主義 (Christianity and socialism). *SM* 6.5 (February): 1-6.

WANG, Hsing-kung 王星拱
   1927   "Tsung-chiao wen-t'i chih-i" 宗教問題之一   (The problem of religion, I). In *KNCS*, pp. 59-71.

1966   *K'e-hsüeh fang-fa lun* 科學方法論 (Discussion of scientific method). Peking, 1920; reprint edition Taiwan: Shiu Niu Press.

WANG, Li-chung 王理中
   1927   "Chi-tu-chiao yü ssu-hsiang chieh" 基督教與思想界 (Christianity and the intellectual). *CLYSM* 2.1 (January): 14-16.

1927   "Chi-tu-chiao tui-yü chiao-yü ti t'e-shu kung-hsien" 基督教對於教育的特殊貢獻 (The special contribution of Christianity to education). *CLYSM* 2.3: 58-60.

WANG, Ming-tao 王明道
    1970   *Chi-tu ti hsin-fu* 基督的新婦 (The bride of
            Christ). 1926; reprint edition, Hong Kong:
            Bellman House.

    1962   *Yeh-su shih-shei* 耶穌是誰 (Who is Jesus). 1927;
            reprint edition, Hong Kong: Hung Tao Press.

    1967   *Ch'ung-sheng chen-i* 重生眞義 (The true meaning
            of rebirth). 1933; reprint edition, Hong Kong:
            Alliance Press.

    1962   *Jen neng chien-she t'ien-kuo ma?* 人能建設天國麼？
            (Can the kingdom of heaven be established by man?)
            1933; reprint edition, Hong Kong: Alliance Press.

    1962   *P'u-shih jen-lei tu shih shen ti erh-tzu ma?* 普世人
            類都是神的兒子麼？(Are all men sons of God?)
            1934; reprint edition, Hong Kong: Alliance Press.

    1963   *Chen-yi fu-yin pien* 眞僞福音辯 (Debate between
            the true and the false Gospel). 1936; reprint
            edition, Hong Kong: Sung En Press.

    1967   *Wu-shih nien lai* 五十年來 (These fifty years).
            1950; reprint edition, Hong Kong: Bellman House.

WU, Chih-hui 吳稚暉
    1924   "Ch'iang-nu chih-mo ti chi-tu-chiao" 强弩之末的基
            督敎 (Christianity on the verge of collapse).
            Chüeh-wu (August 19).

WU, Lei-ch'uan 吳雷川
    1920   "Wo tui-yü chi-tu-chiao-hui ti kan-hsiang" 我對於
            基督敎會的感想(My feeling toward the Christian
            church). *SM* 1.4 (November): 1-4.

    1923   "Chi-tu-chiao yü Ju-chiao" 基督敎與儒敎 (Chris-
            tianity and Confucianism). *CL* 1.43 (January 12).

    1923   "Chi-tu-chiao ching yü Ju-chiao ching" 基督敎經與
            儒敎經 (The Christian scripture and the Confucian
            documents). *SM* 3.6 (March): 1-6.

1923 — "Chi-tu-t'u chiu-kuo" 基督徒救國 (National salvation by Christians). *CL* 1.4 (April 22).

1923 — "Lun Chung-kuo chi-tu-chiao-hui ti ch'ien-t'u"論中國基督教會的前途 (Discussion on the future of the Christian church in China). *CL* 1.11 (June 10).

1924 — "Chung-hua chi-tu-chiao chi-szu tsu-hsien ti wen-t'i"中華基督教祭祀祖先的問題.(The problem of ancestral sacrifice by Chinese Christians). *CL* 2.3 (April 13).

1924 — "Chiao-hui hsüeh-hsiao yü Chung-kuo chiao-yü ti ch'ien-t'u"教會學校與中國教育的前途 (Christian schools and the future of China's education). *CL* 2.20 (August 11).

1924 — "Tsung-chiao pien-huo shuo shu-pien" 宗教辯惑說疏辯 (A critique of the "Criticism of religious heterodoxy"). *CL* 2.30 (October 19).

1924 — "Chi-tu-chiao yü Chung-kuo shih-chü"基督教與中國時局 (Christianity and the situation in China). *CL* 2.36 (November 29).

1924 — "Sheng-tan chieh ti lien-hsiang--Yeh-su yü K'ung Tzu" 聖誕節的聯想一耶穌與孔子 (Related thought during Christmas--Jesus and Confucius). *SM* 5.2 (November): 4-11.

1924 — "Jen-ko--Yeh-su yü K'ung Tzu"人格一耶穌與孔子 (Personality--Jesus and Confucius). *SM* 5.3 (December): 5-11.

1925 — "Kuo-chia chu-i yü chi-tu-chiao shih-fou ch'ung-t'u"國家主義與基督教是否衝突 (Are nationalism and Christianity conflicting?) *SM* 5.4 (January): 4-5.

1925   "Lun Chung-kuo chi-tu-t'u tui-yü kuo-chia ying-fu
        ti tse-jen" 論中國基督徒對於國家應付旳責任 (Discus-
        sion on the responsibilities of Chinese Christians
        toward the country). *SM* 5.5 (February): 5-7.

1925   "Hu-an yü Chung-kuo chi-tu-chiao ti ch'ien-t'u"
        滬案與中國基督教旳前途 (The Shanghai Case and the
        future of Christianity in China). *SM* 5.9 (June).

1925   "Hu-an yü chi-tu-chiao ti lien-hsiang" 滬案與基督
        教旳聯想 (Some thoughts on the Shanghai Case and
        Christianity). *CL* 3.13 (June 28).

1925   "Hsin-chiao yü ai-kuo" 信教與愛國 (Having reli-
        gious beliefs and being patriotic). *CL* 3.18
        (August 2).

1925   "Fan chi-tu-chiao yün-tung yü kuo-chia chu-i" 反基
        督教運動與國家主義 (Anti-Christian movement and
        nationalism). *CL* 3.39 (December 27).

1926   "Chi-tu-chiao chih sheng-ling yü Ju-chiao chih
        jen" 基督教之聖靈與儒教之仁 (The Spirit in Chris-
        tianity and *jen* in Confucianism). *SM* 6.5 (Feb-
        ruary): 11-18.

1926   "Yü ai-kuo ch'ing-nien shuo Yeh-su" 與愛國青年說
        耶穌 (Talking with the patriotic youth about
        Jesus). *CLYSM* 1.1 (April): 2-4.

1926   "Cheng-chü yü ch'ing-nien" 政局與青年 (The poli-
        tical situation and the youth). *CLYSM* 1.3 (May):
        60-61.

1926   "Chung-kuo ch'ing-nien pu-tang hsiao-fa Yeh-su
        ma"? 中國青年不當效法耶穌麼？ (Should not the Chi-
        nese youth imitate Jesus?) *CLYSM* 1.8 (September):
        221-24.

————— 1927 "Chi-tu-chiao chiao-yu yu kuo-chia chiao-yu ti
kuan-hsi"基督教教育與國家教育的關係 (The relation
between Christian education and national education). *CTCNC*, pp. 59-63.

————— 1926 "Yü hsien-tai ch'ing-nien shang-liang chiu-kuo ti
wen-t'i"與現代青年商量救國的問題(Discussion with
today's youth about the problem of national salvation). *CLYSM* 1.11 (November): 310-14.

————— 1927 "Tsung-chiao yü jen-sheng" 宗教與人生 (Religion
and life). *CLYSM* 2.1 (January): 31-34.

————— 1927 "Chi-tu-chiao ti lun-li yü Chung-kuo ti chi-tu-
chiao-hui"基督教的倫理與中國的基督教會(Christian
ethics and the Chinese church). *CLYSM* 2.2: 31-34.

————— 1927 "Chi-tu-chiao ch'i-tao ti i-i yü Chung-kuo hsien-
che hsiu-yang ti fang-fa"基督教祈禱的意義與中國先哲
修養的方法(The meaning of Christian prayer and the
method of self-cultivation of Chinese sages).
CLYSM 2.6: 145-50.

————— 1929 "Lun chi-tu-t'u tang ju-ho hsiao-fa shang-ti" 論基
督徒當如何效法上帝 (How should the Christian
imitate God)? *CLYSM* 4.9 (December): 8-11.

————— 1930 *Chi-tu-t'u ti hsi-wang* 基督徒的希望 (The Christian Hope). Shanghai: Association Press of China.

————— 1930 "Ts'ung Ju-chia ssu-hsiang lun chi-tu-chiao" 從儒
家思想論基督教(Discussing Christianity from the
standpoint of Confucian thought). *CLYSM* 4.13:
3-6.

————— 1931 "Chi-tu-chiao yü ke-ming" 基督教與革命 (Christianity and revolution). *CLYSM* 5.4 (February):
1-5.

1932   "Chi-nien Yeh-su tan-sheng ti wo-chien" 記念耶穌
誕生的我見(My view of commemoration of Jesus
birth). *CLYSM* 7.3 (December): 1-6.

1936   *Chi-tu-chiao yü Chung-kuo wen-hua* 基督教與中國文化
(Christianity and Chinese culture). Shanghai:
Ch'ing-nien hsieh-hui shu-chü.

1958   *Wu-ssu shih-ch'i ch'i-k'an chieh-shao* 五四時期期
to   刊介紹 (An introduction to the periodicals of the
1959   May Fourth era). 3 vols. Peking.

WU, Yao-tsung 吳耀宗
1924   "Yeh-su--wo-men" 耶穌一我們 (Jesus and we). *CL*
1.45 (February 3).

1924   "Chin-jih chi-tu-chiao yun-tung ti ch'ü-shih chi
ch'i wei-chi"今日基督教運動的趨勢及其危機(The trend
and crisis of the Christian movement today). *CL*
2.5 (April 27).

1929   *Wo so jen-shih ti Yeh-su* 我所認識的耶穌 (The Jesus
that I know). Shanghai: Ch'ing-nien hsieh-hui
shu-chü.

YEH, Sheng 葉聲
1928   "Tsung-chiao wen-t'i: ho Chang-Niu liang hsien-
sheng tso i-ko shang-ch'üeh"宗教問題：和張鈕兩先生作
一個商榷(The religious problem: a discussion with
Mr. Chang and Mr. Niu). *WS* 3.5 (March): 49-52.

1928   "Kei Chang Shih-chang chün i-ko chien-tan ti ta-
fu" 給張仕章君一個簡單的答覆(A simple answer to
Chang Shih-chang). *WS* 3.5 (March): 62-64.

YING, Yüan-tao 應元道
1922   "Chung-kuo chiao-hui ti tzu-li" 中國教會的自立
(The independence of the Chinese church). *CNCP* 52)
(June): 45-48.

1922   "Chi-tu-chiao ho she-hui chu-i" 基督教和社會主義
(Christianity and socialism). *CNCP* 54 (October):
61-66.

1922   "Chi-tu ho k'e-hsüeh" 基督和科學 (Christ and science). *CNCP* 55 (November): 1-7.

1923   "Tsung-chiao ho jen-ch'ün ti kuan-hsi" 宗教和人群
的關係 (The relation between religion and the
people). *CNCP* 60 (February): 1-21.

1926   "Erh-shih-nien-lai chih Chung-kuo chi-tu-chiao
chu-tso-chieh chi ch'i tai-piao jen-wu" 二十年來之中國
基督教著作界及其代表人物(The literary world and
its representatives of the Chinese church during
the last twenty years). *WS* 1.5 (April): 6-34.

1926   "Chin wu-nien lai Chung-kuo chi-tu-chiao ssu-hsiang
chih shih-tai pei-ching ho ch'i nei-jung chih ta-
kai" 近五年來中國基督教思想之時代背景和其內容之大概
(A general survey of the background and content of
Christian thought in China during the past five
years). *WS* 1.9-10 (September): 1-32.

YÜ, Chia-chü 余家菊
1923   "Chiao-hui chiao-yü wen-t'i" 教會教育問題 (The
problem of Christian education). *Shao-nien Chung-
kuo* 4.7 (February).

1927   "Chi-tu-chiao yü kan-ch'ing sheng-huo" 基督教與
感情生活(Christianity and emotional life). In
KNCS, pp. 272-354.

1925   "Shou-hui chiao-yü-ch'uan wen-t'i ta-pien" 收回
教育權問題答辯 (Reply to the question of Restoration of Educational Rights). *CHCYC* 14.8 (February).

YÜ, Jih-chang (Yui, David Z. T.) 余日章
1924   "Chung-kuo tsai kuo-chi chien chih ti-wei" 中國在
國際間之地位 (China's position among the nations).
CNCP 73 (May): 1-4.

1926   "Chin-jih Chung-kuo cheng-chih hsien-hsiang ti
kuan-ch'a" 今日中國政治現象的觀察 (Observations of
the political situation in China today). *CNCP* 91
(March): 1-6.

1926   "Chi-tu-chiao tsai Chung-kuo tang ch'ien chih wu-
        ta wen-t'i"基督教在中國當前之五大問題 (The five big
        problems confronting Christianity in China today).
        CNCP 97 (November): 1-6.

1926   "Chi-tu-chiao yü cheng-chih" 基督教與政治 (Chris-
        tianity and politics). *CNCP* 98 (December): 8-13.

1927   "Kuo-chia chu-i yü kuo-chi chu-i" 國家主義與國際主義
        (Nationalism and internationalism). *CNCP* 99 (Jan-
        uary): 1-6.

YÜ, Mu-jen 余牧人
  1923   "Chi-tu-chiao kai tsao she-hui ti fang-fa"基督教
        改造社會的方法(The Christian method of social
        reform). *CNCP* 66 (October): 28-38.

YÜAN, Yeh-yü 袁業裕
  1928   "Lun ch'ü-hsiao ta-tao tsung-chiao k'ou-hao" 論取
        消打倒宗教口號 (Discussing the abolition of the
        slogan 'Down with religion'). *WS* 3.5 (March):
        52-54.

1928   "San Min Chu I che tui chi-tu-chiao t'ai-tu chih
        yen-chiu"三民主義者對基督教態度之研究 (A study of
        the attitude of the advocates of San Min Chu I
        toward Christianity). *WS* 3.5 (March): 67-74.

Index

About the Author

Dr. Wing-hung Lam was born in Hong Kong. After graduating from the University of Hong Kong in 1969 with a B.Sc. in physical sciences, he joined the staff of Fellowship of Evangelical Students, Hong Kong, for two years. He went to Trinity Evangelical Divinity School in Deerfield, Illinois, for the M.Div. training and graduated *summa cum laude* in 1974. In 1978, he earned the Ph.D. in historical theology in Princeton Theological Seminary, Princeton, New Jersey.

During his Princeton days he took up pastoral duties in the Princeton Chinese Church, and later on became interim pastor in the Chinese Ling Liang Church in Toronto. Since 1978 Dr. Lam has served as lecturer in China Graduate School of Theology, Hong Kong, where he teaches theology and church history. He has also written *Wang Ming-tao and the Chinese Church*, a popular and important work in indigenous Chinese theology.